A Brief History of Women in Quebec

Studies in
Childhood and Family
in Canada

A broad-ranging series that publishes scholarship from various disciplines, approaches, and perspectives relevant to the concepts and relations of childhood and family in Canada. Our interests also include, but are not limited to, interdisciplinary approaches and theoretical investigations of gender, race, sexuality, geography, language, and culture within these categories of experience, historical and contemporary.

Series Editor:
Cynthia Comacchio
History Department
Wilfrid Laurier University

Send proposals to:
Lisa Quinn, Acquisitions Editor
Wilfrid Laurier University Press
75 University Avenue West
Waterloo, ON N2L 3C5
Canada
Phone: 519-884-0710 ext. 2843
Fax: 519-725-1399
Email: quinn@press.wlu.ca

A Brief History of Women in Quebec

Denyse Baillargeon
Translated by W. Donald Wilson

WILFRID LAURIER UNIVERSITY PRESS

Wilfrid Laurier University Press acknowledges the support of the Canada Council for the Arts for our publishing program. We acknowledge the financial support of the Government of Canada, through the National Translation Program for Book Publishing for our translation activities. We acknowledge the financial support of the Government of Canada through the Canada Book Fund for our publishing activities.

LIBRARY AND ARCHIVES CANADA CATALOGUING IN PUBLICATION

Baillargeon, Denyse, 1954–
[Brève histoire des femmes au Québec. English]
  A brief history of women in Quebec / Denyse Baillargeon ; translated by W. Donald Wilson.

(Studies in childhood and family in Canada)
Translation of: Brève histoire des femmes au Québec.
Includes bibliographical references and index.
Issued in print and electronic formats.
ISBN 978-1-55458-950-0 (pbk.).—ISBN 978-1-55458-952-4 (epub).—ISBN 978-1-55458-951-7 (pdf)

  1. Women—Québec (Province)—History. 2. Women's rights—Québec (Province)—History. 3. Feminism—Québec (Province)—History. I. Wilson, W. Donald, 1938–, translator II. Title. III. Title: Brève histoire des femmes au Québec. English. IV. Series: Studies in childhood and family in Canada

HQ1459.Q8B34213 2014   305.409714   C2014-900209-2
                                              C2014-900210-6

Cover design by Sandra Friesen. Front-cover image from iStockphoto. Text design

© 2014 Wilfrid Laurier University Press
Waterloo, Ontario, Canada
www.wlupress.wlu.ca

This book is printed on FSC recycled paper and is certified Ecologo. It is made from 100% post-consumer fibre, processed chlorine free, and manufactured using biogas energy.

305.
409
714
BAI

Printed in Canada

Every reasonable effort has been made to acquire permission for copyright material text, and to acknowledge all such indebtedness accurately. Any errors and omission publisher's attention will be corrected in future printings.

No part of this publication may be reproduced, stored in a retrieval system, or transmitted, in any form or by any means, without the prior written consent of the publisher or a licence from the Canadian Copyright Licensing Agency (Access Copyright). For an Access Copyright licence, visit http://www.accesscopyright.ca or call toll free to 1-800-893-5777.

French edition
Copyright © 2012 by Éditions du Boréal
Brève histoire des femmes au Québec

Contents

INTRODUCTION vii

1. Amerindian and French Women during the French Colonial Period 1

2. The Early Years of British Rule (1780–1840) 25

3. A Society on the Path to Industrialization (1840–1880) 49

4. A New Capitalist Industrial Order (1880–1920) 73

5. Women in a "Modern" Society (1920–1940) 103

6. A Society Undergoing Profound Transformation (1940–1965) 129

7. The Feminist Revolution (1966–1989) 157

8. Women in a Neoliberal Society (1990–2012) 189

CONCLUSION 217

SELECTED BIBLIOGRAPHY 223

INDEX 235

Introduction

What part have women played in the history of Quebec since the French first settled the St Lawrence River Valley? What positions did they occupy in this society, and what is the explanation for the changes that have been noted? Such are essentially the questions at the heart of this book. In other words, it sets out to illuminate the historical experience of all Quebec women by bringing out the economic, social, political, and ideological forces that have shaped that experience, and to allow an understanding of its major dimensions. Similarly to what occurred in other Western societies, this historical experience has been deeply marked, by the development first of merchant, and later industrial, capitalism, while it has also been shaped by a patriarchy that sought to restrict women's rights and the scope of their activity. Contrary to a stubbornly persistent myth, Quebec has never been a matriarchal society in which women supposedly dominated men and wielded the real power. Furthermore, the history of Quebec women has been affected by a few special features: the strong presence of the Roman Catholic Church, which made itself felt from the colonial period on, and, beginning in the nineteenth century, the centrality of the National Question, both of which contributed substantially to forming the institutions and structuring the social relations – gender relations in particular – that frame the context of this history. Making use of the research and interpretations of historians interested in women's and gender history, this brief synthesis therefore sets out to provide an account of the history of women in Quebec showing what makes that history distinct and leading to a better understanding of it.

Our overview builds on a number of concepts and key ideas developed by feminist historians during the past few decades. On the one hand, it deems that far from constituting two separate, watertight universes, the private or domestic sphere that has been considered the special domain of women's activity and the public sphere occupied by men have been two fields with fluid, shifting borders, irremediably bound together and acting one upon the other. This view of the relationship between the private and public spheres posits that the role, status, and place of women in society cannot be understood apart from the organization of society as a whole, hence the attention devoted to it. On the other hand, the book looks at women's history from a gendered perspective: in other words, it views sexual identities as social constructs subject to change over time. While maintaining a focus on women it therefore takes into account the ways in which femininity and masculinity have been conjointly and hierarchically defined in different periods, and the male-female power relations that have been the result. Finally, special attention is devoted to other markers of identity – especially social class, ethnicity, and race – that in conjunction with gender have helped to fashion women's historical experience, at least insofar as this can be gleaned from a reading of the sources.

Like any work of synthesis, this book has obviously been shaped not only by previously published work and by the space available, but also by a number of choices that should be clearly articulated. The first concerns the territory to be covered, since the borders of New France and the Province of Quebec as it was in the early days of the British regime were not those of present-day Quebec. For practical reasons, and at the risk of adopting a teleological perspective, we have nevertheless chosen to use the latter geographical framework. As with any historical work, the organization of this survey also rests on a division of time into distinct periods. This is always a delicate undertaking, especially when providing an account of the experience of a heterogeneous group that, far from existing in isolation, has been acted on by the overall economic and political environment, affecting its members to varying degrees and often in very different ways. To effect a meaningful segmentation we had to determine the watershed moments that set the lives of a majority of women on a new course, doing so for reasons that can sometimes be attributed to a single factor but that in most cases were due to a combination of factors, economic, ideological, political, etc. The result is a division into eight chapters covering increasingly shorter periods, reflecting not just the amount of scholarship available but also the speed of the changes that have affected society and women's lives since the last third of the nineteenth century.

The first chapter deals with the period of the French regime and the beginning of British rule, a time when the arrival of French settlers in the St Lawrence Valley transformed the way of life and the organization of First Nations societies – particularly

INTRODUCTION

relations between the sexes – and when a pre-industrial economy created the conditions under which women lived and which were not immediately disrupted by the British Conquest. The second chapter, dealing with the period between 1780 and 1840, opens with the arrival of new women immigrants from the British Isles, altering the composition of the White female population and allowing the new settlers to become permanently established. It studies in particular the consolidation of British colonial society, which led to many changes in women's lives, especially where their political and legal status was concerned, as a consequence of the ongoing economic transformation and the rise of a liberalism that sought to impose a new social order. The period dealt with in chapter 3, from 1840 to 1880, was characterized above all by the completion of the transition from a pre-industrial to an industrial economy, bringing substantial changes in class and gender relations, and by the Catholic Church's assertion of its power, which would exert considerable influence on the lives of French-Canadian women until the mid-twentieth century. Chapter 4 is devoted to the period from 1880 to 1920, during which industrialization and urbanization were intensified, and when women (mostly unmarried) were more largely integrated into the job market. This period was also marked by the appearance of the feminist movement, which along with Quebec nationalism (though the relationship between them was somewhat strained), became one of the most visible social and political movements of the time. The interwar years, studied in chapter 5, saw the appearance of new female role models associated with "modernity," such as the "flapper" and the female athlete, and the period was characterized by a marked decline in the fertility rate, especially among French-Canadian women, by a greater visibility of women in the public arena, and by the adoption of the first social measures affecting women in particular. Chapter 6 covers the next twenty-five years. The winning of female suffrage at the provincial level in 1940 was certainly the outstanding event of this period and justifies the choice of its starting point. However, these years were also characterized by a series of phenomena that heralded a resurgence of feminism in the second half of the 1960s. The most notable of these were the entry of married women into the job market after the Second World War, the social debates about the education of girls and young women, and the demands related to the legal status of married women and women's activism within various associations. The "feminist revolution" that was launched in 1966 with the creation of new organizations, and its relationship to the National Question, were certainly the distinguishing feature of the following period, which ends in 1989 – a year marked by the Daigle-Tremblay case and the massacre at Montreal's École Polytechnique. Finally, chapter 8 examines the following decades, during which neoliberal government policies, the challenge to the "Quebec model," and the diversification of immigration against a background of nationalist debate made for an explosive cocktail that had a profound impact on society and obliged the feminist movement to redefine itself by extending its activity to issues of poverty and the inclusion of immigrant women.

This periodization is not watertight, however, for a number of developments did not lend themselves to enclosure within such precise temporal confines. As a result, the treatment of certain aspects of women's lives occasionally spills across the chronological boundaries of the chapters, in both directions. We should add that the wealth of research available made it impossible to undertake an exhaustive synthesis. We have therefore chosen to emphasize six themes: demographics, education, domestic work and paid employment, religion, the law and the relationship between women and the state, and the social and political activities of women, including the feminist movement. Finally, we should point out that not all of these themes are necessarily considered in every chapter, for in order to economize on space or to develop them more fully certain questions were only dealt with at certain junctures. As with every attempt at a synthesis, therefore, this one offers a partial view of the topic and is, furthermore, presented from an avowedly feminist point of view.

Magda Fahrni and Paul-André Linteau of the History Department of the Université du Quebec à Montreal, and Michèle Gélinas of the Collège de Maisonneuve read an initial version of this manuscript, while my colleague Thomas Wien of the Université de Montreal reviewed chapter 1. I am most grateful to them for their comments and suggestions, though the ultimate responsibility for the text is of course entirely mine.

CHAPTER ONE

Amerindian and French Women during the French Colonial Period

The different places occupied by French and First Nations women in their respective societies during the period when the St Lawrence Valley was settled in the seventeenth century provides an excellent indication of the distance separating them. No less than in their material cultures, there were radical differences between the two groups in the way their societies were organized. These included the relations between the sexes that were much commented upon by explorers, and particularly by the missionaries who arrived along with the first settlers to spread the Catholic faith in the Americas. In their writings, especially the *Relations of the Jesuits*, they expressed great astonishment, and perhaps a lack of understanding tinged with contempt, at the relative equality of the sexes prevailing in certain Aboriginal societies. These men, products of an extremely hierarchical and deeply patriarchal society in which religion not only dictated behaviour but also legitimized the exercise of power and the place allotted to each, have provided accounts that, while imbued with androcentric prejudice, nevertheless, in combination with more recent

CHAPTER ONE

anthropological and archaeological findings, allow us to paint a fairly clear picture of the condition of First Nations women.

At the time when the French settled what would become the land of modern Quebec, the Aboriginal peoples who lived there fell into three large linguistic groups: the Algonquians, the Iroquoians, and the Inuit. The Algonquians, comprising eight different nations (Abenakis, Algonkins, Atikamekw, Cree, Maliseet, Mi'kmaq, Montagnais, and Naskapi), were hunter-gatherers, while the Iroquoians, comprising among other groups the Huron (Wendat) and Iroquois (including the Mohawk), lived, like the Inuit, in semi-sedentary communities. Each of these "nations," as the French called them, were dependent on the work of their women, who made an essential contribution to the survival of the group, since they supplied a significant portion of its diet. Among hunter-gatherers they collected berries and plants and shared in the fishing and even the trapping of small animals. In agricultural societies it was the men who prepared the soil but it was the women who tended the corn, squash, beans, and sunflowers and harvested the crops. Among sedentary tribes, as well as in nomadic ones, it was the women who oversaw the distribution of food. If they did not join in major hunting expeditions (except among the Inuit), it was their task to butcher the meat and prepare the skins to be used for making clothes, moccasins, or tents. Indeed, the women made most of the objects in daily use (containers, baskets, mats, etc.) whether of clay, tree bark, or wicker. They also made the fishing nets and snowshoes and stitched bark to make canoes. In nomadic societies it was also the women who set up and took down the camp and who conveyed the equipment from one location to the next.

This heavy workload of the women was sometimes decried by European observers, who took it as evidence that women were held in low esteem. Yet these same observers also noted the independence the women enjoyed in carrying out their responsibilities, as well as the matrilineal nature of Iroquoian society, in which children belonged to their mothers, who conferred clan identity and honorific titles on them. Missionaries were particularly scandalized by the sexual freedom enjoyed by the young women, by the ease with which divorce was possible, and by husbands' lack of authority. Several nations, especially among the Iroquoians, were matrilocal, meaning that after marriage the man went to live in his wife's family and hunted with it. In addition, families living together in longhouses were headed by women, who were responsible for the management and distribution of foodstuffs, including the produce of the hunt, and for socializing the children.

Indigenous women did not become clan chiefs, but at least among the Iroquoians the most senior among them (elders of matrilineal lines) took part in choosing the chiefs and provided a source of wisdom in the making of collective decisions. Women also had a say over whether prisoners of war would live or die, for they could claim one to replace a dead relative or, on the contrary, hand him over for torture. Where religion was concerned, several First Nations peoples attributed mankind's presence on earth to a mother goddess whom the Huron called Aataentsic, and allotted an important role to women in certain rituals. Moreover, their knowledge of medicinal plants made them respected among their communities.

While it was based on a fairly rigid division of labour along sexual lines, the organization of Aboriginal societies in the American North-East was not hierarchical. Men and women were sovereign in their respective spheres of activity, none of which were especially valued over the others, for each made an essential contribution to the survival of the group. If it cannot be said that Indigenous woman ruled the men (which would have made their societies matriarchal), they certainly enjoyed a degree of independence and a status to which European women of the same period could not aspire. Their major contribution to the subsistence economy of these communities and the control they exercised over the management of the food supply were the basis for the considerable autonomy that they enjoyed. This independence was manifest in the free exercise of their sexuality, in the recognition of a mother's rights over her children, and in certain cases by the part played by clan mothers in political life. The positive reaction to the birth of a daughter, the feminine character of Indigenous creation myths, and the responsibility of women for rituals related to birth, death, and caring represent a number of elements that allow us to conclude that Indigenous women were held in high esteem in their communities.

The arrival of the Europeans had a major impact on the way of life of the First Nations peoples and on the work and status of First Nations women. In addition to spreading viral diseases that wiped out entire populations, the fur trade, by increasing barter, introduced new articles such as copper pots, cloth, etc., replacing items made by Aboriginal women and thus transforming their role. It is true that in some respects these new tools made their workload lighter, but the time saved had to be reinvested in preparing a greater quantity of skins to be used as a currency of exchange. In addition, this upheaval in the material culture was accompanied by missionaries' attempts to redefine gender relations to conform to the Roman Catholic teaching that women should be subordinate to men. Initially, this patriarchal concept of the inequality of the sexes and the male dominance the missionaries were trying to impose met with strong resistance, especially from the women, who had most to lose. However, as time passed, the number of conversions increased, particularly in communities that moved close to the French settlements. Some of the new female converts, such as Catherine Tekakwitha, became fervent Catholics and would be held up by the Church as models of saintliness.

Yet in spite of all this it cannot be said with any certainty that the arrival of the Europeans with their manufactured goods and religious beliefs translated into a loss of status for First Nations women. According to some scholars, the fur trade, which led to more hunting expeditions and intertribal wars, meant that the men were more and more absent from their villages and were also dying in greater numbers, resulting in a strengthening of women's influence. With the men away, women played a greater role in managing the community's affairs and assumed responsibility for integrating the increasingly numerous prisoners that served to replenish the decimated ranks of the tribes. According to this analysis, advanced most notably by the anthropologist Roland Viau, it was the industrialization that began in the mid-nineteenth century that really brought about the loss of status for First Nations women, as female activities became devalued in favour of men's paid employment.

Until the arrival of the "filles du roy," starting in 1663, there were very few White women in the colony, for the fur trade, the basis of its economy, did not require that families be established. It would thus be some time before a settled population became a priority for the home country, with the result that during the early decades the European society implanted along the shores of the St Lawrence remained an essentially male universe. Numbers of coureurs de bois married Aboriginal women, creating family bonds useful to their commercial activities, but these unions were formed and lived out far from what was then called "Canada." Such marriages *à la façon du pays* ("after the custom of the country"), whose number it is impossible to estimate, played a fundamental part in the fur economy and continued throughout the French regime, despite being frequently denounced by the missionaries, who viewed them as a serious offence against Catholic teaching, and also in spite of the uneasiness they caused among the civil authorities, who feared that the Europeans would "go native." In fact, until the 1670s the colonial authorities took quite a favourable view of interracial marriage on condition it was blessed by a priest and not only contributed to increasing the population but also "civilized" the Aboriginals – an undertaking that turned out to be impracticable.

Marie Rollet, who arrived in 1617 with her husband Louis Hébert, an apothecary, is considered the first French woman to have set foot on the soil of New France. But it was not until 1634 that other women gradually began to join her. These included the first nuns, a number of Ursulines and Augustinians, who came ashore at Quebec City in 1639. However, the initial attempts to create a European population, undertaken in particular by the Company of One Hundred Associates, fell far short of restoring demographic equilibrium, since in 1663 there was still only one woman of marriageable age for every six men, making the future of the colony seem to be in serious jeopardy.

The establishment of Royal government in 1663 brought added impetus to immigration. Louis XIV, in his determination to populate this corner of his empire, sent the filles du roy, some 770 young girls, more than half of them coming from the Salpêtrière Hospital in Paris, according to estimates by the demographer Yves Landry. The arrival of these "wards of the King" signified the real beginning of colonial society, for most of them soon married and founded families, ensuring a permanent Francophone presence in the Americas. There has been much speculation about the "virtue" of these immigrant women, suspected of being prostitutes and sometimes compared to merchandise displayed to satisfy the settlers' carnal appetites. However, according to Marie de l'Incarnation, the founder of the Ursuline convent in Quebec City, they were, rather, girls who chose their future spouses with care, preferring men who had already built a home on one of the concessions granted under the seigneurial system. The high fertility rate of these unions resulted in a much more rapid growth of the population, which rose from about 3,000 in 1663 to around 10,000 by 1681. Following this effort to increase the population, which ended in the 1670s, immigration continued throughout the eighteenth century, though less intensively.

By the end of the French regime, the St Lawrence Valley contained between 65,000 and 75,000 inhabitants – an increase due basically to the natural growth of the 10,000 settlers who had made their permanent homes there. Of all those born in France who spent time in the colony, almost 30,000 individuals, only a third remained, compared with 90% of the filles du roy. In the seventeenth century, when men were far more numerous than women, most women married early, before they turned 20, and at 22 on average for the entire period – that is, three years earlier than women in France at the same time. The early marriage age, the greater frequency with which both members of the couple survived until the end of the woman's fertile life, the high proportion of remarriage among widows (at least in the seventeenth century), the availability of land (which allowed everyone an adequate diet), and the infrequency of epidemics in what was a relatively scattered population were all factors that account for the large number of children women gave birth to: eight or nine on average before 1700, and seven after that. Nevertheless, the high infant mortality rate, with one child in four dying before the end of its first year, meant that the average number of children in "complete" families (i.e., those in which both parents survived until the woman's menopause) was 5.6, one more than in France. Yet this large number of children was not uncommon in New World societies, as the case of New England confirms. The availability of land and the need for children to work it (since children were viewed primarily as a potential family workforce) explain these high fertility rates, which therefore seem to have had very little to do with the religion of the settlers or with the natalist policies of the intendant, Jean Talon – who in the seventeenth century rewarded those who married young and had large families and fined those who remained single. Nevertheless, with a birth rate of 50 and even 55 per 1,000, New France seems to have been a particularly fertile part of the world.

Settling in New France meant a life of toil for married couples. For the pioneers it was quite simply a matter of transforming forest into arable land, no easy task since trees had to be cut down, stumps removed, bush burned, stones gathered, and the soil levelled. On lands granted by the local seigneur, the settlers would first construct a one-room log cabin with a roof of branches and bark. Only some years later would it become possible to build a second dwelling, larger and slightly more comfortable, whereupon the first would become a cowshed. In the following years, furniture, dishes, tools, and cattle would be acquired as the cleared area was expanded, becoming an initial inheritance for the offspring who would carry on the farm.

In this pioneering context the women's work was, in many respects, similar to that of the Aboriginal women. But if the unusual circumstances prevailing at the start required that women help with clearing the land (physically demanding work more suited to men), once the family was well established their responsibilities became centred on the children and on producing food. As birth followed birth (one every second year on average during the fertile years), farmers' wives tended the cattle, the poultry, and the vegetable garden and, whenever possible, sold surplus eggs and vegetables at a nearby market, baked the bread, butchered the meat, did the canning, and cooked the meals over an open fire. As they grew up children would help their mothers with these tasks, while the older boys went to work alongside their fathers in the fields. But mothers and daughters would also share in the field work when required, especially at harvest time.

In the towns, which at the time were little more than large villages, it was not unusual for a woman to grow a vegetable garden and raise a few hens or even a few pigs or a cow, practices that would endure well into the nineteenth century. The wives of artisans and small shopkeepers would help with the family business, serving customers, keeping the accounts, and overseeing the apprentices and servants who joined the household. Indeed, so necessary was the woman's contribution to the family enterprise, whether in town or country, that a man could not think of setting up in business without first taking a wife, with the result that widowers, even more than widows, lost no time in remarrying. Day labourers (men hired and paid on a daily basis) doubtless had no inheritance to grow, but they still counted on their wives working as laundresses, seamstresses, or keeping lodgers to help put food on the table. Suzanne Gousse, who has studied the account books of Alexis Lemoine (known as "Monière"), a Montreal merchant, found that he regularly placed orders with seamstresses for various articles such as clothing and tents for use in the fur trade, showing that some women contributed directly to the efficient working of the colony's main economic activity. These occupations, with the addition of midwifery and domestic service, were the main careers open to laywomen until the last third of the nineteenth century.

However, some activities in which women engaged were not always remunerated. If in the mid-eighteenth century there were four midwives in the colony, supported by the king, one for each district in New France, the vast majority of women who engaged in this profession were chosen by the women of their community and might provide their services in return for other than monetary forms of payment. As for domestic servants, usually they did not receive any wages. Whether born into large, economically deprived families or orphaned wards of the king, girls would be placed in service at a very early age and work in return for their keep and a trousseau provided them when they married. Among the domestic servants there were also widows who took employment for a few years and were paid wages, as well as Aboriginal and Black slaves. The economy of the St Lawrence Valley was not dependent on the intensive exploitation of a slave workforce in the same way as the plantations of the American colonies; nevertheless, slavery was not unknown, with the owners of slaves – civil and military officers, merchants, artisans, and religious communities – using them mostly as domestic servants. According to the historian Marcel Trudel, between the creation of the colony and the abolition of slavery in 1834 at least 4,200 individuals lived in slavery. From this group, 52.5% of which were women, history has especially recorded the case of Marie-Josèphe Angélique, a Black slave owned by Thérèse de Couagne, who was accused in 1734 of setting a fire that gutted her owner's house before spreading to the Hôtel-Dieu de Montréal hospital and convent and forty-odd houses. Found guilty, Marie-Josèphe Angélique was hanged and her body burned. According to Denyse Beaugrand-Champagne's analysis of the trial, however, her condemnation was based on rather questionable proof, in particular a confession obtained under torture as well as the evidence of a 4- or 5-year-old. So, rather than an act of revolt by a slave against her condition, as Afua Cooper has interpreted it, it seems quite possible that the fire was completely accidental.

Many households employed a single domestic to help the mother and her daughters with the chores, though upper-class women – the wives of administrators, military officers, merchants, and seigneurs – had an entire staff to relieve them of domestic duties. Yet these women still contributed to the smooth functioning of their households by organizing and supervising the work of the household personnel. More than in any other social group, however, their primary role as upper-class women was to ensure the continuation of the family line. Thus they had numerous children – all the more so since, unlike women of other social groups, they very often enjoyed the services of paid wet-nurses, thereby depriving themselves of the contraceptive effect of breastfeeding. Other responsibilities that fell to them were maintaining social relations useful to their husband's career or business, and establishing their children. If these women were not able to assume public office, they nevertheless kept abreast of the political and commercial dealings that preoccupied colonial high society, for if they were to fulfil their role as mediators properly they needed to be familiar with the interests at stake in the relations between members of the elite. Finally, they paid close attention to the smooth functioning of the family concern, whether a seigneurie or a business, would represent their husbands in court or in commercial transactions at the notary's if the men were unable to attend, and sometimes even took over matters after his death, like the seigneuresse Marie-Catherine Peuvret, studied by Benoît Grenier. Some were fairly successful in business, like Marie-Anne Barbel, who, after the death of her husband Jean-Louis Fornel, carried on his activities in commerce and real estate and also launched out into brick making, or Agathe de Saint-Père, the wife of Legardeur de Repentigny, who established the first Canadian textile industry, or Marie-Thérèse Baby, the widow of Claude Benoist, and her daughter Ursule Benoist, also a widow, who founded Veuves Benoist et Makarty, quite a flourishing wholesale trade. Other examples of female entrepreneurship were provided by single women such as Louise de Ramezay, daughter of the governor of Montreal, who administered seigneuries, sawmills, and tanneries, or the Desaulniers sisters, who kept a store for forty-four years and are even said to have dabbled in the illegal fur trade.

Women of the elite were not the only ones to carry on the family business, for the same could be observed among the widows of artisans, innkeepers, and small shopkeepers. We can assume that this allowed such women to enjoy an economic independence unattainable within marriage; nevertheless, widowhood was not necessarily an enviable condition in a society that considered marriage the natural state of women and allowed them very little latitude to satisfy their needs on an autonomous basis. For many, widowhood meant an impoverishment that, if they lacked a family network to support them, could lead to begging or even prostitution. If colonial society did show compassion towards impoverished widows who were in no way responsible for their fate, it kept a close watch on their behaviour and never failed to show intolerance of those whose sexual behaviour it considered scandalous. The number of abandoned children, which grew along with the population, certainly provides proof of the difficulty of escaping the prevailing moral climate for unmarried mothers (whether widows who conceived after the death of their husband, prostitutes, servants abused by their employers, or young single women seduced by their lovers), even if some of these babies may well have been born to women who were legally married but too impoverished to care for them.

The double standard in sexual matters, the unwritten law that required absolute chastity of women outside of marriage while excusing men's extramarital relations, was only one manifestation of the inequality that characterized their relations. From the point of view of the civil and religious authorities, the "natural" inferiority of women, both physical and moral, destined them to live under the governance of a man, father or husband, who was alone competent to exercise authority within the family. This patriarchal vision, which was shared by the entire society including women themselves, authorized the Church and the law to force them to submit to their husband's will, to obey him, and even to tolerate uncomplainingly the "moderate" physical punishment he might consider it necessary to inflict on them. When Antoine Déat, parish priest of Notre Dame, in a sermon pronounced in 1751, counselled patience and abnegation to those who might have to suffer because of a violent husband, he was in fact merely expressing a broad consensus that still remained unchallenged.

The matrimonial regime of community of goods, which prevailed in New France in accordance with the Paris Custom, which came into force in 1664, confirmed this primacy of the male within the couple while allowing women a measure of economic protection. If the couple had not signed a marriage contract stipulating the separation of goods – which few seem to have done – the law provided that both spouses shared ownership of any movable property brought into the marriage, such as personal effects or tools, as well as any immovable or real property (i.e., land or buildings) purchased after the marriage or inherited from brothers and sisters or from non-relatives. Unless otherwise stipulated in the notarized contract of marriage, each retained ownership of the immovable property they brought into the marriage, as well as inheritances from their parents.

Though the couple's assets belonged equally to both, and though married women did not lose their legal personhood as they did under English law, the fact remains that the husband had sole control, for the Custom considered him the head of the communal estate and the best judge in matters concerning it. This exclusive decision-making power also extended to property belonging exclusively to the wife: though she retained ownership, by virtue of the principle of the legal incapacity of married women which forbade them to make contracts (except in making everyday purchases) or to initiate legal action, only the husband could administer it. Even women who obtained a legal separation from their husbands on grounds of conjugal violence (there was no divorce in New France), or because he was squandering the goods of the community, could not recover their full legal capacity. In such cases, which, according to Sylvie Savoie, numbered little more than 160 throughout the entire French regime, a wife would be allowed to administer her property, but not to dispose of it (i.e., sell or mortgage it) without permission from her husband or a judge. The husband could, however, agree by notarized deed to confer the status of public merchant on his wife, thus allowing her to manage her business independently, or to delegate the management of family business to her, generally during his absence.

Married women, even those legally separated, regained full legal capacity only on the death of their husband. When one of the spouses died, the surviving spouse inherited half the community possessions while the other half went to the children. If a community was deeply in debt, the woman, but not the man, could renounce it: recovering her personal property, she left the creditors to pay themselves out of whatever she left them. Furthermore, under customary law, on the death of her husband a widow was entitled to a dower derived from the income generated by half of the goods brought into the marriage by the husband and half of his inheritances, that is, of his personal possessions that were not part of the joint estate. The marriage contract could permit couples to choose to substitute a predetermined dower (i.e., a sum of money) for the customary dower, or allow the widow to choose between the two. These advantages granted to women were intended to compensate to some extent for the economic dependency in which they found themselves during the years of marriage; furthermore, the husband could not escape the obligation to provide a dower any more than he could disinherit his daughters, for the Custom provided, in principle, for the community to be shared equally between all of the children. It was rare, however, for daughters to inherit land, which was generally left to the sons, one of whom would often compensate his brothers and sisters by buying them out or offering compensation in the form of cattle or tools.

While laywomen were defined by a patriarchal ideology and a legal framework that placed them in a subordinate position, their condition was closely tied to that of their family. Apart from the legal, moral, and religious restrictions that applied to all women, the work they did, the role they played, and the way of life to which they could lay claim depended on the wealth and status of their fathers and husbands, making it impossible to paint a uniform picture of their place in colonial society. The great majority – the wives of habitants, artisans, or small shopkeepers – worked ceaselessly to ensure the survival of the family and their children's future, while only a minority lived a comfortable existence that, though not utterly shiftless, was exempt from physical labour. Many were forced into domestic service during some period of their lives and were subjected to another woman's will; as for slaves, they were completely subservient to their masters and mistresses. Though it was experienced in very different circumstances, motherhood nevertheless represented a common denominator, for it was considered the function of all married women to bear children.

Unmarried women were rare in New France, and usually they were nuns. Driven by a mysticism nurtured by the seventeenth-century

Counter-Reformation, the first nuns, who arrived at Quebec City in 1639 – three Ursulines led by Marie Guyart de l'Incarnation and two Augustinians from Dieppe, Marie Grunet and Marie Forrestier – set out to teach and care for the Aboriginal peoples in the hope of converting them to the Catholic faith. However, this undertaking turned out to be more challenging than they expected. The Augustinian hospital, initially established at Sillery, close to the Amerindian mission, was abandoned in 1644 because of attacks by the Iroquois, forcing the nuns to move to the citadel and offer their services mostly to settlers. In 1672 they were in charge of an establishment with twenty-odd beds; twenty years later, at the archbishop's request, they opened a general hospital, an establishment that, during the *Ancien Régime*, took in orphans, the elderly, the mentally ill, the handicapped, and other disadvantaged persons without discriminating, in order to get them off the streets where they were begging and, in the eyes of the authorities, a threat to public order. As for the Ursulines, they met with stiff resistance from the young Amerindian women they hoped to "civilize." Even if they continued to accept some Native women until the early eighteenth century, they very soon devoted themselves to educating settlers' daughters, who fell into two groups: boarders, who paid for their schooling and thus came from more well-off families, and day pupils from less privileged backgrounds, who were given free schooling in a separate establishment subsidized by the fees of the wealthier students. In both cases, however, the period of schooling remained very brief, amounting at best to one or two years and in most cases to just a few months – long enough to prepare for first communion. Moreover, religious instruction was considered fundamental, along with the domestic arts and the "ornamental branches" for the better-off, with the three Rs making up the remainder of the syllabus.

The Ursuline and Augustinian nuns belonged to established religious orders and were subject to the law of cloister, meaning that they lived and worked inside the convent, to the relief of the religious authorities, always distrustful of women not subject to direct male oversight. In this context, it is not surprising that Jeanne Mance and Marguerite Bourgeoys, two single laywomen who settled in Montreal in 1643 and 1653, respectively, intending to found establishments devoted to care and education, faced considerable opposition from the Church hierarchy. Jeanne Mance, who opened a dispensary, had to battle Mgr de Laval, the bishop of Quebec City, who would have preferred that the Augustinians take charge of it. During a trip to France, determined to keep control of her little hospital, Jeanne Mance recruited a number of nursing sisters from Saint-Joseph-de-la-Flèche; in 1659 the administration of the hospital, named the Hôtel-Dieu de Montréal, came under this community. As for Marguerite Bourgeoys, who wished to devote herself to the education of young girls, both White and Aboriginal, she set out to found a secular institution, a community of pious women devoted to God's service but without taking permanent vows, wearing a habit, or living within convent walls. With a few companions recruited initially in France, and later in the colony, she created a half-dozen small schools, and in 1671 was able to obtain Royal letters patent granting her association legal recognition. However, the status of the "Filles de la congrégation" within the Church remained precarious. Mgr de Saint-Vallier, who succeeded Mgr de Laval, wanted to cloister them and on several occasions insisted that they merge with the Ursulines, which they refused to do. It was not until 1698, two years before the death of its founder, that the Congregation of Notre Dame was canonically established as a lay community (meaning that its members were not cloistered), the first of its kind in Canada and one of the first in the Roman Catholic world.

Marguerite d'Youville was the first Canadian woman to found a lay religious community. Becoming a widow in 1730, she opened a notions store to provide a living for her two sons and with three other young women began visiting the poor in their homes. In 1737 they took a vow to live together in order to devote themselves entirely to caring for the poverty-stricken, though without taking the veil. Historians generally trace the foundation of the Montreal Sisters of Charity to that date, but the Church did not officially recognize the new community until 1755, that is, almost twenty years later. In the meantime, the first four "Sœurs Grises" or "Grey Nuns,"[1] as they were called by the people of Montreal in reference to the colour of their habit, but also to the illegal trade in brandy carried on by Marguerite's husband and father-in-law,[1] began to shelter impoverished women. Their charitable work and their devotedness led the authorities to entrust them with responsibility for the Montreal General Hospital, an establishment founded by the Charon brothers at the end of the seventeenth century that was deep in debt and literally falling into ruin. However, the agreement signed with the colonial government in 1747 was merely provisional, and shortly afterwards, the intendant of New France and the governor, with the approval of Mgr Pontbriand, issued a new order transferring responsibility for the hospital to the Augustinians. The support

---

1 *Gris* in French means both the colour grey and "drunk."

of the people of Montreal and of the Sulpicians would be needed for the Grey Nuns to obtain Royal letters patent in 1753. These recognized the legal existence of the community, and officially and definitively entrusted the administration of the establishment to it. As in Quebec City, the Montreal General Hospital cared for the elderly and for orphans, but it also took in "fallen women," that is, prostitutes and unwed mothers. In times of epidemic or war, when the sick and wounded poured in, this institution also became a real nursing facility.

The fervour and eminently religious purpose of these women should not obscure the fact that they were also uncommonly able administrators. The founding of schools and hospitals in a colony that was barely organized and, in the case of Montreal, living under threat of war with the Iroquois until the early eighteenth century, was indeed a formidable challenge: at a time when the colony itself lacked everything, funding had to be found to construct and expand the establishments, for recruitment, for food, and to provide for the daily life of the community, the pupils, and the sick. Benefiting from political and financial support from France, these female founders also needed to make regular appeals to their protectors to maintain their support despite the opposition they encountered from the colony's civil and religious authorities. All this testifies to their persistence as well as to their political instincts. If they took on so many responsibilities in the name of their religious faith, their achievements nevertheless demonstrate that these women possessed exceptional qualities.

By concerning themselves with children's education, by caring for the sick and the outcast, these religious communities of women provided services essential to the population, as the government recognized in granting them subsidies. In fact it was these early founding women who created the first structures to deal with health, social assistance, and education, structures that would continue to evolve over the next two centuries. These institutions were far from ephemeral; indeed, they would undergo a phenomenal expansion in the second half of the nineteenth century, when the number of religious vocations was very much on the increase. During the period of the French regime, however, their numbers remained small: around 630 women chose a religious life during this period, representing just 3.7% of the entire female population born before 1739. Yet this proportion rose to almost 18% among daughters of the nobility. In comparison, 6% of men from this social class took religious vows, compared with 0.9% of the male population as a whole, for a total of 211 priests and monks. The difference is explained in part by the fact that the Jesuits and the Sulpicians recruited exclusively in France while the female communities very soon became "Canadianized." The high proportion of aristocratic young women in the religious orders was a consequence both of the requirement to pay a substantial dowry on entering a community and of a family strategy designed to avoid splitting inheritances; furthermore, in the absence of an acceptable suitor the nobility considered the religious life a very honourable alternative for its daughters. It should be added that despite the greater prestige enjoyed by the cloistered communities on account of their venerable age, greater numbers of novices were attracted to the lay communities, which did not require such a large dowry. Finally, it should be pointed out that the inequality of worldly society was reproduced within the convents, which housed two classes of nuns: choir sisters, who came from the elite and fulfilled the most prestigious functions as nurses, teachers, and administrators, and converse sisters, of more lowly birth, who looked after the housekeeping duties.

French colonial ambitions in the St Lawrence Valley came to an end with the Seven Years War, which in the Americas was over by 1760. If this ultimate conflict between the French and the British was a particularly trying time for the settlers, especially those upriver from Quebec City on the south shore of the St Lawrence, where farms were systematically burned, the fact remains that, as Louise Dechêne has shown, the entire history of New France was marked by armed conflicts, the brunt of which was borne by the general population. In the seventeenth century, wars with the Iroquois seriously hampered the development of settlements at Montreal, Trois-Rivières, and the surrounding areas, obliging the inhabitants to abandon their farms for safety's sake and take refuge inside the fortifications. Some women did take part in these battles, as is shown by the story of Madeleine de Verchères, who in 1692 almost single-handedly drove off an attack by the Iroquois against the family stronghold. However, such feats of arms were rare. Especially after the 1740s, daughters and wives had to resign themselves to the regular absence of their menfolk when they were called up for fatigue duties and military exercises and expeditions. This was in addition to dealing with the shortages of food, due as much to a lack of hands to work in the fields as to the levies imposed by the army in securing its supplies. The scarcity and astronomic cost of food also became a major problem during the British Conquest, provoking several riots headed by angry women in both Quebec City and Montreal. These food riots, which were equally frequent in Europe during the same period, show that though women were excluded from formal power they did not hesitate to make their voices heard in the public arena when government decisions made a drastic assault on their domestic responsibilities.

The French regime has sometimes been considered a golden age for women, who, according to the interpretation advanced by the historian Jan Noel, received favourable treatment compared with their sisters in the British colonies or modern Europe. It is true that female religious communities played a fundamental part in the development of New France, a role to which the women in the English colonies (where no such communities existed) could not aspire. If the women in charge enjoyed considerable latitude in governing their communities, the fact remains that they were still subject to the power of their bishops, as is shown by Colleen Gray in her study about the first four Mothers Superior of the Congregation of Notre Dame. It can also be said that the legal framework afforded married women better protection than English common law, and that a number of them were called on to replace their spouses when they were absent because of a military expedition, the fur trade, or a trip to France. However, when they acted in their husband's name, women were generally equipped with a power of attorney that clearly defined the limits of their freedom to act, while the case of "businesswomen" – female shopkeepers, merchants, and traders – had numerous equivalents elsewhere. In other words, the women of the French colonial society were just as subject to male domination, even if it did take a different form in French Canada.

The British Conquest did not have the same consequences for all women, as was also the case for the population as a whole.

CHAPTER ONE

Many female members of the elite accompanied their husbands or fathers when they left the colony, but most remained, no doubt hoping that when peace was restored their lives could resume a more normal course. Unlike male religious communities, the women's communities were left alone by the British authorities, who no doubt felt that they made an indispensable contribution to the welfare of the population, as the hospital nurses of Quebec City had demonstrated in caring for British soldiers. Shortly after the change of regime the authorities recognized the principal institutions that had shaped the lives of the French settlers: the civil law, the Catholic Church, and the French language. The establishment of this new political order, combined with major economic changes, would eventually have serious repercussions on women's lives, while after the end of the eighteenth century their ethnic composition would change gradually with the influx of a significant minority of women from England, Scotland, and later Ireland.

CHAPTER TWO
....

The Early Years of British Rule (1780–1840)

Until 1783 the fact that there was a new colonial power did not fundamentally alter the sociodemographic character of the Francophone Catholic society that existed along the shores of the St Lawrence. The Royal Proclamation of 1763, which established the territorial and administrative structures of the new entity called the Province of Quebec, aimed to make the colony more "British" by imposing common law and favouring the Anglican Church and its members. However, the small number of people of British extraction – a few hundred merchants, administrators, and soldiers residing in Quebec City and Montreal – was an impediment to such an undertaking. In 1774, given the low rate of British immigration into this new possession and the growing discontent of the inhabitants of the Thirteen Colonies that would become the United States of America, Great Britain finally abandoned the policy. In 1774, to ensure the loyalty of its new French-speaking subjects, the United Kingdom passed the Quebec Act, recognizing the Roman Catholic Church and retaining French civil law and the seigneurial system of tenure, while failing to create the elected assembly called for by the British merchants.

It was the end of the American Revolutionary War rather than the British Conquest that brought about a decisive change in the ethnolinguistic character of Quebec. In the early 1780s approximately 2,000 Loyalists took refuge in Quebec, with a few hundred settling in the region of Montreal and around Sorel, while most became established in the south of the province. This first group of migrants also included a number of Iroquois who had remained faithful to the British Crown as well as a few Afro-Americans, some of them slaves brought by their masters, while others had regained their freedom by fleeing to the New England colonies. Beginning in 1791 they would be followed by thousands of American settlers from New England who settled mainly in the Eastern Townships, causing the number of English-speakers to swell from 500 in 1762 to 50,000 in 1815, out of a total population of over 340,000. These new arrivals had to start again from nothing, clearing the land granted them by the government. As in the past the women played an indispensable part in establishing their families. Like the pioneer women of New France, they shared in the various types of labour required to transform forest into arable land; later they would contribute to the development of the family farm by tending the vegetable garden, the poultry, and the cattle, and helping with the field work, in addition to feeding and clothing their families and caring for the children.

The arrival of these English-speaking settlers did not merely alter the demographic portrait of Quebec and expand the territory's cultivated area: it also made an important impact on the political future of the colony and on women's rights. Coming from states with elected assemblies, the new arrivals, supported by members of the emergent Francophone bourgeoisie, would very soon call for the creation of a similar institution in the new British colony. The pressure they exerted on the colonial authorities led to the Constitutional Act of 1791, establishing both a new political structure and a new division of the territory. The Province of Quebec, which had previously included the upper valley of the St Lawrence and Lake Ontario, was divided into two new colonies separated by the Ottawa River. To the west was Upper Canada, which after Confederation would become Ontario, and to the east was Lower Canada, which after 1867 would again be called Quebec. Henceforth, each of these two colonies was able to elect an assembly, though its powers were strictly limited, executive authority being concentrated in the hands of a governor, a legislative council, and an executive council, none of which was answerable to the Legislative Assembly. In Lower Canada the control exerted by the representatives of the Crown over the elected assembly was very soon castigated by its members, the majority of whom were French-speaking, and it would become one of the causes of the Rebellions of 1837–38 (to which we shall return). The property qualification established by the Constitutional Act of 1791 was, however, set very low, granting the vote to most rural property owners and tenants aged 21 and over who were British subjects, as well as to a substantial proportion of urban artisans. In addition, given that the law granted the vote to "persons" satisfying these requirements, several female property owners – mainly widows, but also single women who had reached the age of majority and women married under the regime of the separation of property or wives legally separated from their husbands – were able to avail themselves of this right, at least until 1849. However, the Constitutional Act specified that only men could be elected: in other words, though they could vote, women could not be candidates.

After 1815 the Anglophone population that settled in Lower Canada, and which numbered about 50,000 up to 1851, came essentially from the British Isles. The industrial and agricultural crisis that befell Great Britain after the Napoleonic Wars set off a wave of emigration to the British colonies in North America that would last through a good part of the nineteenth century. English, Scots, and Irish (the last driven from their country in great numbers by the famine that raged there in the late 1840s), they swelled the Anglophone ranks, while the increase in the Francophone population was basically the result of natural growth. However, a high birth rate was typical among all families in Lower Canada, whatever their origin, for children represented an indispensable workforce for the mostly rural population, while among the better-off they ensured the continuation of the family line and fortune. As a result, families of seven or eight children were common during this period, with numerous births occurring at regular intervals in the lives of married women, who were expected to combine pregnancy, giving birth, breastfeeding, and caring for young infants, with work on the farm, or in the workshop, or with the social responsibilities required by their rank.

Until 1850 barely more than 15% of the total population lived in towns and cities. However, Anglophones became urbanized faster. While they represented a little less than a quarter of the inhabitants of Lower Canada in 1844, by 1831 they already comprised 33% of the population of Quebec City, and in Montreal 50%. It should be pointed out that the administrators, magistrates, entrepreneurs, and merchants who presided over the political and economic destiny of the colony were concentrated in the towns and that a substantial proportion of them were of British extraction. Yet the majority of urban-dwelling Anglophones were not members of the elite: in Quebec City 39% of the artisans and 51% of the day labourers were English-speaking, while in Montreal they amounted to 55% and 53% of those same groups, respectively.

Lower Canada remained an essentially pre-industrial society with an economy based on agriculture, artisanal production, and local, regional, and international trade, with wood the main resource exported to Britain during this period. Beginning in the early nineteenth century, forestry created a great deal of employment for men, whether in logging camps or in the sawmills, which grew rapidly in number. In the 1820s thousands of workers were hired to construct the Lachine Canal, the completion of which facilitated trade with Upper Canada. The dockyards of Montreal, but especially of Quebec City, the ports, and a few manufacturing industries (breweries, distilleries, flour mills, and foundries) also employed male labour. As for the women, they continued to work in the domestic environment, even when they had jobs.

Thus, just as in the eighteenth century, a considerable number of girls were put into domestic service by their parents, while some, often immigrants, placed small advertisements in Quebec City and Montreal newspapers looking for employment. In one of these ads, which appeared in the *Quebec Mercury* in 1817, an Irishwoman of medium age, recently arrived from Dublin, offered her services as a cook, governess, general help, laundress, or farmhand, stating she was able to make butter "in a superior stile [*sic*]" and proclaiming her readiness to work in town or country. The text of this request for employment provides a good glimpse of the range of tasks entrusted to servants, though it is far from an exhaustive list. Lighting fires in the morning and putting them out at night, looking after the children, sewing and mending, shopping, and serving clients, in the case of families of artisans or small shopkeepers, were all potential additional duties. In fact, most often, domestic servants were general helps, for most families – 60% according to Claudette Lacelle's estimates – lacked the means to hire more than one servant, even though the families that employed household help were numerous. For instance, in Quebec City almost one household in five had at least one domestic servant in the early nineteenth century, while in the Upper Town, where the elite were concentrated, this proportion rose to 40%. This was also where the highest concentration of households employing more than two servants was found.

Whether they worked alone or were part of a larger staff, women domestics had to work long days (15 hours on average) with hardly any time off (one afternoon a week in the best of cases). So working conditions were poor, but it should be said that in those days most women worked equally hard. For girls from poor families that were unable to provide for their needs, working as a domestic at least brought the assurance that they would be fed and clothed, while for immigrant women who arrived penniless and alone entering domestic service was one of the few ways available to earn a respectable living in a society that offered women very limited options and looked askance on those who led independent lives. Since servants usually lived in their employers' house, this kind of work was considered suitable for women because it kept them in a family setting where, ostensibly, they were safer. But this situation had many disadvantages. Frequently isolated, domestic servants had to put up with the demands of their masters and mistresses, who could take advantage of them with complete impunity. In this respect, though it is impossible to generalize, it can be said that the relations between employers and female servants depended both on the age of the latter (the youngest perhaps being treated like a child of the family) and also on the size of the domestic staff, for families that employed several servants had a contractual rather than a paternalistic relationship with them. Beside those who remained in the service of the same family for many years and so developed an intimate relationship with its members, many others – about two-thirds – took this kind of employment only temporarily when they were between the ages of 16 and 25, and they frequently changed employers, suggesting dissatisfaction on one side or the other. This means that many suffered from a lack of stability and security, since abandoning or losing their employment also meant losing the roof over their heads. If conflicts with employers explain this mobility, it can also be ascribed to the sexual abuse and assaults to which female servants were subjected. A study of court cases involving single mothers in the second half of the nineteenth century, carried out by Marie-Aimée Cliche, does show that female servants were over-represented in them. Whether on account of a pregnancy or not, those who lost their employment and were unable to find another were often reduced to prostitution in order to survive.

According to a census carried out in Montreal in 1835 by Jacques Viger, a future mayor of the city, at least 20% of women had jobs, while they comprised 26% of the population that claimed to be in employment – a higher proportion than at the end of the century. This relatively high participation of women in the formal economy can be largely explained by the large number of domestic servants, who formed 56% of the female workforce, while another 26% were classified as "day labourers." These two occupations alone accounted for 82% of the women who indicated employment, a concentration of the workforce that would long remain one of the features of women's paid work. The other female occupations most frequently reported by Viger – governess, laundrywoman, midwife, seamstress, or milliner – called on the competencies traditionally ascribed to women, though Viger does mention a few that were firmly outside that range, such as blacksmith, coach builder, gardener, or farmer. Innkeeper, merchant, weaver, corset maker, and milliner were also among the women's occupations listed, while about thirty said they were teachers. Viger did not list any landladies, but we can suppose that many women kept boarding houses, another important female activity in towns where many single travellers were arriving or passing through. This may indicate that not all women's activities were recorded systematically, a common problem in researching women's paid employment in the nineteenth and early twentieth centuries. In Quebec City, the 1851–52 census shows that twenty-five women owned such establishments, while almost 13% of them listed an occupation, representing 20% of the city's total workforce. As in Montreal, domestic servants were a clear majority, amounting to 60% of working women compared with 23% for female artisans, labourers, and day workers.

In the great majority of cases, women who were not in domestic service carried on their occupation in the home or in a shop attached to it, allowing them to combine family and professional duties. There was therefore no watertight separation between women's domestic and paid work, for the two kinds of activity were combined within the same space and overlapped in many respects, since women most often used competencies acquired in the course of their socialization as a source of income. Even teachers (other than nuns, a minority at the time) frequently lived and worked in the same place. Anglophone women recently arrived from the United States or Great Britain with a minimal amount of schooling as their only qualification were particularly active in this occupation, even if Francophone women were not completely lacking. At a time when the government played a very small part in education, a simple advertisement in a newspaper could allow a woman to recruit a number of pupils to whom she would teach some rudiments of the three Rs, and in the case of girls (who made up the large majority of their clientele), various types of needlework. However, since there was no law obliging children to attend school, parents could decide to keep them at home for a few days or weeks or take them out of school when they were needed, which perhaps partially explains the ephemeral existence of many such establishments. Yet this lack of stability does not seem to have discouraged candidates, since the number of lay teachers grew, keeping pace with immigration: according to Andrée Dufour, eighty-one were enumerated in Montreal in 1835 (sixty-eight Anglophones and thirteen Francophones) and fifty-two in Quebec City in 1851 (though this figure does appear to include the Ursulines). No doubt teaching allowed immigrant women to earn a living or contribute to their family's budget for a few months or years, long enough to get on a more solid financial footing – a concern that also motivated their Francophone colleagues. However, some did pursue a genuine career as teachers, as is indicated by the existence of boarding schools and academies that catered to a middle-class clientele and survived for several decades. In such establishments girls learned not only the basic subjects but also grammar, history, and geography, as well as dancing, drawing, painting, music, singing, and embroidery – all the accomplishments needed to shine in "good" society.

In rural areas the adoption in 1829 of a law establishing "trustee schools" opened up careers in teaching to laywomen. Two years later women already numbered almost half the teachers, a proportion that grew to 63% by the mid-nineteenth century. According to Andrée Dufour and Micheline Dumont, this feminization of the teaching profession was largely due to a reduction in government salaries, starting in 1832. Seeing the success achieved by these schools, which already numbered 981 only a year after their creation, the government decided to limit the budgets for elementary teachers. The result was that many men chose to leave the profession, especially since teaching at the primary level was not viewed as a very prestigious career. For women, on the other hand, the conditions were still appealing for, unlike the men, their opportunities for employment were rare in rural areas and because they considered teaching a good preparation for marriage and their future role as mothers. Teaching young children at the primary level thus became an occupation closely associated with the attributes of femininity, something that was not without consequences for the future of the profession.

Prostitution was a last resort to which a substantial minority of women were reduced in order to survive. The phenomenon was not unknown in the days of New France, but it expanded anew thanks to the growth in commercial and port activity and the increased presence of sailors and soldiers in the colony's two major cities. In 1823 there were at least forty brothels in Montreal; two years later Viger counted twenty "madams" and a hundred or so "streetwalkers" – that is, 6% of the women who declared an occupation. This number certainly grew considerably over the following decades, for in 1843, according to the figures established by Mary Anne Poutanen, it was possible to identify 150 bawdy houses. The growth of the Montreal population, which doubled during this period, added to the presence of large numbers of soldiers and of labourers hired to dig the Lachine Canal and improve the port facilities, provide a partial explanation for this increase. But the identification of a larger number of brothels in the city was very likely also related to the lower tolerance of prostitution by bourgeois society, resulting in an increase in complaints to the police. The 1851 census found thirty or so prostitutes and fewer than a dozen brothels in Quebec City, but just as in Montreal, these figures were probably an underestimate, for many women practised prostitution on a temporary or occasional basis to supplement their incomes or tide them over between jobs, so that they were not counted. It also seems reasonable to assume that not all women were prepared to admit their involvement in prostitution. Patriarchal society, which tolerated sexual misdemeanours on the part of men while at the same time it restricted employment possibilities for women, helped to fuel the sex trade. For the poorest and most isolated women – those who could not count on the help of a family, those ostracized because of an extramarital pregnancy or left penniless when their husbands died – prostitution was frequently the last remaining way to survive and provide for their children.

CHAPTER TWO

Despite their privileged situation, female members of the merchant bourgeoisie and middle classes were not idle. In addition to caring for their children, they always played a prominent part in maintaining family and social relationships and would take over during their husbands' absences. Far from being restricted to the family their responsibilities extended to the community, where they pursued various activities. For instance, starting early in the nineteenth century middle-class women founded numerous organizations that became grafted onto the network of social assistance that the nuns had instigated under French rule. The urban poverty engendered by seasonal unemployment, epidemics, and the arrival of penniless immigrants provided the impetus for this philanthropic activity, which was also motivated by the religious conviction that the better-off had a duty to practise charity towards the weak. The fear that the impoverished masses might disrupt public order or spread disease in their wake also had something to do with this phenomenon. In the absence of any sustained public intervention (since the government was content to subsidize their activities only partially) these women banded together, raising funds and launching initiatives to alleviate the direst consequences of poverty in a society that was becoming less and less tolerant towards those it marginalized. Far from being confined to their homes, as was desired by the ideology of separate spheres – which would gain greater currency throughout the nineteenth century – women from the better-off strata of society thus played a fundamental part in caring for the destitute, who continued to grow in numbers as the liberal economy imposed its new rules of the game.

The Female Benevolent Society, founded in 1815 by a group of English-speaking Montreal women including Eleanor Gibb,

H.W. Barrett, and Janet Finlay Aird, was one of the first organizations created by laywomen at this time. In the announcement published shortly before its launch these women spoke of their distress at the poverty they witnessed and affirmed their desire to relieve the suffering of women, infants, the sick, the aged, and the disabled. Thanks to the funds raised through charitable activities such as rummage sales, they distributed food, firewood, clothing, and medicine to the needy. They also opened a house to allow immigrants arriving through Quebec City to rest before travelling on towards Upper Canada, and they assisted women in labour. In 1822 in light of a shortage of beds in the General Hospital and the Hôtel Dieu, they created a small hospital, later to become the Montreal General Hospital (now one of the components of the McGill University Health Centre). That same year they also founded the Protestant Orphan Asylum for Anglo-Protestant children. After ten years of inactivity this organization was reborn as the Montreal Ladies' Benevolent Society, a change of name that reflected the more elite membership of its board, "Ladies" seeming more dignified than "Female." The Society would continue its activities into the twentieth century, providing assistance to impoverished women and children, while the management of the hospital and orphanage was taken over by men.

The Hôtel-Dieu de Montréal and the General Hospital, administered by the nuns of St Joseph and the Grey Nuns, respectively, were two other major establishments that cared for the sick, the aged, and the orphans of Montreal. Their activities grew along with the population and as social problems became more numerous, as is indicated by the number of orphans taken in by the Crèche d'Youville, which rose from an average of 50 per annum between 1800 and 1823 to 120 during the following two decades. However, the membership of these two communities remained quite small: in 1840, for instance, there were only thirty-seven Sisters of St Joseph and thirty-three Grey Nuns. Starting in the 1820s they received reinforcements from newly created lay organizations. Thus in 1827 on the instigation of Angélique Blondeau, the widow of Gabriel Cotté, a fur merchant, fifteen women from bourgeois Francophone families founded the Dames de la Charité. Initially, these ladies visited the poor in their homes, distributed aid to them, opened a soup kitchen, and set about finding work for unemployed servant women. Three years later they were also accepting destitute elderly women into a house lent to them by the Sulpicians, and soon added orphaned children, while in 1832, the year of a terrible cholera epidemic that left many children alone in the world, they decided to devote themselves entirely to the orphans and accordingly changed their name to Dames de l'Asyle des Orphelins Catholiques Romains. Beginning in 1889 the Grey Nuns took over the internal management of their establishment, which in 1916 officially changed its name to Orphelinat Catholique. Émilie Tavernier-Gamelin, who had been active in the Dames de la Charité, chose instead to continue her care for aged, disabled women, initially taking them into her own home until in 1836 she moved them to a house donated by Olivier Berthelet, a wealthy Montreal businessman. This soon became known as the "Maison de la Providence." In the very early 1840s this establishment was officially baptized the Asile de Montréal pour les femmes âgées et infirmes. In 1841 the ladies in charge of it created another association, the Société des dames de la Providence, to provide assistance to the poor in their homes. Two years later, at the instigation of Mgr

Ignace Bourget, the bishop of Montreal, this charity would give birth to the Congregation of the Sisters of Providence. This community numbered fifty-one nuns in 1850.

It is true that these women participated in the creation of a double network of private charities along linguistic and religious lines; however, during the first four decades of the nineteenth century their philanthropic activities were actually characterized by a degree of ecumenism. The mixed marriages that took place between members of the elite in the early days of British rule, though not very common, did encourage cooperation between Anglophones and Francophones, while on the Protestant side members of different churches – Anglicans, Presbyterians, and later Methodists – often worked together in the same organizations. In 1831, for instance, Catholic and Protestant women's associations in Montreal organized a joint rummage sale, dividing the profits between them. Marie-Charles-Joseph Le Moyne, the seigneuresse of Longueil and widow of Captain David Grant, became the first president of the Catholic orphanage founded by the Dames de la Charité and the second president of the Protestant orphanage established by the Female Benevolent Society. From the time of the British Conquest nuns had opened their establishments to English-speaking Protestants, and in 1822–23, a year marked by a typhus epidemic that took several hundred victims, the Grey Nuns dealt with more Protestants than Catholics, including a substantial number of Irish orphans. The terrible cholera epidemic of 1832 also united these women in a joint effort to combat the spread of the disease, care for the sick in hospitals and hastily erected makeshift shelters, and assist the families of victims. In Quebec City in 1820, where women from the elite were similarly involved in helping the poor, especially mothers and children, members of both linguistic communities, under the patronage of Lady Dalhousie, the wife of the lieutenant-governor of Nova Scotia, founded a bilingual organization, the Female Compassionate Society of Quebec / La Société compatissante des Dames de Québec, which helped poor women of both French- and English-speaking backgrounds without making any distinction.

The rise of ethnic tensions that began in the 1830s would become an impediment to such collaboration. The events leading to the Rebellions of 1837–38, an episode that marked the culmination of the conflict between the mostly French-speaking members of the Legislative Assembly and the executive powers – composed almost entirely of members of the elite of British extraction – were accompanied by a hardening of religious attitudes on both sides. In response to the proselytizing by evangelical Protestant groups that began in the 1830s, the Catholic Church asserted a stronger hold over Catholics, which in its view required among other things an increase in the number of female religious communities to work with the poor. The founding of the Sisters of Providence was typical of this trend, which gained in strength after 1840, driven by the ultramontanist ideology, which affirmed the supremacy of the spiritual over the temporal and called for the primacy of church over state, and of which Mgr Bourget was one of the most fervent advocates. Among Catholics, the social services, like education, therefore became increasingly dominated by nuns working under the aegis of the Church, while Anglo-Protestants saw certain of their charities, such as the Montreal General Hospital and the Protestant Orphan Asylum, come under male administration. The 1840s seem to have been decisive in this respect. This decade was, indeed, characterized by a marked change of attitude towards women and the place allotted to them in society. This was a consequence of the rise of a wealthy liberal bourgeoisie embodied by the Patriot movement, for the men who led the Rebellions of 1837–38 shared a certain number of prejudices about women and the roles appropriate to their sex. The principles associated with the bourgeois democracy to which they subscribed prompted them to uphold civil liberties, advocate secularism, and call for ministerial responsibility, but they were also agreed in linking the exercise of citizenship to the ownership of property and in affirming that the latter was an inviolable right. Above all, their republicanism led them to try to exclude women from political life. This was because for republicans the exercise of citizenship required detachment from the private sphere, an essential condition if one wished to work for the common good. In their eyes, women, as the reproducers and sustainers of life, could not satisfy such a requirement, for their primary allegiance lay necessarily within the family. This was why they held that the participation of women in political life was contrary to nature – in fact they even saw it as a sign of sexual immorality, since women who flaunted themselves in public could hardly be more worthy of respect than a prostitute, who was after all called a *femme publique*, a "public woman." Indeed, some Patriots did not hesitate to liken Queen Victoria, who had come to the throne in 1837, to a "whore," thereby associating British "tyranny" with the sex and supposed sexual misdemeanours of the new sovereign. This combination shows that men favoured a new perception of women's role in society – a perception that had also imbued the bourgeois revolutions in France and America. In the minds of republicans, men's ability to engage in political action depended entirely on their womenfolk confining themselves to the family, since by running the household and rearing the children they freed men from these chores and allowed them to carry out their civic duties more effectively, while preparing their sons to become good citizens. Women thus filled a role essential to the working of the republic, one they could not abandon without threatening the social order and public welfare, which thus became associated with a new, much more inflexible sociosexual order sanctioned by the ideology of separate spheres. Indeed, the confinement of women to the private sphere became a sign of respectability, while venturing into the public arena seemed evidence of an immodesty bordering on an indecency that was only likely to encourage moral degeneracy, including in political matters.

During the years leading up to the 1837–38 Rebellions this conception of women's place in society took the form of an increasingly vigorous challenge of women's right to vote – a challenge facilitated by the electoral procedures in force. It should be remembered that at the time voters were required to prove before a scrutineer and the candidates that they were qualified to vote; then they announced their choice aloud, upon which it was entered in a register, or poll book. The poll remained open until an hour went by without anyone appearing to vote, so that the election could last several days. According to the analysis of the surviving poll books, carried out by Nathalie Picard, some 900 women took part in elections between the end of the eighteenth century and the 1830s. However, their eligibility to vote was frequently challenged by scrutineers, who could reject voters at their leisure or ask them to take an oath when they doubted their status as property owners. The depth of the controversy surrounding the matter is shown by a petition addressed to the Assembly in 1828 challenging the results of the election held the previous year in the Upper Town of Quebec City on the grounds that widows had been denied their right to vote, while a second petition called for the result to be rejected in another riding (William Henry) because women *had* voted. In the Montreal West by-election of 1832 numerous women, mostly wives who owned property separately from their husbands, but also some single women, were disqualified. Unlike widows, who had less difficulty in exercising their right to vote, these women were held to be living under the tutelage of a male, whether father or husband, so that in the view of scrutineers and candidates the proofs of independence that were recognized in the case of widows were not acceptable in theirs.

The ability of women to cast an informed vote without interference from the male members of the household was much debated in the newspapers of the colony from the early 1820s on. For those opposed to granting women the vote, their presence in polling stations was an aberration and even represented a threat to democracy, for like drunkards they were more liable to be influenced by the candidates or induced to vote for the sole purpose of preventing the polling stations from closing, thus blocking the election of a candidate who had already won a majority. The parties and the political press on each side accused one another of exploiting the female vote and tried to denigrate their opponents by claiming they had become so desperate that they had been obliged to turn to women for support. This kind of discourse was especially pernicious, not only because it cast doubt on women's independence of thought and action and defined the legitimate voter as a male, but also because, in the same breath, it cast doubt on the manhood of those who accepted women's right to vote.

CHAPTER TWO

The by-election of 1832 in the riding of Montreal West, the longest in the entire history of Lower Canada and the one during which the largest number of women tried to record their votes – 226 in all – was followed two years later by the adoption of a law intended to deprive women of the vote. The inquiry into the violent demonstrations that followed the by-election and resulted in three deaths on the Patriot side did turn a spotlight on the female vote, as Bettina Bradbury has shown. At the conclusion of the inquiry, John Nielson, a moderate Patriot member of the Assembly, submitted a draft law that among its other provisions deprived women of the vote. Louis-Joseph Papineau supported it in these terms: "As for the practice of letting women vote, it is just that it be destroyed. It is ridiculous, it is odious, to see women dragged to the hustings by their husbands, daughters by their fathers, often even contrary to their will. The public interest, decency, and the modesty of the sex require that such scandals be no longer repeated." Using a typically republican logic, Papineau was thus lumping together the public interest, female decency, and the exclusion of women from the vote – an argument that met with the Assembly's approval. So it cannot be said that the Patriots withdrew the vote from women solely in order to prevent Anglophone women from supporting the government party, even if we can also read between the lines of Papineau's words an attack on Marie-Claire Perrault (the wife of Austin Cuvillier, a member of the Legislative Assembly and former member of the Patriot Party who had defected), who had voted for the colonial establishment's candidate. However, the law abolishing female suffrage would not be adopted until 1849, for the version presented in 1834 was rejected, though for unrelated reasons. It is very revealing that the exclusion of women from the vote did not elicit any protest from them: by the end of the 1840s the ideology of separate spheres had done its work so well that women themselves seem to have accepted a strictly male definition of citizenship.

The Patriots' desire to exclude women from political citizenship did not prevent them from calling on their support during the events of 1837–38, as long as they respected the norms restricting them to the domestic sphere. Thus women were urged to support the cause by boycotting British imports, especially cloth, which they were encouraged to manufacture themselves. In other terms, they were appealed to not only as consumers but also as producers, since their domestic production was supposed to replace the purchases from which they would abstain. In these appeals to female industry the Patriots were also establishing a link between female modesty and the national cause, portraying the preference for imported fashion over simple, locally made materials as a threat to the colony's prosperity as much as to feminine virtue. The Patriots also encouraged the creation of patriotic women's associations such as the Association des dames patriotiques du comté des Deux-Montagnes, though these seem to have played quite a marginal role, for if we can be sure that women did attend revolutionary meetings, make banners, melt spoons to make munitions, and hide fugitives, no examples have been found of them taking any active share in the fighting or even giving massive support to male revolutionary activities. Quite to the contrary, it seems that many women implored their husbands or sons not to take part in a battle that they considered doomed to failure. It has to be said that in the final analysis the Patriots did very little to include women in their national project, their position on women's suffrage acting instead as a deterrent. The two rare examples of woman bearing arms during the risings, Hortense Globensky and Rosalie Cherrier, were supporters of the government forces who were attempting more than anything to defend their person and property against the attacks of Patriots outraged at their choice to side with the Crown. As for female participation in meetings, it is interesting to note that as in the polling stations their presence was represented by the Constitutional Party as tangible proof of the small support the Patriots were able to attract and of the weakness of their movement.

The 1830s also witnessed a change of attitude among the Patriots towards the dower, which initially they had defended. On their arrival in the colony, the British merchants objected to this inalienable right granted to women by the Paris Custom, considering it an infringement of their freedom of contract. The dower – in other words the right of widows to derive income from half of their husband's property at the time of their marriage or acquired subsequently through inheritance – actually remained attached to the land, even if the husband decided to sell it. Since women could not renounce this customary dower without signing a marriage contract, and since the dower took precedence over any other debt, it provided significant protection for widows, but it was also a real headache for anyone wanting to carry out real estate transactions, for a buyer could discover several years after the fact that a widow had a claim on his property. Because of the growing population and successive changes of ownership, this situation was more common in the towns than in rural areas, where the inhabitants knew the identities of previous owners of the land they wished to acquire. From the point of view of the British merchants, however, the customary dower was equivalent to a hidden lien that discouraged the sale of lands and the accumulation of real estate for speculative purposes, so that from the early nineteenth century they had been combatting this practice. If they were not simply able to obtain the abolition of the customary dower, they demanded the creation of registration offices so that anyone could have access to reliable information about the liabilities attached to real estate.

Until the mid-1830s the major French-speaking political leaders were opposed to this measure, for they thought that the customary dower proved the superiority of French law in protecting widows and their children. Subsequently, however, their position shifted closer to that of the British merchants. With a membership composed of professionals, landowners, and merchants in the process of consolidating their economic base, the Patriot Party also came to see the customary dower as a serious curb on men's ability to deal in land with total peace of mind, as well as an obstacle to capital investment and the creation of industries in the colony. In any case, the Declaration of Independence that was proclaimed in 1838 by the Patriot Robert Nelson called for the abolition of the customary dower and the creation of registration offices.

Yet it was the special council appointed after the defeat of the Patriots to govern the colony pending the election of a new assembly that made fundamental changes in the law concerning the dower. On the one hand, the council's order required the registration of pre-established dowers (i.e., those determined by a marriage contract) to ensure that a widow would have precedence over any other creditor in benefiting from the usufruct of properties inherited from her husband. In addition, lands to which this dower applied had to be clearly identified. On the other hand, the order entitled women to consent to the alienation of the property to which the customary dower would otherwise apply. Finally, it also stipulated that the customary dower could apply only to land owned by the husband at the time of his death. This order, therefore, did not entirely abolish the customary dower, something that would not happen until 1866 with the adoption of the Civil Code. However, it did do away with its inalienable character by allowing women to consent to the sale of lands to which it applied, meaning that their rights over such lands would be extinguished, since from then on the dower would apply only to lands owned by the husband at his death.

By restricting the application of the customary dower in this way, and requiring that pre-established dowers be registered, these measures made it easier for investors to accumulate property with the intent of profiting from its purchase and resale. So the older idea according to which women enjoyed inalienable rights in return for their subordinate status within marriage was swept aside in favour of a concept based on the freedom of individuals, essentially males, to make contracts. In this way, the widow's entitlement to a dower, as well as the relationship between husband and wife within marriage, were reshaped to facilitate the development of an emergent capitalist economy. However, it was during the second half of the nineteenth century that this economy would shift into top gear, bringing new changes to which women, like their families, would have to adapt.

CHAPTER THREE

A Society on the Path to Industrialization (1840–1880)

Around the middle of the nineteenth century Quebec had not yet become an industrial society, but it was clearly about to do so. Railway construction, which really began at the end of the 1840s, gave a major boost to this economic restructuring. Not only did the ability to convey freight by rail facilitate commercial exchange, it also led to the creation of factories and workshops (to manufacture rails, rolling stock, and locomotives, and for maintenance) employing a growing workforce and requiring a supply of many kinds of equipment, making it a driving force for the production of manufactured goods as a whole. While railway construction underwent a spectacular development, foundries, metal workshops, as well as flour mills, sugar refineries, and other manufacturing concerns related to food production, forestry, tanning, and textiles, were constantly growing up along the Lachine Canal and nearby, so that by 1871 they numbered around sixty and employed almost 5,000 workers. Beginning in the 1860s the introduction of new techniques and new manufacturing processes (most notably the steam engine) accelerated the rate of production, with some establishments employing hundreds of workers. In return, this urban working class provided a market for manufactured goods, which gradually replaced certain products that had previously been homemade.

Of course, these changes occurred at very different rates depending on the type of production and the region. Montreal, the home of a wealthy Anglophone bourgeoisie that owned a very large share of the capital required for the development of infrastructure and means of production, certainly took first place among the province's industrial towns and cities and was already doing so by the 1840s. But entrepreneurs also established factories, especially in the fields of textiles, leather, and timber in several towns and cities such as Hull, Sherbrooke, Trois-Rivières, Valleyfield, and Saint-Hyacinthe, in addition to Quebec City, where the footwear industry replaced the shipyards that were in decline due to the advent of metal steamships, replacing wooden ships.

Rural areas also underwent numerous upheavals during these years. Some farms became specialized in order to respond better to the needs of the local urban or even international market, while others faced increasing marginalization, due among other things to the overpopulation of the seigneuries resulting in migration to the industrial towns of Quebec and New England or to new settlement areas where agriculture and forestry went hand in hand. Despite the opening up of these new settlement regions, the proportion of the rural population shrank constantly during the second half of the nineteenth century, falling from 80% in 1851 to 72% in 1871 and to 60% in 1901. Obviously, these figures do not take account of the thousands of families who left the province to find work in the United States, a trend that began in the 1840s and grew markedly after 1870, when the manufacturing sector was no longer able to absorb the surplus of agricultural labour. Towards the end of the century more than half a million French Canadians had left the province in this way, with the result that there were as many living in the United States as in Quebec. As for migration to the cities, it more or less followed industrial development, with Montreal attracting the largest body of rural dwellers and immigrants. Between 1851 and 1901 the city's population grew from 57,000 to 325,000, making it by far the most populous urban centre. In comparison, Quebec City, which was next in size, suffered economic and demographic stagnation with 42,000 and 68,000 inhabitants in those same years. Other towns where industries developed had populations of around 10,000 by the turn of the century.

This transition from a pre-industrial economy to an industrial one that we have sketched out very briefly had a profound effect on class and gender relations and on the way of life in general. Most notably it was during this period that the rhetoric of separate spheres, according to which women were expected to confine themselves to their domestic responsibilities because of their biological destiny, was asserted with increasing vigour. Industrialization, which created a clear distinction between workplace and home, helped to reinforce the identification of women with the family and consolidate the association of men with the market economy, the duty to provide for the financial needs of the household being henceforth considered a male prerogative. As a result, in addition to justifying the abolition of women's voting rights, this discourse legitimized the marginalization of women on the job market and the very inferior wages they received compared with men. Indeed, the patriarchal ideology of separate spheres, which held that a woman's place was in the home, provided a vindication for the extreme exploitation from which women suffered under industrial capitalism in its quest for cheap labour.

The social discourse that confined women to the domestic environment did not in fact prevent them from joining the workforce, but instead justified the different way in which they were integrated into the labour market. Moreover, the greater numbers of women in cities like Montreal and Quebec City in the second half of the nineteenth century provides conclusive evidence of their presence in the workplace, though we do find that in Montreal their involvement declined, falling from 26% in 1825 to 20% in 1891. Single women actually migrated in greater numbers than men from rural areas to the cities in order to earn a living. The demographic imbalance that was already noticeable in the 1840s grew with time. After 1871 there were more than 110 women for every 100 men in Montreal and Quebec City, and as many as 140 in the 15–30 age group, an age at which they had a better chance of finding employment. The breakdown of this data also shows that the ratio of women to men was higher in neighbourhoods surrounding factories as well as in middle-class neighbourhoods, where a higher proportion of households employed domestic help.

This type of work, which ranked first among women's occupations, became even more feminized throughout the nineteenth century. For instance, in Montreal, while young women represented two-thirds of domestic servants in 1835, they had increased to 90% by 1871, since men preferred factory work. However, the actual proportion of women working as domestics was in decline, dropping from 9% of the female population of Montreal in 1844 to slightly below 8% in 1881. In Saint-Hyacinthe, where footwear and textile factories were founded in the 1860s and 1870s, the decrease was even more marked, with domestics representing almost 70% of the female workforce in 1861, but falling to only 20% thirty years later, according to Peter Gossage's data. In fact, exactly like men, women left their employment as domestics whenever they could, for even though factory work was onerous, poorly paid, and the hours were almost as long, at least their time was their own once the workday was done. Unlike men, however, they had only a limited number of industrial jobs located in very specific manufacturing sectors available to them, which explains why they found it more difficult to escape domestic service.

Those who were able to join the ranks of female factory workers found themselves mostly in textile, footwear, and tobacco manufacturing, in which they comprised between 30% and 60% of the employees, and in the clothing industry, where over 80% of the workforce was made up of women and children. Female workers, the great majority of them single, earned on average half the wages of a man and thus supplied employers' demand for a cheap workforce. Employers justified such wage differentials by arguing that the young female workers they hired had no domestic responsibilities. This ignored the fact that most of them were required to contribute to the family budget and that many others had to earn their own living. The idea that women workers were earning "extra income" thus became a convenient excuse for their exploitation, a practice most flagrant in the clothing industry. Indeed, garment manufacturing, which at the end of the nineteenth century employed thousands of seamstresses working at home, paid starvation wages for exceptionally long working hours. Remunerated on a piecework basis, these women had to sew continually from morning to night, despite which they earned much less than factory workers – a form of exploitation known as the "sweating system." Women who agreed to sew at home for a manufacturer, or more precisely for a subcontractor, were often married women or widows with a young family who were trying in this way to combine their family responsibilities with the need to earn a wage. With the coming of railways this kind of work even expanded into rural areas. This involvement of rural women in the subcontracting that was usual in the garment industry can be attributed to the specialization and commercialization of agriculture, which tended to exclude them from agricultural production, dairying in particular, leaving them free to pursue other activities.

Apart from sewing in the home, married women and even widows rarely took paid work, for industrial society held that they should devote themselves completely to caring for their homes and children. In fact, in the nineteenth century even the presence of unmarried girls in factories was regularly criticized, including by labour leaders. In the eyes of the latter, allowing women to work in industry seemed not only to endanger their morals and health but also to represent unfair competition, depressing wages, and preventing men from completely fulfilling the role of breadwinner on which their masculine identity depended. There can be no doubt that the wages earned by men were most often totally inadequate to provide for a family, so that the breadwinner-housewife couple that was held up as the model was an ideal out of reach of the great majority of working-class households. Daughters therefore had to set off for the factory, though in a lower proportion than boys, while their mothers struggled to make ends meet by taking advantage of every opportunity they could grasp.

The contribution of working-class housewives to the domestic economy actually went far beyond simply providing services. To compensate somewhat for their husbands' inadequate wages, they had to employ various strategies depending on the stage in the life cycle of the family and the number and ages of the children: taking in boarders, keeping a garden, or raising animals like chickens or pigs for the family table or for sale, doing laundry, ironing, and cleaning or mending for neighbours – such were some of the activities to which they could turn to keep the wolf from the door and which they undertook in addition to their household duties of cooking, washing, cleaning, and sewing clothes for the family – in addition of course to looking after the children. Activities such as growing vegetables and raising animals could mean substantial savings on the family's food bill, which consumed the major part of its budget. However, these standbys were declining in Montreal – starting in the 1860s – because of the densification of the urban space and also because, for public health reasons, the City prohibited keeping pigs within the city limits. Nevertheless, we can surmise that elsewhere in the province, where industrial towns developed more slowly, such practices lasted throughout the nineteenth century. What is certain is that urban working-class housewives engaged in many productive tasks that were interwoven with other activities related to the sustenance of daily life. The extent of their responsibilities, and the time they had to devote to them in the absence of any efficient domestic technology, explain, no less than the ideology of separate spheres and male pride in being the sole breadwinner, why very few such women sought regular employment outside the home.

The absence of electricity, indoor toilets, or baths, in addition to the use of wood- or coal-burning stoves that required constant feeding and coated the walls with soot, made women's daily tasks time-consuming and tiring, and housing conditions uncomfortable. Only cold running water, which became available to most dwellings in Montreal from the 1870s on, made household chores a little easier, but generally each lodging had only a single tap, located in the kitchen. This meant that summer and winter water had to be heated for cooking, laundering, or washing. Nor was this water free, for a tax had to be paid in return for being connected to the supply, or else the service would be cut off – something that happened frequently in poor working-class households in which lengthy spells of seasonal unemployment were common, or that were severely affected by major economic crises like the one that occurred in 1873.

Teaching, which became more and more closely associated with the feminine sphere, was another occupation taken up by large numbers of women. The status attached to the profession of primary teacher, which was higher than that of domestic servant, explains why many young women preferred it as a career prior to marriage, especially in rural regions where the possibilities for employment were limited. In 1857 women made up over 65% of the teaching profession, a figure that rose to almost 90% towards the end of the century. Schoolmistresses, who were frequently hired while still quite young, were required to demonstrate good morals – as crucial to securing a position as their training. Furthermore, in the *écoles de rang*, or small rural schools, where they were responsible for both the teaching and the upkeep of the school (which also served as their residence) they could never be sure their contracts would be renewed. In return they received a ridiculously low wage, much lower than their male colleagues. Generally, they were paid half the salary of a man – a disparity as great as in industry. However, women who taught in model schools (positions that required longer training) earned as much as three times less than their male colleagues; in the Montreal Catholic School Board in the 1880s it was as much as five times less. Yet, as is shown by a study by Marta Danylewycz, more than a third of these women were aged over 30 at the time, suggesting that in the cities, contrary to what is widely believed, a sizable proportion of female Francophone urban teachers made teaching a true career and had several years of experience to their credit.

The training of male and female teachers provides a partial explanation for these disparities in salary. For instance, towards the end of the 1880s 60% of Francophone Catholic male teachers held a diploma from one of the two normal schools that by the middle of the nineteenth century had been established to train teachers, while this was the case for only 6% of female teachers. This was because very few parents could afford to have their daughters trained by the Ursuline nuns, who offered an equivalent program. Others held a certificate awarded by a board of examiners, a system the educational authorities had introduced by the middle of the century. But these inequalities can equally well be ascribed to the general discrimination suffered by women in the workplace, for even those who were as well qualified as men and had reached the same educational level were always paid less. Similar differentials existed in the Protestant school system, though there salaries were, on average, twice as high. This difference reflected the way of financing the school system that was adopted in 1869: in that year the government began to allocate the education tax according to the taxpayer's religious affiliation, providing a considerable advantage for Protestant schools, the value of the property owned by Anglophone Protestants being on average much higher than that of Francophone Catholics. Furthermore, almost 25% of the female teachers in the Protestant system held a diploma from the normal school affiliated with McGill University. Starting in 1884, the year in which McGill opened its doors to women, some even obtained a university degree, enabling them to command a higher salary. It was also possible for Anglophone women to pursue a teaching career at the high school level, which was added in the 1880s, thereby increasing the possibility of a higher salary, an option not available to Francophones.

On the Francophone side, the public education system developed much more gradually. The model schools, which offered a fifth and a sixth grade, and the academies, corresponding to the next two years, which were added in 1888, were still few in number and had few students, for most children left school after their first communion (that is, following the first four years of school that constituted primary education). It was in the private convent schools, founded by nuns, that girls could benefit from lengthier schooling. However, unlike the *collèges classiques* for boys, which were founded during the same period, these institutions did not lead to a university education, which remained closed to Francophone women until the early twentieth century. On this topic it should also be mentioned that though McGill began to admit women in the 1880s they could only take courses offered in the Normal School and the Faculty of Arts, but not in the Faculties of Medicine or Law; in any case the doctors' and lawyers' professional associations refused to admit women into their ranks. In the Montreal Catholic School Board, founded in 1846 after legislation was passed entrusting education to such bodies, the low priority accorded to the education of girls can be seen from the fact that the grants to schools that admitted them were between six and ten times lower than those for boys' schools. What is more, during the first fifty years of its existence, the Montreal Catholic School Board did not construct a single school for girls, being satisfied to incorporate into its system the private schools women had established early in the century or simply to leave girls' education to the nuns.

Starting from the second half of the nineteenth century, Francophone laywomen teachers had to contend with the increasing presence of nuns, who established convent schools all across the province at the request of school boards or ran public schools at a very low cost with which it was impossible to compete. This meant that a career in teaching became less accessible to laywomen, making it much more difficult for them to make any claim for better working conditions. Thus, while nuns comprised 18% of teachers in the 1860s, by the end of the century they amounted to 30%, distributed among a score of religious communities, most of which had come into existence during this period. Their concentration was even stronger in the towns and villages, for nuns were largely absent from the *écoles de rang*. By the turn of the century they had created some 200 private convent schools, often paired with a free public school funded by boarders' fees.

CHAPTER THREE

The clericalization of the teaching profession under the Francophone school system came about in a context in which political, economic, and social upheavals provided an opportunity for the Church to exert an increasing hold over Quebec society. The failure of the 1837–38 Rebellions and the Act of Union of 1840 with its assimilationist agenda, along with the rise of industrialization and urbanization, which impoverished large sectors of the population and destroyed traditional community solidarity, were actually propitious for the strengthening of an institution that claimed to unite French Canadians under its banner. The Church's task was all the easier since the liberal state accepted no responsibility for public services and was glad to abandon the sectors of education, health, and aid to private bodies, apart from making them grants or adopting laws which, however, rarely attempted to restrict their activities. Beginning in the 1840s, therefore, the Catholic Church was given free rein to control the lives of the faithful, who greatly appreciated the services it was able to render them in such troubled times and displayed a new-found religious fervour. The latter stimulated many women's vocations, which in turn supplied the Church with the workforce it needed to tighten its grip on society. In these conditions, the number of nuns exploded, rising from 650 towards the middle of the nineteenth century to over 6,600 fifty years later – a figure equal to 6% of all unmarried women aged over 20. This trend continued until the early 1920s, when nuns, who by then numbered 13,500, represented 9% of single women aged 20 or above – a record for the Western world.

If the women who entered a religious order did so mainly for religious reasons, the fact is that the socio-economic conditions that prevailed during the second half of the nineteenth century also encouraged such a rapid increase. The difficulty of finding a husband – which reflected the economic difficulties experienced by a growing share of the population – the limited opportunities for employment, the wage discrimination that women suffered often condemning them to extreme poverty, the impossibility of gaining admission to French-language universities and the more lucrative professions, and the low social prestige suffered by single laywomen, not to mention the subordinate status of married women, were all factors that may have encouraged taking the veil. Having done so, some of these women were able to exercise functions and occupy positions of responsibility that would have been out of their reach in a secular existence, and this was certainly an additional attraction. To all of them, however, religious life provided at least the assurance of an existence free of material concerns, since the community took care of all their needs. Additionally, in a society over which the Church was extending its influence farther and farther, nuns enjoyed a social status and an authority to which very few laywomen could aspire without a battle for recognition. However, though numerous possibilities for careers in teaching, caregiving, social services, and administration were opened up to a number of these women, and though they enjoyed considerable independence in managing their communities, schools, and health and welfare organizations, they still had to act within the framework defined by the Catholic Church and respect its hierarchy. This meant that they were not completely free of the male power of the bishops, even though, unlike laywomen, they did have the advantage of enviable room for manoeuvre, however limited by the obedience they owed their superior. A true mainstay of the Catholic Church, nuns enjoyed great consideration on the part of the ecclesiastical authorities, while they could not escape their control entirely because they embodied religious power among the population and conveyed the Church's message.

The importance the Church placed on the role of nuns in exerting control over the province's French-speaking population was demonstrated, among other things, by the eagerness with which it brought religious communities from France and encouraged new foundations. Ignace Bourget, the bishop of Montreal from 1840 to 1876, was the principal architect of this trend. Not only did he bring in some French religious communities, including the Sisters of the Good Shepherd, who in 1844 came from Angers to assume responsibility for the rehabilitation of delinquent girls, he also tried to convince laywomen to establish new communities in order to better fulfil their social apostolate. This is how the Congregation of the Sisters of Providence (already mentioned in the preceding chapter) came into being, as well as the Congregation of the Holy Names of Jesus and Mary, the Congregation of the Sisters of St Anne, two teaching orders born out of the educational ministries of Eulalie Durocher and Esther Blondin, as well as the Institute of the Sisters of Mercy, founded by Rosalie Cadron-Jetté, which continued the work with single mothers that she had undertaken as a laywoman. The establishment of this last community bears witness to a growing intolerance towards unmarried mothers (referred to as "*filles-mères*"), who suffered the ostracism of their immediate circle and of society as a whole and therefore needed a place of refuge where they could conceal their pregnancy and give birth in secret. If the phenomenon of extramarital pregnancy has always encountered some kind of social disapproval, in the context of the nineteenth-century religious renewal and the tightening of patriarchal rule it meant real dishonour for both the girl and her family. Indeed, the Sisters of Mercy were themselves stigmatized by a portion of the population that accused them of encouraging vice by being complicit in such "debauchery," making it very difficult for them to raise funds to support their work.

Children born in secret were usually given up, as much because of the condemnation aimed at unmarried mothers as because, given the wage inequity from which they suffered, these women could never have earned enough to support them. Until 1898, when the Sisters of Mercy opened a crèche to care for them, the babies born in their maternity wards were channelled towards the establishment maintained by the Grey Nuns, where they joined a constantly growing number of little ones, mostly "illegitimate" (i.e., born out of wedlock). Thus during the first twenty years of the nineteenth century, from 1801 to 1820, the Crèche d'Youville took in 907 infants, while between 1851 and 1860 alone the number rose to almost 6,000, a third of them from outside Montreal. According to Peter Gossage, that kind of increase shows that in the context of a society on the way to industrialization, characterized by economic instability and increased geographical mobility, it became easier for a young man to evade his responsibilities, so that whereas previously most extramarital pregnancies would have been legitimized by the subsequent marriage of the couple, now the usual result was rejection for the girl, who was left with little choice but to reject her child in its turn. It is worth pointing out that almost 90% of the children entrusted to the Crèche d'Youville died before the age of one year, a catastrophic mortality rate due to the mediocre state of their health on their arrival in the Crèche and by the crowded conditions that prevailed there.

CHAPTER THREE

Of all the religious communities in Montreal, the Grey Nuns probably diversified their aid activities the most. In addition to the General Hospital and the Crèche d'Youville they also managed orphanages for Irish and French-Canadian children, shelters for young domestics, several clothing depots for the poor, "kitchens" where food was distributed, some clinics and infirmaries, a homeless shelter (the Hospice Saint-Charles, which would later become the Accueil Bonneau), homes for the elderly and disabled, and several *salles d'asile*, which provided child care for mothers unable to cope with their workload. These places, where parents could send their children during the day in return for a minimal fee, were established, starting in 1858, on the suggestion of a Sulpician named Victor Rousselot. By 1900 there were five of them in Montreal alone, handling around 1,500 children, and a half-dozen others established on the south bank of the St Lawrence and in other towns such as Quebec City, Sorel, and Saint-Hyacinthe. Their existence and popularity, which have sometimes been attributed to the high number of mothers in employment, were mainly due to the lack of space in working-class housing and the economic activities carried on by women in the home.

Also on the suggestion of Victor Rousselot, who himself had serious problems with his eyesight, the Salle Nazareth, which opened in 1861, was devoted to children suffering from blindness. This was the seed from which the Nazareth Institute grew, an establishment specialized in teaching blind children using the Braille alphabet, which was introduced to Canada by the Grey Nuns. Giving pride of place to musical training, the Nazareth Institute also prepared young boys to practise a trade such as organist or piano tuner to allow them to survive in society. A community clinic for eye ailments was attached to it in 1873. Finally, in 1880, the Grey Nuns also took over the administration of the Notre Dame Hospital, founded a short time before by a group of French-Canadian doctors, and for which they also supplied the nursing staff. By the end of the century they were in charge of seventeen establishments in Montreal and nearby, in addition to those they had opened in other towns in the province, in Canada, and even in the United States.

The Sisters of Providence were no less active. In addition to caring for elderly infirm woman (the vocation that had inspired Émilie Tavernier-Gamelin to begin her charitable work) as well as caring for the poor in their homes like the Grey Nuns, during the second half of the nineteenth century these nuns established several orphanages and schools, several shelters, clinics, and hospitals, and created the Oeuvre de la soupe and the Oeuvre du dépôt, where the destitute could come to obtain food and clothing, respectively. In 1851 they founded the Montreal Institut des sourdes muettes, while in 1873, at the request of the government, they took over the care of the mentally ill in the Asile Saint-Jean-de-Dieu, which they had built and which they operated with the help of government funding. By the end of the century they were in charge of twenty-two establishments in Montreal alone, in addition to about fifteen in various towns throughout the province. Like the Grey Nuns, they also expanded across Canada, even reaching as far as the State of Oregon.

The example of these two communities provides an eloquent illustration of the extent to which nuns were involved in providing care and assistance: indeed, very few categories of the impoverished and marginalized escaped their attention. At the same time, the creation of so many charities devoted to the care of the poor, delinquent girls, unmarried mothers, the frail, young infants, handicapped children, the aged, the disabled, the sick, and the mentally ill bears witness to the social exclusion experienced by a growing number of people, especially women and children, in a society undergoing industrialization. The nuns who cared for these outcasts provided basic support for them by offering a shelter of last resort, enabling them to survive, receive an education, or die a "Christian death" (to borrow the title of an article by Bettina Bradbury), even though one may well think that in this way they also helped to uphold the social order and spread the Catholic principles that helped to justify it.

As in education, one consequence of the omnipresence of the nuns in the provision of aid was that it hindered social action on the part of Catholic laywomen, an obstacle with which Anglophone women did not have to contend. Within their respective churches they helped the poor by distributing aid to their homes in the form of clothing, food, and firewood. They were also active under the aegis of the Ladies Benevolent Society, the Female Compassionate Society, and the Montreal Lying-in Hospital, founded in 1843, to provide assistance for single mothers or women too poor to give birth at home. In Montreal, as in Quebec City, they ran a number of private orphanages, to which were added shelters for elderly or immigrant women like the Ladies' Protestant Home and St Bridget's Asylum in Quebec City. In Montreal in 1874 and in Quebec City the following year, they established local branches of the Young Women's Christian Association (YWCA), an organization that originated in England and that had previously become established in Toronto. The objective of the YWCA, which was evangelical in inspiration, was to preserve the morals of young single women recently arrived in the city by offering them lodging for a modest sum and helping them to find employment, particularly as domestic servants. Strictly supervised, the residents of the YWCA, an interdenominational body, were strongly urged to attend one of the Protestant churches in the city regularly and to join Bible study groups. Eventually, these associations also provided reading rooms, libraries, and cafeterias for their clientele. They organized evening courses to develop the skills of young working women and, towards the end of the century, even offered them an opportunity to participate in physical training and sports. In 1879, on the suggestion of Emily F. De Witt, who headed a committee to organize hospital visits (another aspect of its activities), volunteers from the Montreal YWCA helped to found the Montreal Diet Dispensary, which specialized in the preparation and distribution of healthy meals for the sick and destitute when recommended by a doctor or clergyman. The YWCA also took under its wing the Montreal Day Nursery, a daycare founded on the instigation of a Protestant clergyman at the end of the 1880s. Until the 1890s the association was also founding homes for the rehabilitation of prostitutes, called "Magdalene Homes."

Finally, despite the meagre support its campaign received from Quebec Catholics or Anglicans, the prohibition movement, of which portents could be found as early as the 1820s, led to the creation of several Quebec branches of the Woman's Christian Temperance Union, an organization born in the United States in 1874, and which first emerged in Canada in small Ontario communities. Convinced that alcohol was the root of many social problems, including poverty and conjugal violence, the female members of this association tried to convert young people, especially young men, to abstinence, persuading them to sign a pledge never to consume alcohol, and petitioned governments to outlaw the production and sale of alcoholic beverages. At the turn of the century they would also be in the forefront of the anti-smoking campaign, and they were among the first to come out in favour of women's suffrage.

Founded after Confederation, bodies like the YWCA and the Woman's Christian Temperance Union represented a new kind of women's organization in the sense that they were active all across Canada and brought together women belonging to several Protestant churches, giving them greater independence from the male clergy. Nevertheless, just like Catholic nuns, these middle-class women were very much motivated by religious considerations, for their major concern was the moral regeneration of their protégées and of society as a whole. Like the Catholic women's communities, especially those involved in education, they helped to spread a model of female respectability based on attachment to the domestic sphere, even if, clearly, their social involvement led them themselves to cross the boundary between the private and public domains.

The changes in gender relations brought about by the onset of industrial society were also apparent in the legal arena in the tightening of laws concerning women, their property, and, above all, their bodies. For instance, the new Civil Code that was adopted in 1866 required that the customary dower, which had been spared by the changes made in the 1840s, should now also be subject to registration. The general principle of the legal incapacity of married women was fully built into the new Civil Code, even though it stipulated that women responsible for charitable organizations could obtain special permission to deal with the business of those organizations without the express authorization of their husbands. The same applied to female public merchants in business matters, except that they were obliged to obtain their husbands' previous authorization in order to request this status, unless they had married under the separation of property regime. Also included was a rule according to which a woman could only ask for legal separation on the grounds of adultery by her husband if he kept his mistress in the conjugal home, while a husband merely needed evidence of his wife's infidelity. The Code also stipulated that children should remain in their father's custody pending the court's decision, with final custody going to the parent obtaining the separation, unless the judge decided otherwise. The law still allowed young women to bring a civil suit for "seduction" against the father of their child and to receive damages if he had obtained their consent to sexual relations by promising marriage; in future, however, fathers would also be able to sue their daughter's seducer for damage to the family honour. Furthermore, in the case of paternity suits, the law now stipulated that only a child's guardian could initiate legal proceedings, thus excluding mothers who were still minors, so that in their case only the girl's father could bring the suit.

There were also important changes in criminal law. In the case of infanticide, the law of 1803, which had laid down that any woman who concealed the birth of an illegitimate child found dead would be held responsible for its death and receive the death penalty unless a witness provided evidence that the child was stillborn, was replaced in 1812 by a less severe law, with the avowed aim of obtaining more convictions. It was now stipulated that women could benefit from the presumption of innocence, so that it became incumbent on the prosecution to show that a murder had been committed – a very difficult proposition, considering the state of medical knowledge at the time. But the law also provided that such women could be condemned to two years imprisonment if they had tried to conceal their pregnancy, which was much easier to establish. Infanticide, which was more often than not committed by young unmarried women, was dealt with leniently by judges and juries (entirely composed of men at the time), as well as by the doctors and coroners called as witnesses. Taking advantage of ambiguities in the law, they appeared to take into account the material and psychological distress of the accused, her fear, and above all the shame she claimed to feel for having breached the prevailing sexual norms.

Yet the sympathy for mothers found guilty of infanticide did not prevent legislators from tightening the laws related to abortion, seduction, rape, and contraception. The discovery of the human ovary in 1832 led to the elimination of the distinction between an abortion carried out before or after the child had moved in its mother's womb, which had been the basis for a difference in sentencing. Starting in the 1840s all attempted abortions were criminalized, whatever the stage of pregnancy, meaning that the abortionist, the sole guilty party in this kind of matter, risked a life sentence. However, in 1869 a new law introduced by the federal government laid down that a woman who had an abortion also risked a life sentence, while a woman who aborted herself was liable to seven years' imprisonment. Where seduction (an offence that could also lead to a criminal charge) was concerned, a law adopted in the 1840s specified that the abduction of a girl aged under 16, or under 21 in the case of an heiress, was punishable by imprisonment or a fine, the father being considered the injured party. Whether it was a civil or a criminal matter, the provisions concerning seduction insisted on the need to establish the girl's chastity beyond all possible doubt if there was to be any chance of obtaining damages or a conviction, but this was very difficult to prove. Especially in civil suits the courts no longer considered the birth of a child sufficient proof that a promise of marriage had been made, as had previously been the case; now written documents impossible to produce were required. The existence of maternity hospitals for unmarried mothers and orphanages to receive their children probably contributed to a renewed questioning of young women's virtue with the aim of absolving men of their liability. In the case of rape, a criminal "offence" punishable by death or imprisonment, women not only had to demonstrate their good reputation but also prove that physical constraint was used. Since women were generally subjected to strenuous cross-examination aiming to show that they were of loose morals, very few were willing to bring a charge.

This increased severity of the courts towards female victims of sexual abuse while infanticidal mothers won the sympathy of juries points to the fact that in the latter case only the woman was involved, and that she could justify her deed by the desire to preserve her reputation. Women who accused their aggressors were, on the contrary, attacking the male prerogative that allowed men to exercise their sexuality freely and use women's bodies as they wished – an affront more difficult for patriarchal society to tolerate, hence the increased severity of the law and especially of its application. The adoption of the federal law of 1892 making it illegal to distribute information about contraception or to sell contraceptives, crimes liable to two years' imprisonment, constituted, like the abortion law of 1869, another aspect of the male desire to control women's bodies, in this case by restricting their control over their fertility. Almost a century would have to pass before these laws would be repealed and the freedom of women to exercise their sexuality be recognized.

The rights of Native women also became a target for lawmakers during this period. In 1851 the Parliament of United Canada decided that a non-Native man who married a Native woman could not claim Indian status as it had been defined by the law adopted a year previously, while a non-Native woman who married a Native man did acquire that status. Eighteen years later, the federal government would go even further when it decreed that a Native woman automatically lost her Indian status, including the ability to transmit it to her descendants, if she married a non-Native, whereas men retained that prerogative. Additionally, the law of 1869 stipulated that a married woman had to take the tribal identity of her husband, and that if her husband was expelled from the reservation she was banished with him. In 1874 another law laid down that a Native woman could inherit only a third of her husband's possessions, while the other two-thirds went to the children – an improvement over the law of 1869, which disinherited women entirely. Adopted when White governments were trying to assimilate the First Nations peoples by restricting them to reservations, these legal provisions came in response to demands from Native men looking for a way to prevent lands intended for them from falling into the hands of non-Natives at a time when mixed marriages were becoming more common. If such a concern was well founded, the fact that they made such demands shows how the condition of Native women, previously considered men's equals, had been reversed. The discrimination that lay at the heart of these laws would give rise to a struggle that began in the 1960s and which has not yet come to an end.

CHAPTER FOUR

A New Capitalist Industrial Order (1880–1920)

The period between 1880 and 1920 saw an acceleration of the economic change that had been taking place since the mid-nineteenth century, as industrial capitalism underwent an even more pronounced expansion. Especially from the late 1890s on society saw the development of new sectors related to the exploitation of natural resources (water, forests, and mines) that relied mainly on a male workforce, while the established manufacturing industries became electrified and increased their production by introducing a greater division of labour and further mechanization. These changes depended on the concentration of ownership of companies, making it possible to assemble the necessary capital to create new factories, enlarge the old ones, or adapt them to new technologies. As a consequence, real monopolies appeared in certain areas – in the textile industry, for instance, where in 1905 Dominion Textile Inc acquired ownership of all the Quebec factories except one. This phenomenon, which also affected the banks and public services, would later result in the ever more complex bureaucracies required to keep track of activities that had become centralized, leading to a phenomenal increase in office employment, involving a growing number of women.

The process of urbanization also continued, though not with any consistency. Montreal, with almost 700,000 inhabitants in 1921, still stood out from the other urban centres, which, except for Quebec City (95,000), Hull (24,000), Sherbrooke (23,000), and Trois-Rivières (22,000), still had fewer than 10,000 inhabitants. Data from the 1921 census of Canada showed that Quebec society had become largely urban; however, this should be taken to mean that over 50% of the population was now living in towns with more than 2,500 inhabitants, a rather low threshold. Furthermore, Montreal stood out from most other towns and cities for its ethnic diversity. In 1911, for example, a little over 15% of its inhabitants were not of French (55%) or British and Irish (30%) origin, while in the province as a whole the proportion was only 4%. Having fled czarist Russia in great numbers, where they had been victims of persecution from the end of the nineteenth century, the 30,000 or so Jews living in Montreal in 1911 formed the third-largest community, comprising 6% of its population. People of Italian origin, numbering 7,000 in the same year, occupied fourth place, while at the other end of the scale the Chinese and Black communities numbered fewer than a thousand, the great majority of them men. But, whatever their numerical importance, as the years went by these groups developed their own institutions, associations, businesses, and places of worship and leisure, enabling them to preserve their cultural and religious identities while endowing Montreal with a cosmopolitan character that differentiated it clearly from other conurbations in the province.

If immigration contributed to the process of urbanization, especially in Montreal, the latter occurred essentially because of the attraction of the city for rural dwellers seeking employment. Beginning in the mid-nineteenth century and throughout the period, the depopulation of rural areas intensified as farmers' inability to enlarge and mechanize farms to make them more profitable led more and more of them to abandon their land. Even though it attracted far fewer candidates than the city, the creation of new settlements that had begun in the 1850s also continued, reaching into regions less and less suitable for agriculture, so that these new farms rarely developed beyond a subsistence level, leaving families dependent on forestry, fishing, or mining for their survival.

The urban and rural environments, very diverse in themselves, conditioned women's lives in several respects. From a demographic point of view, for instance, fertility rates remained very high in rural areas, especially in recently settled ones, while they tended to decline in the towns, especially in those with a larger population. For example, Gérard Bouchard has found that in the Saguenay during the first thirty years of the twentieth century women gave birth to around ten children on average, a rather exceptional fertility rate that was encouraged by the availability of land on which to establish younger generations and also by the strict oversight of the priests, for the Catholic Church was adamantly opposed to contraception and kept a close eye on women. But, as Marie Lavigne has pointed out, only 20% of married Quebec women born around 1887 and who survived until 1961 gave birth to more than ten children, a proportion that shrank to 13% for those born around 1903. In Quebec as a whole, women born at the end of the 1880s had 5.5 children on average, a figure that rises to 6.4 if only Francophone Catholics are considered. Apart from the living environment, the ethnic origin, language, religion, class, and educational level of mothers were also factors that helped to determine the number of children that women brought into the world. In other words, where fertility was concerned, as in many other areas, the deciding factor was mainly the diversity of circumstances, even if it can be said that in general Francophone Catholics had more children than the others and that they would be slower to have smaller families.

Living in a settlement area, on a farm not far from an urban centre, or in a town or city (especially a large city like Montreal) also determined the nature of women's lives and work. If the railway, and very soon the automobile, the postal service (which delivered department store catalogues even to rural homes), mass circulation newspapers and magazines, tourism, and new means of communication like the telephone facilitated economic and cultural exchanges between the various regions, making it easier for urban manners and values to spread to the most distant corners of Quebec, the fact remains that where they lived was a determining factor in women's lives. In settlement areas, for instance, they participated in clearing the land and later helped with the farm work while tending the garden, the farmyard, the cows, and of course the household tasks, all in addition to caring for the children. Unlike urban women, rural women were unable to benefit from conveniences such as running water and electricity, and they had to produce just about everything that the family consumed, from food to clothing, for money was short in these regions. Forestry work or fishing, like selling firewood or farm products to the neighbouring lumber camp, brought in a little income, but not enough to make a substantial improvement in families' standard of living. It should be stressed, moreover, that it was mainly young men, whether single or recently married, who found employment in lumbering, so that it was rare for the mother of an already numerous family to have to look after the farm on her own during the long winter months.

New settlements like mining, lumbering, and the construction of the first large hydroelectric dams, especially in Mauricie, were constantly taking over a little more land from the First Nations peoples, who were forced to find new means of subsistence. From the point of view of government authorities the solution to this problem was to settle them on reservations so that they might be more easily turned to farming, but very few of them adopted the White man's lifestyle. Instead, the men preferred to work as guides for prospectors, hunters, and tourists, while the women were active in crafts such as basket weaving, which in some areas brought in appreciable revenues.

In the more established agricultural areas the women would also grow a vegetable garden, feed the poultry and collect the eggs, milk the cows, care for the pigs, and sometimes keep bees, in addition to sharing in the field work whenever required. Selling various produce at the nearest urban market allowed them to earn a little money, but the commercialization of agriculture gradually excluded them from certain types of production, such as making butter and cheese, which had been taken over by specialized factories, thus becoming a male preserve. According to Martine Tremblay, after the 1880s agricultural periodicals practically ceased any discussion of the types of production traditionally associated with women; the articles written for them dealt instead with their roles as mothers and housekeepers, a sign that they were no longer considered true producers. The end of domestic butter and cheese making, evidenced by the increase in the number of butter and cheese factories throughout the period, no doubt meant a lightening of women's workloads, but their exclusion from such activities also shows that the modernization of agriculture was accompanied by a contraction of the feminine sphere, which at least in public discourse became reduced to the domestic. In fact, it seems that as soon as they became profitable and socially valued, agricultural activities, even those considered suitable for women, came under the control of men, who had long dominated the most prestigious forms of production.

In the industrial towns increasing numbers of young girls took employment until they married. Hence, in 1891 women provided 20% of the workforce in the province as a whole, rising to 30% in Quebec City and Montreal. At the end of the nineteenth century they still held a large number of jobs as domestics, though the female workforce became increasingly concentrated in manufacturing. In Montreal, for instance, manufacturing accounted for 40% of female workers in 1911, while personal services, in which 90% were domestic servants, represented 32% of the total.

This growing presence of young women in factories became a cause for disquiet among members of the clergy, reformers, and union leaders, both Francophone and Anglophone. Until the First World War they viewed this as a genuine "social problem" that had to be restricted, or even eradicated, in particular by increasing men's wages. More than the shameless exploitation to which they were exposed, concern for young girls' morals underlay these reservations, as is shown by the questions about the existence of separate toilets or the presence of unmarried mothers in factories that members of the Royal Commission on the Relations of Labour and Capital (1886–89) put to the women who appeared before them. For many labour leaders, the presence of women on the job market helped to depress the wages of all workers, hence the appeals for them to be paid at the same rate as men. In their mind, such a measure would encourage employers to get rid of their female workers and so free up jobs for men, who could then claim a "family wage," that is, one substantial enough to support a family. Since it was rare for women to do the same work as men, pressure was also brought for laws to be introduced to protect them in order to restrict the most flagrant abuses. Thus in 1885 the Quebec government adopted the Manufacturers' Act, which forbade the hiring of girls before the age of 14 (12 in the case of boys) and limited the women's workweek to sixty hours. But, given the lack of an adequate number of inspectors to enforce the law, it was frequently breached, and since very few female workers belonged to unions it was difficult for them to obtain their rights.

Indeed, with the exception of the Knights of Labour, an association that originated in the United States and achieved a measure of success in Quebec in the 1880s and 1900s, the labour movement showed very little concern for women. In the context of the labour relations of the time, in the absence of a law forcing employers to negotiate with unions, the absolute priority seemed to be the organization of workers in skilled trades, who were easier to defend. In the eyes of union leaders it was much more difficult to unite female workers, not only because they were rarely skilled but also because their working lives lasted only a few years until they married, making them less interested in practising solidarity and less combative.

CHAPTER FOUR

Yet during this period there were several examples of spontaneous work stoppages either initiated or strongly supported by female workers, unionized or not, especially in the textile industry. In 1880, 500 female workers from the Hudon factory in Hochelaga, at the time a suburb of Montreal, led the first sizable strike in this sector, demanding better wages and a reduction in the number of working hours. In 1908 the henceforth unionized female workers of this same factory, together with those from the St Anne textile mill, both then owned by Dominion Textile, stopped work to protest against harassment by a subforeman – quite a frequent complaint at the time. Between these two dates mills in Montreal, Valleyfield, Magog, and Montmorency also experienced work stoppages initiated by women or in which women played a leading role. According to the historian Jacques Ferland, the organization of production in the textile sector, where men and women often worked alongside one another on the same shop floors and operated the same machines, created a solidarity that transcended the gender barrier and opened the way for these female workers to become militant. Ferland notes that in the footwear industry, on the other hand, in which men and women were assigned very different tasks and operated very different machines, female workers were generally considered unskilled and consequently excluded from the shoemakers' and leather-workers' unions and, as a result, from the labour conflicts they initiated. In other words the example of the female textile workers shows that in the right circumstances women were less passive than union leaders liked to think and that their short- or medium-term involvement with the labour market was not in itself an obstacle to their taking action.

The increase in white-collar jobs, whether in government or business offices, was certainly the major new feature of this period. For instance, in 1880 the Bell Telephone Company began to hire women as telephone operators, the young boys it had previously employed having turned out to be rather undisciplined and even rude to customers. As Michèle Martin has observed, the patience, calmness, docility, and discretion ascribed to women, together with their pleasant voices, their dexterity in operating the switchboard, and the speed with which they connected users, made them, according to the company, better intermediaries with its clientele. Telephone operators, who were present in both the great city exchanges and the smaller exchanges established in rural or semi-urban locations, soon became an icon of this modern means of communication, at least until the advent of automated exchanges in the early 1920s.

A similar feminization of the workforce was observed in offices when, after 1900, considerable numbers of young women were hired as typists and clerical workers. However, unlike the telephone operators they did not replace the existing male employees, instead occupying new, more routine positions created as a result of the "administrative revolution." The concentration of businesses, giving rise to ever more impressive bureaucracies, required a more populous workforce to carry out the more standardized and consequently less prestigious tasks that were entrusted to young women. While there were fewer than 500 of them working in this field in Quebec in 1891, their number had reached 17,500 by 1921 – a figure that shows the extent of a phenomenon that exploded in just a few decades. By the latter date, in Montreal alone, where the head offices of the large Canadian industrial, commercial, and financial companies were clustered, they represented over 18% of the female workforce.

Trained in specialized private schools like O'Sullivan's Business College, the Institut Sténographique Perreault, or the secretarial school run by the Congregation of Notre Dame, office workers came from families sufficiently well-off to pay for this type of training for their daughters – though this did not mean that they all came from the middle class. In addition to typing and stenography, a mastery of English was a decided advantage in finding employment, for the great majority of the companies hiring women were Anglophone and worked mostly in English, the language of business at the time. This made it difficult for monolingual Francophones to break into the field, especially since French-Canadian companies like the Bank of Hochelaga, studied by Michèle Dagenais and Ronald Rudin, took longer to feminize their personnel. As for women from the other ethnic communities in Montreal, they seem to have been almost entirely excluded from this type of work, which conferred a certain status on its practitioners.

If they were mostly confined to subordinate and routine positions, office employees did earn higher wages than factory workers and had a shorter workweek. Better educated, they performed tasks that were less physically demanding and enjoyed a healthier working environment, one considered more suitable for young women. In addition, even if the higher ranks of the administrative hierarchy were beyond their reach, working in an office, as in the case of telephone operators, offered women possibilities for promotion that were rarely found elsewhere, so that as a whole their wages came to over 70% of the men's – a great improvement over industry. Yet, as in the case of factory workers, the morals of these young women were a source of social concern, as Kate Boyer has shown, not merely because every day they rubbed shoulders with young men in the workplace, but also because their higher incomes seemed to allow them greater economic independence, making it possible for them to indulge in pleasures available in the cities and to spend time in spots like cinemas and dance halls, often considered places of perdition.

The existence of secretarial schools to train for office careers testifies to the broader trend towards specialization in girls' education that developed throughout this period. Thus the end of the nineteenth century saw the appearance of schools of home economics intended to equip young women to acquit themselves more fully and effectively of their future roles as mothers and housewives. The first of these schools, opened in Roberval by the Ursulines of Quebec City in 1882, also aimed to prepare settlers' wives to confront the vicissitudes of a frequently harsh and unattractive existence. This initial foundation was followed in 1905 by the opening of an École ménagère agricole in Saint-Pascal-de-Kamouraska, and then by several others which eventually constituted a real network across the province. Managed by nuns and subsidized by the Ministry of Agriculture, these schools aimed to halt the rural exodus by raising families' standard of living thanks to the training of an elite of farm women well able to support their husbands and keep their sons on the land. This trend also reached the cities, where classes in home economics were ultimately incorporated into all the programs of study for girls when cooking and sewing classes were added to the basic syllabus. In 1906 members of the future Fédération nationale Saint-Jean-Baptiste (to which we shall return) opened the École ménagère provinciale for working-class women in Montreal. Like the YWCA, which offered similar classes, this school set out to remedy the lack of competent domestic servants (a cause for much complaint among middle-class Montreal ladies) and also to train model housewives able to make do with the low wages brought home by male factory workers. Offered even inside factories, these classes set out to rectify the inadequate preparation of young girls for motherhood, which was blamed on their participation in the job market before marriage.

What actually underlay this enthusiasm for the teaching of home economics was the fear that industrialization and urbanization would destroy the foundations of the traditional family, the survival of which depended, in the eyes of the elites, on the ability of women to keep their husbands and children attached to the home. While it was obviously seeking to bind women to the domestic sphere, this movement also displayed a desire to raise the status of housewives at a time when it seemed that education was becoming the key to establishing the social valuation of any activity. Several schools of home economics, including the one in Saint-Pascal-de-Kamouraska and the School of Household Science founded by Anglophones in 1907, also trained specialized instructors who subsequently found positions in both the network of schools of home economics and the urban school boards. As a result, while the great majority of girls completed only the elementary-level course in home economics, some others went on to the secondary level to obtain a qualification that fitted them for a career. On the Anglophone side, the domestic sciences, as they were called, also led to the development of dietetics, a female profession that took off during the First World War, when the army required specialist advice on how to feed the troops.

It was also at the turn of the century that the sisters of the Congregation of Notre Dame opened a new normal school for girls in Montreal, which was added to the McGill Normal School and the school operated by the Ursulines in Quebec City. During the following decades other similar establishments were added in the different dioceses of the province, so that it became possible for future teachers to receive training close to home. Yet the Francophone normal schools attracted a very small proportion of girls for, until the practice was abolished in 1936, the Central Board of Catholic Examiners continued to grant teaching certificates to candidates who lacked any college training. The professionalization of Francophone teachers was handicapped by this dual system of certification, since the holders of a certificate received no training in pedagogy. This was the case for almost 70% of women teachers as late as the 1940s. It should also be said that school boards preferred to hire these certified teachers despite their lack of training, for they could pay them less. This penny-pinching by boards did little to encourage young women to attend normal schools, especially since doing so entailed an expense that, in the eyes of many parents, was not justified for such a short career. Furthermore, women who attended teachers' college were generally satisfied to obtain the lower-level diploma that allowed them to teach only at the elementary level; in any case, only schools in urban areas offered schooling beyond the eighth grade, and these positions were monopolized by nuns, most of whom held only a teaching certificate. On the Anglophone side, in contrast, beginning at the end of the nineteenth century the Protestant Central Board of Examiners required all candidates sitting the examination, both male and female, to have a diploma from the McGill Normal School, while the establishment of high schools for girls opened up careers to these woman teachers elsewhere than in the *écoles de rang*.

The turn of the century also saw the establishment of schools of nursing, a female profession that was developing rapidly at the time. These schools, which were attached to hospitals following the model conceived by Florence Nightingale in the mid-nineteenth century, aimed to turn out a more highly trained hospital staff able to provide a standard of care that conformed to the demands of modern, post-Pasteurian medicine. Practitioners who were won over to the new scientific principles of medicine felt they needed the support of a specialized staff not entirely composed of untrained domestic servants yet submissive to their authority, and thus liable to augment their own prestige. Women, traditionally responsible for tending the sick within the family, appeared to be the natural candidates to fill this role of compliant yet competent subordinates. As a result, beginning in the 1890s several schools of nursing came into being, first at the Montreal General Hospital in 1890 and then at Notre Dame Hospital in 1898. Before long any hospital worthy of the name had its own nursing school, for it was no longer possible to imagine the delivery of care without the assistance of trainee nurses. In addition to taking the theory courses taught by the medical staff, students acquired practical experience in various wards as part of their training, providing hospitals with a free workforce that became indispensable to their proper functioning. This apprenticeship system meant that despite their training very few nurses ended up working in hospitals, for new students replaced those graduating, who on qualifying often had no alternative but to join the army of nurses that provided private home care. Only a few were able to envisage a hospital career, filling the supervisory positions required to oversee the student nurses. On the Francophone side, it was generally nuns who fulfilled these functions, resulting in the exclusion of laywomen.

In addition to working in private care, qualified nurses could also find employment with the public health services that were becoming more numerous during the early decades of the twentieth century to combat widespread problems such as tuberculosis and infant mortality. Initially created in England to care for the working-class population of the large industrial cities and look after their health, the profession of public health nurse or visiting nurse was introduced to Canada in 1897 by the wife of the Governor General, Lady Ishbel Aberdeen, who founded the Victorian Order of Nurses (VON), a philanthropic association, to provide home care to the poor. As early as the following year the VON became active in Toronto, Ottawa, Halifax, and Montreal. Montreal was therefore one of the first Canadian cities to become acquainted with this service, and by 1917 ninety-three nurses were working for the VON in the city, where they cared for the poor, with no discrimination on grounds of language, race, or religion. The example of the VON quickly snowballed, so that very shortly municipal health services, especially in Montreal, various private charitable associations, and even businesses, most notably the Metropolitan Life Insurance Company, were using visiting nurses to supervise the health of pregnant women, infants, and schoolchildren, carry out screening, and educate the masses about hygiene. The special nature of their work, which focused on prevention and education, encouraged the development of specialized programs of study, offered initially by McGill University beginning in 1920, and then, starting in 1926, at the University of Montreal. Better paid than their colleagues in private employment and benefiting from enviable professional autonomy and social status, public health nurses constituted a kind of elite within the profession and also represented a form of authority to the population that they served.

If society encouraged the education of women in areas traditionally associated with them, like teaching or nursing, it found it much more difficult to accept that they might aspire to conquer some masculine strongholds. Admission to university was therefore carefully controlled, and it was only very gradually that young middle-class women found the doors of the most prestigious faculties such as Law and Medicine open to them. McGill University, for instance, admitted women starting in 1884, but only to the Faculty of Arts. Five years later Donald Smith, a railway magnate, made a large donation to McGill on condition that it create a college for women. Royal Victoria College, which opened in 1899, thus encouraged the segregation of the male and female student bodies, for they followed separate classes, but at least it had the merit of legitimizing the presence of women on campus. For the time being, however, the professional faculties remained male preserves. Indeed, it was not until 1911 that women were allowed to study law at McGill, though it was still impossible for them to practise, for women would not be admitted to the bar until 1941. Annie MacDonald Langstaff, who in 1914 became the first woman law graduate, would be in the forefront of women's struggle to change this rule; she was finally admitted posthumously to the bar in 2006 in recognition of her contribution.

Bishop's University, founded in the mid-nineteenth century to cater to the Anglophone students of the Eastern Townships, was the first to accept women into medicine, probably because it had greater need than McGill of the income generated by female students' fees. In 1891 Grace Ritchie, a well-known Montreal feminist, who had begun her studies at Kingston Women's Medical College, became the first woman to obtain a medical degree from Bishop's, a year after the program was opened to women. Maude Abbott, who would gain worldwide recognition for her work on congenital heart disease and her research on the history of medicine, and Regina Lewis-Landau, the first Canadian woman of Jewish origin to qualify in medicine, were also among its most famous graduates. However, when the Bishop's Faculty of Medicine and that of McGill University merged in 1905 it meant an end to the admission of women to medicine in Quebec, at least temporarily, for McGill would not admit them until 1918.

Since there were no female *collèges classiques* it was even more difficult for Francophone women to gain access to postsecondary studies. In the early twentieth century nuns from the Congregation of Notre Dame and some middle-class Francophone women were beginning to agitate for the creation of such an establishment, but it was not until 1908 that they obtained the consent of the civil and ecclesiastical authorities, whose reluctance was finally overcome by the announcement of the opening of a secular secondary school over which the Church would have no control. However, the founding by the Congregation of Notre Dame of the first *collège classique* for girls (it would become the Collège Marguerite-Bourgeoys in 1926) did not resolve all the problems, for Laval University (of which the University of Montreal was only a branch until 1920) was particularly loath to admit women. It was not until 1925 that Marthe Pelland became the first woman to be admitted to the University of Montreal's Faculty of Medicine, while Laval University did not open its doors to women until 1936. Irma Levasseur, the first French-Canadian woman to practise medicine, obtained her degree from St Paul University in Minnesota in 1900. On her return to Quebec three years later she was obliged, like her Anglophone colleagues, to apply to the Quebec Legislative Assembly to obtain a licence to practise, for it was not until 1930 that the Quebec College of Physicians decided to admit women.

If women were able to make inroads into medicine more rapidly than into law, though not without difficulty, this was because acting as a caregiver seemed more suitable for women than working as an attorney. As was stated by one of the judges in the case of Annie MacDonald Langstaff in 1915, the presence of a woman at the bar was considered totally alien to public morality and order – an argument already used in the nineteenth century to withhold the vote from women. On the other hand, practising medicine in a doctor's office, a clinic, or a hospital remained a discreet activity that did not offend against morality – quite the opposite, in fact: since their patients were mostly mothers and children, female physicians helped to preserve female modesty while confirming their own femininity.

Journalism was another profession that women could practise without violating the frontier between the two sexes. According to Line Gosselin, at least 150 women exercised this profession in Quebec between 1880 and 1930. The emergence of the mass circulation press, which tried to attract female readers by devoting columns or even entire pages to them, facilitated their entry into this new professional field. If most women journalists were restricted to "female" subjects, some, like Robertine Barry, who was hired by *La Patrie* in 1891 wrote columns of more general interest, while others founded their own newspapers or magazines. Examples of this are *Le Coin du feu* (1893–96), created by Joséphine Marchand; *Le Journal de Françoise* (1902–09), established by Robertine Barry; *Pour vous Mesdames* (1913–15), edited by Gaétane de Montreuil; *La Revue Moderne* (1919–60), launched by Anne-Marie Gleason; and *La Bonne Parole* (1913–58), the organ of the Fédération nationale Saint-Jean-Baptiste. But only rarely was it possible for women to pursue a career as a reporter or correspondent, and it was even rarer for them to rise to a senior editorial position. One exception was Ida Siegler, who in 1917 became editor-in-chief of the weekly *Canadian Jewish Chronicle*. Just like their nineteenth-century colleagues, many female journalists, such as Anne-Marie Gleason, who signed her articles "Madeleine," resorted to pseudonyms to conceal their true identity, leaving them free to broach sensitive or controversial topics without drawing attention to themselves. Some, like Éva Circé-Côté, who contributed to several newspapers and magazines, even used several different pen names depending on circumstances and on what they wanted to say. In *Le Monde Ouvrier*, to which she contributed a regular column from 1916 to 1942, Circé-Côté signed herself "Julien Saint-Michel," no doubt to cover her tracks when taking a stand on especially contentious questions such as women's suffrage. However, she was not alone in defending women's rights, for numerous women journalists from well-off or at least literate backgrounds were very active in the emerging feminist movement or supported its various causes.

Among those who pursued a writing career there were also a number of women novelists. Probably the best known figures among this little female literary circle are the British author Frances Moore Brooke, who wrote the first Canadian and even North American novel, *The History of Emily Montague*, during a visit to

Quebec in 1764; Rosanna Mullins-Leprohon, whose novels were published in both English and French in the 1860s; and Laure Conan (the pen name of Félicité Angers), who in 1884 published the first Quebec psychological novel, *Angéline de Montbrun*. By the start of the twentieth century the number of women writers was growing, but on the whole their works, like those of Marie-Claire Daveluy or Michelle Le Normand (Marie-Antoinette Tardif), were anything but subversive. According to Lori Saint-Martin, *La Chair décevante* by Jovette Bernier, published in 1931, with its heroine a single mother who decides to keep her child, marked the true emergence of anti-establishment women's writing, even if the eponymous character of *Angéline de Montbrun* also stands out from the women of her day for choosing to remain single without entering a convent.

Some women made their mark in the arts, most notably the singer Albani, née Emma Lajeunesse, who starting in the 1890s enjoyed an international reputation, or Pauline Donalda, another soprano who appeared on the European stage during the first decades of the twentieth century before turning to a teaching career. Five years after her definitive return to Quebec in 1937 she founded the Opera Guild of Montreal, remaining its president and artistic director until 1969. Indeed, between 1919 and 1935 as many as fifty or so Quebec women singers and musicians, winners of the Prix d'Europe, lived and pursued careers abroad after completing their training, contributing to Quebec's reputation overseas.

The creation of organizations agitating for women's rights, especially the right to vote, was certainly one of the most significant phenomena of this period, even if that demand alone did not represent the entirety of women's involvement in the public sphere – far from it. In fact the campaign for civic and legal equality and for access to higher education and the liberal professions that was waged by several associations, soon to be called "feminist," was just part of a much wider social and political involvement on the part of women. Indeed, the negative consequences of the industrialization and urbanization that became intensified after 1880 encouraged an increase in women's initiatives to contend with the growing problems of poverty and public health. Like other reformers such as doctors, clergy, and intellectuals, women from the middle and upper classes were concerned about the living conditions of the masses, especially the fate reserved for women and children, even if it was only because of the social disorder which, in their view, might result from them.

While older organizations, like the Montreal Ladies Benevolent Society, the YWCA, the Montreal Diet Dispensary, and the charities established by nuns in the nineteenth century, carried on their activities, others were created to confront new challenges, the founding of the VON, mentioned above, being a case in point. But this initiative was far from the only one, for in 1901, in order to curb rampant infant mortality in Montreal, Anne-Marie Gleason, then a journalist with *La Patrie*, created, with the support of some doctors, the first "Goutte de lait," where poor mothers could obtain pasteurized milk. A similar service was introduced at the Montreal Foundling and Baby Hospital that same year. During the following decades clinics of this kind became more numerous, thanks to initiatives by women or with their collaboration, especially in Montreal, Sherbrooke, and Quebec City, where Frances Barnard Tessier took over their organization in 1915. Grace Julia Drummond devoted herself to the Montreal Park and Playground Association, an organization formed to create playgrounds for children in poor neighbourhoods of the city as a protection against the physical and moral perils from which, according to these ladies of the social elite, they were at risk. In 1907 Dr Irma Levasseur, with the support of a committee of ladies from the wealthy Francophone middle class, founded the Sainte-Justine Hospital for children with Justine Lacoste-Beaubien in charge, as she would remain for almost sixty years. Five years later Caroline Leclerc Hamilton created the Assistance maternelle de Montréal, an organization that set out to provide material and medical support to impoverished pregnant women. It was not long before similar services existed in Quebec City and Sherbrooke. In 1902 women from the tiny Montreal community of African descent banded together to found the Coloured Women's Club of Montreal in order to provide material assistance to new arrivals and to help them cope with the discrimination from which they suffered.

The founding of these organizations and establishments, of which we could list many more, bears witness to the intense activity on the part of women, mostly from the middle and upper classes, who in this way were seeking an outlet for their abilities in the field of public service. Without openly challenging the ideology of separate spheres that was intended to restrict them to their role as mothers, these women reformers and philanthropists believed that the attributes of femininity, especially the "innate tendency" of all women to care for the weak, actually *required* them to intervene in the public sphere, particularly to provide assistance to poor mothers and their children. In their opinion, women, as those most responsible for the well-being of families, had a duty to make their positive influence felt in society, since it was really an extension of the family. In other terms, they subscribed to a maternalist ideology that stood the dominant patriarchal discourse on its head, using the argument that women have a special nature that justified their incursions outside the domestic sphere. However, this conception of their role, which won them the support of some members of the masculine elite, as long as they took it no further, put them in a false position vis-à-vis the female population to whom they devoted their energies. Concerned above all with the morals of working-class families and wishing to inculcate in them the middle-class, bourgeois values that they themselves embodied, the volunteers, nurses, and other activists who constituted the personnel of these associations often displayed a total lack of understanding of their economic situation, as well as a propensity to view poverty as the result of individual shortcoming rather than of social inequality. In short, if their desire to support impoverished mothers did point to a measure of female solidarity, the relations they established with their "protégées" were often characterized by an authoritarian, moralizing attitude that reflected the class relations running through the entire society.

Many women's organizations founded at this time were affiliated with the Montreal Local Council of Women or the Fédération nationale Saint-Jean-Baptiste. These coalitions were created in 1893 and 1907 to give women's action greater power and visibility and to exert a stronger influence over governments. The creation of a court to deal with young delinquents, the pasteurization of milk, the adoption of a law obliging stores to provide seats for saleswomen, the appointment of female factory inspectors and policewomen, the payment of a government pension to widows, and the limit placed on the number of liquor outlets were only a few examples of the legislative changes that these two organizations wanted to see adopted and which, in some cases, they even managed to obtain. The same two organizations also agitated for the admission of women into higher education and the professions, for the legal equality of married women, and for women's suffrage. This last demand, which echoed that of other feminist groups all over the Western world, was in a way the logical outcome of their various struggles, for, as in most industrialized countries, it was because they saw women's suffrage as the only way to obtain greater influence over elected representatives and achieve the reforms they considered necessary that women were finally convinced to claim the vote.

In Quebec the struggle for women's suffrage, which really began in 1913, developed at a moment when ethnic tensions were becoming more acute, affecting its evolution and outcome and also leading to the existence of two feminist umbrella groups in Montreal, one Francophone and one Anglophone. Various factors, such as the exodus of French Canadians to the United States, the treatment of Francophones in the other Canadian provinces, and the imperialist sentiments of some Anglophones, all coming on top of the industrialization that seemed an outright attack on the traditional way of life and values of French Canadians, helped to exacerbate nationalist feelings among the latter. The Catholic Church, which since the 1840s had claimed to protect the French-Canadian identity, displayed a particular distrust of "modernity," viewing it as a consequence of the economic domination of the province by Anglophones, and sought actively to curb any initiative on the part of this movement that might threaten to undermine the traditional family, which it saw as the foundation of its power over the society as a whole. The Church considered feminism especially pernicious, for it was viewed by numerous nationalists as an Anglo-Saxon import with its objective nothing less than the destruction of the family as an institution.

So, from the foundation in 1893 of the Montreal Local Council of Women, itself a local section of the National Council of Women of Canada (NCWC), created that same year, the archbishop of Montreal, Mgr Fabre, forbade Catholic women's associations to affiliate with it on the grounds that the NCWC was a Protestant organization. Nevertheless, a few Francophones became members on an individual basis and even held important offices on the executive committee, for example, Marguerite Lamothe-Thibodeau, president of the Association des dames patronnesses de l'hôpital Notre-Dame; Joséphine Marchand, a daughter of the future Premier Félix-Gabriel Marchand (1897–1900); and Marie Lacoste-Gérin-Lajoie, a self-taught jurist and future president of the Fédération nationale Saint-Jean-Baptiste. However, clerical pressure, the emergence in France of a Christian feminism in which they could recognize themselves, and the unease they felt in an Anglophone environment that showed little sensitivity to their special situation, led them to leave the organization and create another that was more in their own image. The foundation of the Fédération nationale Saint-Jean-Baptiste in 1907 was, therefore, an indication not only of Francophone women's desire for autonomy and of their wish to draw together all the Catholic women's associations, including the numerous charities run by nuns, but also of the discord within feminist circles about the National Question.

CHAPTER FOUR

The creation of the Fédération nationale Saint-Jean-Baptiste did not prevent these two groups from working together on a number of issues, especially women's suffrage. However, it was particularly difficult for Francophone feminists, being ardent believers and respectful of their Church, to wage a campaign condemned by the high clerical authorities and by several prominent traditionalist nationalists like Henri Bourassa. So the Montreal Suffrage Association, created in 1913 by the Montreal Local Council of Women under the presidency of Carrie Derick, the first Canadian woman to hold the rank of full professor at McGill University, had almost no Francophone members, even if in 1915 Marie Lacoste-Gérin-Lajoie, who by then had become president of the Fédération Nationale Saint-Jean-Baptiste, accompanied Derick and Grace Ritchie England to Quebec City in order to submit a demand for women's suffrage to Premier Lomer Gouin. It was not until 1917, when the Canadian government granted the right to vote to the female relatives of soldiers (wives, daughters, mothers, and sisters) and to nurses serving in the armed forces, that Marie Lacoste-Gérin-Lajoie publicly supported women's suffrage, for she considered that granting the right to vote to some categories of women alone was highly inequitable. Indeed, by granting suffrage only to such women, Prime Minister Robert Borden was obviously hoping to ensure the victory of his coalition in the December 1917 federal election, in which the principal issue was that of conscription, a particularly unpopular measure in Quebec. It should be pointed out that Grace Ritchie England, the president of the Montreal Local Council of Women, was equally opposed to compulsory military service and to allowing targeted groups of women the vote, for she considered these measures discriminatory and incompatible with her ideals of justice and equality. Interpreted as a lack of patriotism towards the British Empire and a betrayal of the soldiers in the front lines, her position earned her serious opposition even within her own organization, with some member associations of the Montreal Local Council of Women calling for her to be replaced.

The contribution of Canadian women to the war effort finally overcame the last reluctance of the federal government, which in 1918 granted the right to vote to all women except Asian and Native women. In fact all across Canada the First World War led to a vast mobilization of feminine and feminist organizations that exerted considerable energy throughout the four years of the conflict. If the Canadian army was able to count on more than 3,000 nurses joining up, of whom 2,500 were sent overseas, and on the contribution of 1,000 women recruits who helped to run the supply corps, it benefited equally from the women volunteers who prepared over four million packages for soldiers at the front, made thousands of bandages for the Red Cross, collected funds to support the operation of military hospitals, encouraged people to buy Victory Bonds, and created the Canadian Patriotic Fund to collect donations to supplement the separation indemnity paid to soldiers' families by the state. This last initiative, which was launched in Montreal and in which the Fédération nationale Saint-Jean-Baptiste played an active part, succeeded in collecting almost $43 million from all across Canada between 1914 and 1918 – a colossal sum for the time. It should be pointed out that in addition to these voluntary contributions over 3,500 women, mostly single but including some married women and widows, worked in munitions factories, mostly located in Montreal, while many others replaced men on farms and in offices. It was indeed because of the First World War that the number of female office employees underwent the most rapid growth.

Yet the war was a difficult period for working-class families because of the galloping inflation that mainly affected groceries and fuel. In 1917 housewives in Quebec City, following the example of women in other North American towns and cities, created a league with a membership of almost 6,000 to combat the stunning price increases, which reached 32% for basic necessities. Convinced that the high prices were mostly due to the greed of farmers and shopkeepers and to speculators, they organized boycotts of certain products or stores, made arrangements for bulk buying, encouraged the use of substitute products such as margarine, and called for governmental control over the price of essential commodities. This kind of activism, which echoed the protests of women in the days of New France, shows how the war affected the lives of Quebec women in the smallest details. In 1918 the granting of suffrage to the great majority of Canadian women, including of course those in Quebec, provoked a real uproar among nationalists. In a series of articles published in *Le Devoir*, Henri Bourassa virulently denounced granting the vote to women, predicting that the "woman elector" would soon give rise to the "man-woman, a hybrid, repugnant monster who will kill the woman as mother and the woman as woman." So, it was in the name of women's calling as mothers that Bourassa assailed this feminist advance, while most women claimed this right precisely because it allowed them to fulfil that role better. In fact in Canada as a whole, very few feminists invoked the equality of all human beings as a justification for their demand, since the different and complementary natures of the sexes seemed perfectly obvious to them. If we cannot exclude the fact that some feminists turned to this type of argument for strategic reasons, it remains the case that for most of them women were entrusted with a very special mission that made it crucial that they have the vote, essentially in order to carry out that mission more effectively.

By 1918, when the federal government passed legislation granting women's suffrage, most of the provinces, except Quebec, New Brunswick, and Prince Edward Island, had already done so. By 1922 only in Quebec were women still unable to vote at the provincial level. At the instigation of Idola Saint-Jean, a young feminist, the Fédération nationale Saint-Jean-Baptiste set up the Comité provincial pour le suffrage féminin / Provincial Franchise Committee, which was joined by some Anglophone activists. They believed that conditions were favourable for the Quebec government to show some flexibility, but their petition, presented to Premier Louis-Alexandre Taschereau just as an antisuffrage movement was being organized, was rejected. While the bishops proclaimed their strong opposition to women's voting rights, forcing Marie Lacoste-Gérin-Lajoie to resign the presidency of the committee she had recently founded, some women, especially members of the Cercles de fermières du Québec, an organization created in 1915 by the Ministry of Agriculture, signed petitions declaring their refusal to vote. In fact outside Montreal very few Francophone women supported the demand; nor could the feminists count on the support of the nuns who headed the charities, which were a ferment of feminism elsewhere in Canada. It would only be twenty years later that Quebec women finally gained the vote, though it should be pointed out that in Montreal single women and widows had been able to vote in municipal elections since 1887. However, after the First World War a wind of change was blowing through Quebec society, as is shown by the emergence, in the years between the wars, of new models of womanhood.

CHAPTER FIVE

Women in a "Modern" Society (1920–1940)

The interwar years – a contrasting period from an economic point of view – were characterized by the emergence of new models of womanhood, an increased presence of women in the urban public space, a redeployment of women's organizations, an appreciable growth in state interventions in women's lives, and the culmination of the campaign for suffrage. Without any fundamental change in gender relations, these developments nevertheless impacted women's lives on many levels. Despite the financial crisis, and sometimes because of it, their daily existence seemed more and more shaped by a "modernity," which according to the conservative elite threatened the foundations of "traditional" society, an opposition often raised without any consideration of the many changes in lifestyle that had occurred since the mid-nineteenth century.

Even the relative prosperity of the 1920s was particularly favourable to these upheavals, for it helped to integrate a growing proportion of the population into consumer society. Greatly influenced by American culture, it offered women new fashions, new kinds of behaviour, and new canons of beauty that were a radical departure from the Victorian ideal of the femininity that had predominated until then. Straight, short dresses, the Marcel wave hairstyle, makeup, nail varnish, plucked eyebrows, cigarette smoking, drinking, and driving in cars (sometimes with young women behind the wheel) became emblematic of the "modern" woman whose image was propagated by movies and women's magazines, including Quebec publications such as *La Revue Moderne*, *La Canadienne*, and *Mon magazine*. Often presented as the symbol of the emancipated woman who was not shy about showing off her sex appeal, the image of the flapper was especially attractive to young urban women, who tried to imitate it in spite of virulent denunciations by the Catholic Church and French-Canadian nationalists alarmed at the Americanization of the culture and the infatuation with "indecent" fashions. The creation in 1927 of the Catholic Women's League, which took as its mission to ensure the triumph of modesty in dress, showed that some women, especially in rural regions, also thought that immorality had gone far enough. In 1933 this association had a membership of 70,000 spread over eighteen dioceses throughout Quebec, showing the extent of its influence in certain environments. However, the model of a "decent" swimming costume that was promoted by the League met with only moderate success – showing that the minority of women who went bathing were not reluctant to show off their bodies.

Participation in sports, encouraged by the new social and medical norms that associated slimness and good health, became another symbol of women's emancipation during these decades. The phenomenon was not entirely new, since upper-class ladies had been cycling, snowshoeing, or playing tennis since the nineteenth century, but the 1920s saw a greater democratization of female sporting activities, lending them greater visibility and increasing the attention they received. In Montreal, for instance, the YWCA and the Palestre nationale, a fitness centre for both sexes founded by a group of French-Canadian businessmen that opened its doors in 1918, attracted several hundred young women each year, especially office workers and professional women sufficiently well-off to afford the membership. Even though only a limited number of women, French-Canadian ones especially, as yet practised sports, and though it was encouraged by a number of doctors, women's involvement in sports stirred considerable apprehension. As Élise Detellier has shown in her research, a number of observers feared that the physical efforts exerted by women athletes would give their bodies a masculine appearance and damage their reproductive function, while the priests and the most conservative were concerned to see them wearing trousers or shorts, a fashion considered reprehensible because it was felt that it blurred sexual difference and threatened the gendered social order.

Even if very few women completely adopted the habits and behaviour of the flapper or the female athlete, the mere existence of these two archetypes was enough to sow alarm, for it was interpreted as an indication that the old ideals of femininity defined by chastity and modesty were being eroded and that gender relations based on the subordination of women were undergoing an unprecedented upheaval. The victory of Canadian feminists in obtaining the vote, like the legislation passed by the federal government in 1925 allowing women to sue for divorce simply on the grounds of adultery in the same way as men, or the new ideal of conjugal relations based on love and the personal development of both partners as propagated by the mass media seemed indeed to confirm that the foundations of male power in society and within the family were in serious jeopardy. The financial crisis of the 1930s, which deprived thousands of breadwinners of their livelihood, undermining the basis of their manhood, merely exacerbated this sort of concern and provoked violent reactions against working women.

Tolerance of women taking paid employment outside the home followed a rather tortuous course during this period, depending on the economic cycle. One effect of the First World War was to make it more acceptable for young single women to take paid work because they were filling positions left open by men who had gone to the front, and because it was viewed as support for the war effort. However, once the war ended and the country was in the throes of a major recession, voices were raised, by Catholic trade unions in particular, demanding that women return to the domestic sphere. During the 1920s, once prosperity had returned, there was no longer any great opposition to single women earning a living, even if it still provoked ambivalent comments. Some feared that it would be an impediment to the training of future mothers or that it might encourage a taste for luxury and independence not at all compatible with motherhood, but calls for the exclusion of women from the job market became less frequent, since the younger working woman had come to be seen as an inevitable reality. During that decade, if we can go by the data available for the city of Montreal, the proportion of women in the workforce did not increase substantially. However, a declining percentage of working women were employed as domestics, something that was less apparent socially, while the presence of women was increasingly evident in factories and offices, and this no doubt helped to normalize the phenomenon. In the 1930s, however, when male unemployment was on the rise, women who took paid work again became the object of virulent denunciations. In the eyes of some they were engaged, neither more nor less, in "stealing" the jobs of hard-working fathers, making them directly responsible for the poverty that affected thousands of homes – ideas that show very well that the entitlement of women to paid work was still far from accepted. To correct what they considered an aberration, the conservative elites, and also union leaders, called loudly for their dismissal, especially in the case of married women who were not yet very numerous in working for a living. In 1935 the Liberal MLA Joseph-Napoléon Francoeur even went so far as to introduce a bill in the Legislative Assembly (though it was never adopted), requiring women or girls seeking employment to prove that they genuinely needed to do so. This, like other proposals of the same kind, disregarded the fact that on account of the compartmentalization of the job market the vast majority of women took employment that men would not have wanted anyway.

It was also the case that women were less affected by unemployment, which was most widespread in construction, natural resources, and heavy industry, where the workforce was predominantly male. But factory closures and the slowdown of production in the light industries where women workers were concentrated were nevertheless significant enough to cause a redeployment of female labour. In Montreal, for instance, the proportion of women working in the manufacturing sector fell by 10% between 1921 and 1931, while the service sector, which included domestic servants, grew by a similar percentage. In other words, no longer able to find work in manufacturing, many young women tried to find jobs as domestics in better-off households, less affected by unemployment. Those who kept their jobs were forced, like the men, to accept lower pay or a shorter workweek, resulting in a proportionate decline in their income. The difficult economic circumstances of the 1930s did not, however, prevent several thousand women workers in the garment industry from triggering two significant strikes in Montreal, in 1934 and 1937. During the latter, which was led by Bernard Shane and Rose Pesotta, 5,000 young seamstresses, most of them French Canadian or Jewish, stood shoulder to shoulder for three weeks, at the end of which they obtained recognition for their union, better working conditions, and an increase in wages. But Rose Pesotta was not the only woman to stand out as a union leader. Yvette Charpentier, who also helped to organize women workers in the ladies' garment industry, Jeanne Corbin, who worked on the unionization of loggers in Abitibi, or her Communist colleagues like Annie Buller, Becky Buhay, and Bella Hall Gauld, who in 1920 had helped to establish the Montreal Labour College, devoted to educating workers in Marxism, were also among the women activists who distinguished themselves during this period, as did Laure Gaudreault, a primary teacher from the Charlevoix region who set out to unionize primary school teachers in her diocese in response to the provincial government's failure to keep its promise to increase their pay.

The 1930s were an especially difficult decade for teachers because school boards were suffering the consequences of the financial crisis, and board members did not hesitate to reduce their teachers' already meagre pay in order to balance their budget. In

Laure Gaudreault's mind there was no doubt that the elected representatives were trying to keep their electors happy at all costs by avoiding any increase in property taxes, even if this meant allowing primary school teachers, who had no voting rights, to starve. Unionization seemed to her the only way to improve their situation. In February 1937 the dozen or so different local associations that had already been established came together to form the Fédération catholique des institutrices rurales. This organization's main demands were for better pay, a decent pension scheme, and rules governing the hiring and firing of women teachers. Even though Gaudreault was supported by the superintendent of public education, who considered these demands to be "just and reasonable," much more time would have to pass before the lot of women teachers was improved significantly.

While women teachers became unionized, nurses tried to establish their status by creating a professional association to control their training and ability to practise. The indispensable role played during the First World War by nurses (the only women who served alongside the troops at the front) had helped considerably to raise their reputation with the public, and they intended to take advantage of this. In 1920 they were able to have initial legislation passed to incorporate the recently established Graduate Nurses' Association of the Province of Quebec. This legislation, which had been called for by a group of mostly Anglophone nurses, reserved the title of "registered nurse" to members of their Association, which had as one of its mandates to determine the qualifications for admission to the profession. It was stipulated that to become a member a nurse had to have taken a three-year course in a hospital of more than fifty beds and have passed the provincial examinations set by the Association. During the 1920s changes made to this legislation on the instigation of French-Canadian hospitals and doctors would undermine certain of the new Association's prerogatives, including its exclusive right to approve programs of study and award diplomas. The fact remains that at a time when medical knowledge and treatment were undergoing a significant evolution, the nursing profession was steadily gaining prestige, though this did not mean that nurses' working conditions and wages were improving at an equivalent rate. In 1933, for instance, 1,371 Quebec nurses, including 308 nuns, were employed in hospitals or public health organizations while 1,341 were in private service, meaning that more lay nurses were still earning a living by working "on call" than from a regular salary, a highly precarious situation given the difficult economic times. Furthermore, to provide health services in the settlement areas that were developed following the call for a return to the land that had been instituted by the federal and provincial authorities because of the economic crisis, the Quebec government hired "settlement nurses" to compensate for the absence of doctors in these remote regions, thus opening the door to a demanding but stimulating career, given the professional autonomy they enjoyed.

In 1919 the Quebec government adopted the Women's Minimum Wage Act in order to prevent the exploitation of women workers, but this legislation (which did not apply to primary school teachers or nurses) turned out to be completely useless in protecting women workers, especially in a time of economic crisis. The all-male membership of the Women's Minimum Wage Commission, which was appointed six years after the passing of this legislation, set salary scales according to such a minimal budget that it was practically impossible for someone living on her own to support herself, let alone provide for any dependants. In the early 1930s the various decisions made by the Commission still affected only 15% of the female workforce, a figure that falls to 10% if we take into account the numerous exceptions that employers were able to negotiate. Moreover, since the salary scales gave credit for employees' experience, employers would often ignore such experience in order to pay as low wages as possible, even letting employees go after a few months in order to rehire them as trainees. Tactics such as requesting exemptions that allowed employers to pay salaries below the required minimum became very common in the 1930s. In other cases employers took advantage of the law to reduce wages to the lowest point on the scale, so that the lowest wage actually became the most a female worker could hope for. Widely criticized, the Women's Minimum Wage Act was finally repealed in 1937, when the newly elected Maurice Duplessis government replaced it with the Fair Wage Act, which applied to workers of both sexes. By doing this, the state hoped to raise men's wages at a time when their lack of any protection made draconian wage cuts possible.

The low wages and high unemployment among men, which reached nearly 30% during the winter of 1932–33, were major concerns for the government, for it saw them as a threat to the stability of the family and to the patriarchal social order. The economic crisis therefore led to the introduction of various measures aimed at maintaining the prerogatives of heads of households, especially their special access to a source of revenue. The relief programs launched by the federal government in partnership with the provinces and municipalities, such as the payment of a weekly allowance called "direct relief," hiring for public works, and land grants, were therefore aimed primarily at married men. Single men were instead offered work in camps set up outside the towns and run by the army, a step taken to remove them from urban centres in order to prevent social disorder. However, unemployed single women had almost no entitlement to assistance, even if they were the breadwinners for their families. Nevertheless, the government did implicitly recognize the contribution of housewives to the family economy, for the distribution of direct relief was conditional on the good state of the household, and a grant of land to would-be settlers depended on their wives' ability to adapt to life in an agricultural setting. Interviews with women who lived through this painful period show indeed that without their ingenuity and the privations they imposed on themselves, and without the material assistance provided by other women relatives, the poverty – of which La Bolduc (Mary Travers) was the supreme interpreter – would have been much more extreme. We have to remember that working-class households were most affected by the crisis. Accustomed to making do with highly inadequate wages, even during the prosperous 1920s, these wives and mothers had already learned to cope with poverty, helping them to cushion the most devastating effects of unemployment and compensating for the inadequacy of the relief allowances. In spite of everything, there can be no doubt that the living conditions of the working class deteriorated during this decade, for numerous families had to move to smaller, poorly equipped, or vermin-infested accommodations, share their living space with another family, or choose exile to a settlement area where there was no electricity or running water. However, at a time when there was such opposition to women taking paid employment, it occurred to very few married women to look for a job outside the home – a solution which was in any case unlikely to meet with their husbands' approval. Instead, housewives resorted to tried-and-true solutions such as working in the home, selling homemade products, or taking in a lodger.

The economic situation in the 1930s encouraged many couples to limit the size of their families. The decline in the fertility rate, which had begun in the early twentieth century, accelerated between the two world wars, especially in the 1930s, with the average number of children per woman aged between 15 and 40 falling from 4.4 in 1926 to 4.0 in 1931 and to 3.4 in 1941. This was partly because of a drop in the marriage rate, but it points above all to an increasingly pronounced desire among married couples to have fewer children, especially in a situation where it was becoming more and more difficult to provide a decent life for them and to ensure they had a future. For Catholics this was often an anguished decision for, unlike the Anglican Church, which in 1931 had authorized its members to practise contraception if in their consciences they considered it necessary, the Roman doctrine continued to condemn strenuously anything that hindered conception. Only the "rhythm method," which was developed in the late 1920s by two doctors who had managed to understand the female fertility cycle, seemed acceptable to the Catholic Church as long as the couple first obtained approval from their confessor. In any case, the Knaus-Ogino method, as it was called, was not widely used during this period, so that the vast majority of Catholic couples adopted the withdrawal method instead, despite the risk of being denied the sacraments. Even if this practice involved the man rather than the woman, it was on the latter that the priestly wrath fell, instilling deep feelings of guilt in many.

The poverty arising from the crisis also brought about a renewed growth in prostitution, at least if we are to judge by the rate of women's convictions for serious crimes, which shot up by 190% between 1929 and 1939, compared with 111% for men. However, such data should be interpreted with caution for, as Andrée Lévesque has pointed out, they reflect the intensity of police activity and the severity of judges as much as, if not more than, any genuine evolution of criminal activity. So, if it is true that more women may have been attracted to prostitution because of the lack of employment during this period, we can also presume that economic and social instability led law enforcers to be less tolerant of delinquency, especially on the part of women. As shown by numerous investigations conducted from the end of the nineteenth century on, particularly the inquiry into police corruption carried out in 1924 by Judge Louis Coderre, prostitution had always flourished in Montreal. Towards the end of the First World War the city's red light district contained over 350 bawdy houses, leading to the formation of a group of reformist citizens, the "Committee of Sixteen," which submitted several reports asking the municipal authorities to clamp down on what was both a problem of morals and health, for in the committee's eyes prostitution helped to spread venereal diseases.

The data on the appearances of delinquent girls before the Montreal Juvenile Delinquents' Court, created in 1912, also reveal an increase in their number during this period, rising from 127 in 1923 to 523 in 1941, a rise disproportionately greater than the growth of the population. According to Tamara Myers, the growing concern in families and society about the behaviour of young working-class girls, especially their desire for independence and their real or feared rejection of sexual convention, explains this rise. And indeed the principal charges brought against them were less often for theft than for vagrancy, desertion, immorality, or "incorrigibility," the latter being one of the charges for which they were most often brought before the court in the 1930s, generally by their parents. Covering various types of behaviour, such as a refusal to work or to hand over wages, going out without permission, failing to observe a curfew, or spending the night away from home, this kind of offence is indicative of the conflicts that broke out in some families between daughters determined to gain a measure of autonomy and parents obliged to depend on the girl's wages or their help in the home. In the eyes of the court, however, this resistance by adolescent girls to family discipline, or even to the abuse inflicted on them, seemed above all a symptom of their immorality and the proof that they were surely on the slippery slope to perdition. Indeed, as Myers points out, female delinquency was generally associated with sexual immorality, hence the insistence of probation officers on learning girl's sexual history and a mandatory medical examination to check their virginity. Those who seemed "incorrigible" were sent to one of the two reform schools the Sisters of the Good Shepherd of Angers had been running since the last third of the nineteenth century or, in the case of Protestants, to the Girls' Cottage Industrial School that was founded in 1911.

However, as we have already seen, the obsession with girls' morals and their chastity did not apply only to young delinquents. Nor was it a recent concern, for from the end of the nineteenth century women's organizations had been worried about young single women leaving their families behind and going to work in the city where, they thought, being far from parental supervision they risked becoming debauched or targeted by sexual predators. To avert this threat some of them opened accommodations where young women workers could rent a room cheaply in a respectable and well-supervised environment. In the Montreal of the early 1920s there existed about ten such homes attached to the YWCA or other lay or religious organizations, but despite their number they could not satisfy the demand. To provide guidance to girls arriving in the city and to avoid their becoming "lost," these women's associations also set up kiosks in railway stations. In 1932 Yvonne Maisonneuve founded a shelter called Notre-Dame de la Protection, today known as "Le Chaînon" (The Link), which in eight years would take in over 3,500 women, mostly out of work or homeless, but also pregnant girls who probably wanted to give birth in the Miséricorde Hospital.

According to data provided by Andrée Lévesque, who has studied this establishment for single mothers during the interwar years, so-called illegitimate births throughout Quebec recorded an increase of 37% between 1931 and 1939, but relative to the other Canadian provinces the rate remained low compared with the total number of live births, at under 3.5%. Yet these statistics do not account for all the extramarital pregnancies, since some may have ended in a miscarriage or even a deliberate abortion. The latter phenomenon, which is very difficult to quantify because it was illegal, also seems to have been on the increase during this decade because of urban poverty, to the extent that, in his 1935 annual report, the director of the City of Montreal's Department of Health published a letter to mothers in which he advised maintaining "a strong feeling of repugnance towards those who lack the necessary courage to fulfil their duties as wives and mothers, [and] commit the basest of criminal acts by ending their pregnancy voluntarily."

WOMEN IN A "MODERN" SOCIETY

Such words bear witness to society's preoccupation with motherhood, which became a real public concern in the interwar years. Never before had it been the subject of so much debate or resulted in the introduction of so many measures intended, in principle at least, to improve the lot of mothers and children. This undertaking initially took the form of a vast campaign to lower the infant mortality rate, for which the Canadian record and even the record for the Western world was held by Quebec, and especially by French Canadians. Launched in the 1910s with the creation, sometimes by groups of doctors and priests and sometimes by women's organizations, of infant care clinics (the "Gouttes de lait"), the struggle was carried on even more energetically in the 1920s and 1930s, especially in Montreal, where the City's Department of Health increased their number, making them available to a growing proportion of impoverished mothers. The existence of these infant care clinics, where children were vaccinated and advice was given to mothers on how to feed them, and also – possibly, above all – the requirement that milk sold within the city limits be pasteurized, resulted in a significant reduction in infant mortality, which fell from 185 per 1,000 live births for the period 1916–20 to 74 per 1,000 for 1936–40. We should, however, note that the rates for "illegitimate" children remained catastrophic throughout these periods, coming to 826 and 303 per 1,000 (in 1915–19 and 1935–39, respectively). In Quebec as a whole the infant mortality rate declined from 149 to 83 per 1,000, an improvement partly attributable to the County Health Units that were put in place beginning in 1926. But at the end of the 1930s the infant mortality rate in Quebec was still very high compared with Canada as a whole and with the Province of Ontario, where it was 50 per 1,000. The deeper poverty of the French-Canadian population, the lesser likelihood that French-Canadian mothers would breastfeed their children, the absence of rules forbidding the sale of non-pasteurized milk in several towns and regions of Quebec, as well as the half-hearted measures taken by the Quebec government where public health was concerned were all factors that contributed to this situation.

Private organizations still played a considerable part in the system of public health infrastructures, for the public authorities remained largely reluctant to take charge of them completely. Even in Montreal, where the Department of Health was the most active, those responsible did not allow the City to take over the parish Gouttes de lait run by priests and doctors, even when these became the target of considerable criticism for their lack of efficiency and professionalism. In Quebec City, the Department of Health resolutely refused to establish a network of municipal clinics, or to provide adequate finance for the private clinics run by women's groups, with the result that a high proportion of the female population had no access to such a service. Elsewhere in the province, the towns and villages entrusted this work of prevention and education to the network of County Health Units, though these organizations had to cover vast territories and were unable to follow mothers and babies very closely.

In spite of all this, it can be said that the medicalization of motherhood, which had already begun during the previous period, really took off in the interwar years, with women being urged ever more strongly to consult a doctor when they became pregnant, to call him in for the birth, and to have a doctor monitor their children. If the great majority could not afford to pay for prenatal and postnatal monitoring or for care by a pediatrician, they were still inundated with documentation, most notably by the collection of little "Blue Books" authored by Dr Helen MacMurchy, director of the Child Welfare Division that was attached to the federal Department of Health, which plied them with advice on how to care for their babies. As for the infant care clinics, they provided free access to a medical and nursing personnel that encouraged mothers to adopt new methods in accordance with the most recent scientific discoveries. In essence, the medical discourse of the day and the new practices that it recommended were an attempt to modernize motherhood by putting it on a scientific footing while confirming women in their traditional role as mothers. At the same time, this helped to demolish the networks of older women who had transmitted their knowledge about care and child-rearing and to establish the authority of doctors and the nursing personnel in dealing with mothers.

However, it should be noted that the process of medicalizing motherhood and the increased power that doctors were able to obtain because of it were also based on the consent of mothers anxious to preserve the lives and health of their children, as is shown by the growing use of the infant care clinics and the very numerous requests received by different government agencies such as the Canadian Council on Child Welfare and by private associations for the pamphlets, brochures, and books on infant and child care they distributed. Women's organizations such as the Assistance maternelle that offered free medical care to destitute women also helped to spread the new medical norms related to motherhood. Initially, another objective of this charitable body was to make sure that women gave birth under the supervision of a doctor rather than a midwife, who was usually a neighbour without any training apart from her practical experience. During the Depression, when poverty was widespread, the Montreal Assistance maternelle helped between 3,000 and 4,000 mothers each year, numbers corresponding roughly to a quarter of the births taking place annually within the city boundaries, and to a third if we count only the French-Canadian families who were the target clientele. It would therefore be wrong to minimize its role in the medicalization of birth and motherhood, even if, paradoxically, the opportunity was provided by the economic crisis. Nevertheless, until the end of the 1930s the proportion of Quebec women who gave birth in a hospital setting remained below 15%, whereas in Ontario during the same period as many as 55% of women were having their babies in a hospital.

Apart from the health of mothers and infants, the condition of widows, a substantial number of whom had to put their children into orphanages because they could not provide for them, gave rise to much debate. At the end of the First World War the federal government had introduced a pension for veterans' widows, but initially, despite the repeated demands of several women's organizations, the Quebec government was reluctant to adopt a similar measure for other categories of mothers at the head of single-parent families. The opposition of the clergy and the conservative elite to any "state interference" in the family, and their virulent denunciations of the Public Assistance Act of 1921, provided a convenient excuse for Premier Taschereau to refuse their request. At the dawn of the 1930s, however, a sense that the old forms of relief based on charity and institutional care had become completely inadequate to respond to the needs of an industrialized society forced the government to set up the Montpetit Commission to investigate social insurance. It endorsed the principle of an allowance for single, needy mothers, that is, those who could provide proof of their poverty, though it did restrict the application of the law to widows caring for two children aged under 16 and to those whose husbands were physically handicapped or institutionalized because of mental illness. Women who were separated, divorced, abandoned by their husbands, or whose spouse was serving a prison term, and especially single mothers, who were not even mentioned in the report, were left out. In the case of single mothers, the condition of eligibility, which required that "every needy mother ... be of good character and able to bring up her children in good moral conditions" automatically eliminated them.

Finally adopted in 1937 by the government of Maurice Duplessis – that is, twenty years after the other Canadian provinces – the Needy Mothers Assistance Act, which drew largely on the recommendations of the Montpetit Commission, had the declared purpose of protecting the integrity of the family unit by making it unnecessary for mothers to place their children in an institution so that they would be free to earn a living. But the allowance was so meagre that most women could still not keep their children, for they remained unable to provide them with a decent life even if they were allowed to earn extra income by working at home. As a result, this Act, which claimed to recognize the superiority of rearing children in a family environment, largely missed its target, and until the 1960s orphanages would continue to be full of children separated from their mothers because of the latter's inability to provide for them adequately. Through the additional conditions it placed upon women – obtaining a certificate of morality, and demonstrating their fitness as mothers – the Needy Mothers Assistance Act also revealed the considerable distrust by legislators of women who were not living under the charge of a man. While society proclaimed that women were "naturally" endowed with the qualities required to care for children, it seems that not only the doctors who were heaping advice on them, but also the legislators who were determined to supervise them in place of a husband, either doubted women's ability to act autonomously or feared the empowerment they might derive from it. The family allowance proposed to the Montpetit Commission by Father Léon Lebel was along similar lines: this plan, which was never put into effect, proposed that allowances should be paid to fathers of three children or more as a reward for their contribution to society – but not to the mothers, who were actually responsible for the children's care and upbringing.

The question of family allowances failed to spark the interest of women's organizations, which, apart from the pension for mothers, were more concerned with the legal status of married women and the struggle for the vote. Only the Cercles de fermières kept their distance from these demands, which their leaders condemned on the grounds that greater equality between the sexes was a threat to the stability of the family, the very foundation of the social order. In 1922 this organization supported an initiative by priests to distribute, at church doors, a petition arguing against granting the vote to women; it garnered 25,000 signatures. Devoted to promoting the role of women in the rural world, the Cercles endorsed the conservative, nationalist point of view, which defended the rural way of life as the basis of the French-Canadian identity. Just like the traditional elites, the farm women considered that the city, the very symbol of modernity, encouraged moral depravity. They also thought that the urban environment limited women's activity by confining them to the domestic sphere, while in the countryside, on the contrary, mothers took an active part in developing the farm and the prosperity of their family, helping to keep the rural vocation alive in their sons and daughters and so perpetuate a way of life that would ensure national survival. More concretely, the Cercles encouraged the establishment of small agricultural industries, such as poultry farming and beekeeping, as well as craft industries whose products were sold to tourists who, starting in the 1920s, thanks to the rise of the automobile, were increasingly travelling the roads of Quebec. The Ministry of Agriculture, which had created the Cercles, subsidized these activities and encouraged competition among farm women by organizing contests and shows. This new value placed on women's agricultural and craft production met with great success, for the number of members rose from 5,000 in the early 1920s to over 24,000 by 1939. Assembling the greatest number of women all across Quebec, the Cercles de fermières, which the clergy lost no time in taking under its wing, carried a lot of weight in their opposition to the demands of other women's organizations that were unable to cite such a large membership.

Despite the opposition of the Cercles de fermières to women's sufferage, in 1919 they affiliated with the Fédération nationale Saint-Jean-Baptiste, which was at the forefront of the struggle until the early 1920s. Yet on the occasion of the meeting held in 1922 between the premier and a delegation of 500 women demanding the right to vote, the Fédération nationale Saint-Jean-Baptiste and the Montreal Local Council of Women were able to count on the presence of representatives from the National Council of Jewish Women, the new federation for Jewish women in Montreal, founded in 1918 and of which Amy Stein was president. However, this association, which joined the Montreal Local Council of Women in 1921, was more concerned with the well-being of mothers and children, the creation of summer camps for girls, and the integration of recent immigrants into Canadian society. The other two Jewish women's organizations, Hadassah (1918) and Pioneer Women (1925), sought above all to help Jewish women in Palestine; while they did not oppose it, therefore, these associations did not participate in the renewed call for women's suffrage at the end of the 1920s.

After the resignation of Marie Lacoste-Gérin-Lajoie as president of the Provincial Franchise Committee in 1922, the Fédération nationale Saint-Jean-Baptiste withdrew from the campaign for the vote, though it did not completely abandon its involvement in public affairs; in anticipation of the 1921 federal election in which Quebec women participated for the first time, it organized civics courses to inform women of their new rights and make them aware of what was at stake in politics, an initiative it repeated between 1923 and 1926, attracting hundreds of participants on each occasion. But two other associations took up the torch for women's suffrage: the Alliance canadienne pour le vote des femmes, founded in 1927 and presided over by Idola Saint-Jean, and the Ligue des droits de la femme / League for Women's Rights, established by Thérèse Casgrain the following year. The formation of these two groups points to certain ideological divergences among feminists. Idola Saint-Jean was mainly concerned with working women, whom she wished to draw into the movement, and preached a more radical feminism than Thérèse Casgrain, who came from the wealthy Montreal upper class. Nevertheless, working closely together, the two associations, which united women activists both Francophone and Anglophone, organized various public demonstrations and campaigned in the media, radio and newspapers, especially in the *Montreal Herald*, which in 1929 published a series of bilingual columns calling for women's suffrage and signed by Saint-Jean. At the heart of the feminist strategies there was also an annual "pilgrimage" to the Legislative Assembly, when delegates listened from the visitors' gallery to the debate about a bill to grant women the vote that was introduced by a member sympathetic to their cause. However, this war of attrition was no more able than a petition with 10,000 signatures, which was presented in 1935, to overcome the politicians' resistance.

The breakthrough on the issue of women's suffrage finally came about thanks to Thérèse Casgrain who, taking advantage of her position as vice-president of the Liberal Women's Club and with the support of about forty delegates, was able to have the matter included in the program of the party at its convention in May 1938. Elected in the following year, the Liberals under Adélard Godbout kept their promise, and in April 1940 they passed legislation granting women the vote, despite the clergy's disapproval, as vehement as ever. In the name of the Quebec bishops, Cardinal Rodrigue Villeneuve sent a letter to the premier explaining their opposition to women's suffrage because, it was argued, it undermined the unity and hierarchy of the family and exposed women to all the passions and adventures of electoral politics, and because the great majority of women in the province did not want it – never mind that Quebec women had voted in very large numbers in all the federal elections since 1921. To counteract the bishops, Godbout announced that he could not betray the promise he had made to the women, but that he was ready to hand over his position to Télesphore-Damien Bouchard, a notorious anticlerical. The episcopacy considered that the vote for women was the lesser of two evils, thus ending the debate.

The other great feminist battle of the interwar years was without any doubt the campaign to reform the legal status of married women, who remained in the same situation of legal incapacity as minors and individuals disqualified because of insanity. The Civil Code adopted in 1866 had reincorporated the restrictions on wives' rights inherited from the Paris Custom. Feminists found this situation more and more unjustifiable, particularly since laws granting women control over their property had been in force in the other Canadian provinces since the last third of the nineteenth century. In 1929 the Fédération nationale Saint-Jean-Baptiste, the Montreal Local Council of Women, the League for Women's Rights, the Canadian Alliance for Women's Suffrage, and the Association des femmes propriétaires de Montréal finally obtained the creation of a commission to examine women's civil rights, named the Dorion Commission after its chair, Charles-Édouard Dorion. When they laid out their demands, among the reforms asked for were the recognition of the right of married women to ownership of their earnings and the free use of the goods they acquired with such money; limits on the ability of a husband to dispose of or even dilapidate the goods of the community without his wife's approval; the exclusion from the community of certain categories of liquid property (bonds, shares, and bank accounts) brought into the marriage by the wife; complete freedom for women married separately as to property and wives separated from their husbands to manage their own affairs; the possibility for all women, not just widows, to serve as guardians or trustees; and the obligation to obtain the mother's consent to the marriage of minors. The Association des femmes propriétaires also demanded the abolition of the principle of the husband's authorization, while the Montreal Local Council of Women and the Canadian Alliance for Women's Suffrage insisted on the repeal of the section of the Civil Code that sanctioned a double sexual standard in cases of adultery – namely, the clause stipulating that a husband could ask for a separation from his wife on grounds of infidelity, while a wife could invoke such grounds only if the husband kept his mistress in the couple's home.

The commissioners, all ardent nationalists, rejected a substantial number of these demands using the argument that the Civil Code, inherited from France, represented one of the principal foundations of the nation and that most of its measures, especially those that endorsed the legal incapacity of married women and the marital supremacy of the father, derived from divine law. It did, however, agree to recommend a number of reforms, one of the most important certainly being the recognition that married women should be entitled to ownership of their earnings in order to prevent the husband from seizing them while at the same time refusing to fulfil his duty as a provider. Henceforth, a married woman living under the community of property could exclude possessions acquired before the marriage and veto any decision by the husband to dispose of immovable property owned by the community. Women married under the separation of property were enabled to manage their movable property themselves, while legally separated women regained their legal capacity in the same way as widows. Finally, married women were allowed to act as guardians or trustees in exactly the same way as single women, on condition they be appointed jointly with their husbands. However, where adultery was concerned, the proposed changes adopted in 1931 left the double standard intact, for the commissioners considered that the wound inflicted on a wife's heart was "generally not as painful as that suffered by a husband deceived by his wife," so that it would not be abolished until 1954. They also left paternal and marital authority intact, except for a few specific cases. In short, without attacking the fundamentals of the Civil Code the Dorion Commission introduced just enough reforms to adapt it to the new realities of industrial society. Frightened by the ambient modernity with which they associated feminists' demands, the commissioners were quite determined to preserve one of the last symbols that might have a chance of slowing its advance.

CHAPTER SIX
....

A Society Undergoing Profound Transformation (1940–1965)

From the Second World War to the middle of the 1960s, Quebec women inhabited a society increasingly rent by contradictions. The persistence throughout the 1940s and 1950s of the traditionalist, nationalist discourses that continued to defend the family, religion, and the rural vocation of French Canadians, and for which Premier Maurice Duplessis was an enthusiastic advocate in the postwar years, seems indeed to have been increasingly at loggerheads with the social organization and daily realities of the population, especially its female members. The entry of married women into the job market, the development of a consumerist, mass culture society heavily influenced by the United States, the social and political involvement of women in all kinds of associations, the relative decline of religious fervour and of women's vocations, as well as the Parent Report and the arrival of the contraceptive pill in pharmacies in the early 1960s are just a few examples of the phenomena that simultaneously influenced and reflected the changes taking place in society and in the family. Far from affecting only women, these changes reshaped gender relations and heralded a resurgence of feminism in the second half of the 1960s.

For Canada and Quebec the war that began when Nazi troops invaded Poland in September 1939 brought a return to full employment and a measure of prosperity, though this was tempered by the rationing of a number of foodstuffs and a scarcity of consumer goods resulting from the requisitioning of materials for the war effort. Military production, especially the arms industries, which were mostly established in Quebec, as well as the men volunteering for service in the armed forces, very soon brought down the unemployment rate. After a decade-long economic crisis the workforce quickly became too small to fill all the jobs, even if many rural dwellers, attracted by jobs related to the war, migrated to the cities in such numbers that they caused a serious housing shortage that lasted until the early 1950s, especially in Montreal. This resumption of the rural exodus, which had been practically cut short by the Depression, actually continued after the war, so that by 1961 almost three-quarters of the Quebec population was living in towns.

In 1942, to coordinate the war effort better, the federal government created the Selective National Service to evaluate the country's productive capacities and direct the labour force to where the need was most acute. Single women were offered on-the-job training to enable them to fill strategic jobs as electricians, welders, or mechanics for the construction of tanks and planes. However, most were employed in unskilled work, either in munitions factories or in other industrial sectors such as textiles and footwear, making uniforms and boots. In July 1942 the federal government also changed the income tax law, allowing husbands whose wives earned more than $750 a year to claim the tax exemption for a dependant, and established child care facilities, especially in Montreal, where six of these opened between March and September 1943. These measures, intended to encourage married women to join the "army of industry," provoked such strong reactions from the French-Canadian nationalist elite that one of the two nurseries reserved for Francophones had to close for lack of a clientele. The many denunciations of this federal initiative, which was associated with communism by both lay and religious elites, succeeded in convincing French-Canadian working women with children to find other solutions to their child care needs, such as calling on female relatives, a neighbour, or an elder daughter. Mothers who took employment also had to cope with the fury of the nationalists who denounced them for working outside the home, perceiving this as a threat to the integrity of the family and a cause of social disorder, especially of the juvenile delinquency – which grew during the war, at least according to the statistics. For the most radical among them, the employment of married women was nothing but a federal plot to destroy the French-Canadian family, since it encouraged the emancipation of the women who were its mainstay.

The 1941 census shows that the female workforce in Quebec comprised almost 86% single women, 6.5% widows and separated or divorced women, and around 7.5% married women, with this last percentage increasing markedly after 1943 with the intensification of federal propaganda and war production. In fact many mothers took advantage of the employment opportunities available to them to swell family finances that had suffered from several years of economic crisis, for the high wages (on the female scale) paid by the armament industries were a powerful inducement difficult to resist; the advantages even seemed so considerable that many women teachers and nurses abandoned their careers to work in these factories, despite the long hours and the often unpleasant and dangerous work.

The war effort that the government expected of women was not, however, restricted to entering the employment market, for housewives were also enlisted to salvage all kinds of materials to be reused in production, such as glass, metal, paper, rubber, bone, and leftover cooking oil, and they had to cope with the rationing of foodstuffs such as meat, sugar, coffee, tea, and butter. This measure, adopted to avoid scarcity-related inflation, required women to bring along the ration books of the entire family when they did their shopping, and to pay close attention to the dates on which they could exchange the coupons in them for the products involved, only limited quantities of which were allowed each individual. This meant that, in addition to dealing with the household garbage and the ration books, they had to adapt their recipes to the products and rations available, especially for desserts and preserves. The government also encouraged them to plant a vegetable garden and take in lodgers to alleviate the housing shortage, and it urged women teachers to help out on farms during the summer vacation, replacing the men who had gone to war. Beginning in 1941 single women were invited to join the women's sections of the armed forces in which they were used to handle supplies in the rear, freeing men up for the front; some of them were entrusted with "male" duties in areas such as telegraphy, technical drawing, or engineering, though most performed more traditional office tasks. As it had done during the First World War, the army also recruited nurses, leaving hospitals understaffed. However, because of French Canadians' aversion to enlisting, very few Francophones joined the women's services or became nursing sisters.

The Second World War had a considerable impact on women, not only because they took over functions that lay outside their traditional attributes, but also because the government and society as a whole recognized publicly that their contributions were vital for the war effort and that they were perfectly able to perform their duties with diligence and competence. This was especially the case for the housewives the government asked to cope with rationing without sacrificing a healthy diet for their families, for the health of the population was considered an essential factor in pursuing the war. Never before had women's domestic work, especially their role as consumers, been as clearly recognized as essential to the efficient working of society. In the mind of the federal government and of society as a whole, however, there was no doubt that only the urgency of the situation justified such incursions by women into the public sphere, so that even before the end of the war the federal government was careful to remind mothers that once the conflict was over they would return to their "proper place" at the centre of their households. The closing of the wartime factories and child care facilities, the return to a tax regime that penalized husbands if their wives earned over $250 instead of $750 per annum (as had been the case before the war), the meagre assistance provided to ex-servicewomen to help them return to the job market, the discriminatory rules of the unemployment insurance program (a measure introduced in 1940 by the federal government under Mackenzie King that did not allow payments to be made to married women even if they had been employed before marriage), ensured in combination that women would return to their roles as housewives dependent on a husband provider.

The program of family allowances introduced by the federal government in 1945 was also intended to convince mothers to return to the domestic sphere. Seen as a way to maintain consumption after the war, to trump the hand of the Canadian political left, and to satisfy the demands of women's movements, this allowance paid to women was represented as a kind of replacement for the wage they had earned during the war and as a way of providing them with the means to bring up their children properly without needing to work outside the home. However, the fact that family allowances were paid to mothers rather than to fathers provoked fresh outrage among French-Canadian nationalists, who saw it as a sacrilegious attack on the principle of paternal rule as embodied in the Civil Code. Giving in to their protests, the federal government first agreed to make an exception for Quebec by making out the cheques in the father's name. Finally, however, a coalition of women's groups and unions led by Thérèse Casgrain was able to convince the recalcitrant that, by virtue of a section of the same Civil Code, married women had an unspoken responsibility for the daily management of the family's affairs, and that the payment of family allowances to the mother could be considered part of this mandate. One consequence of this confusion was that Quebec women received the first of their cheques a month later than other Canadian women – but at least they were made out in their names.

The cumulative result of these measures was that in the immediate postwar period the proportion of women in the workforce declined substantially in Canada as a whole, from 33.5% in 1944 – a peak that would not be reached again until the 1960s – to 25.3% in 1946. Yet this decline was only temporary, for by the end of the 1940s married women were returning to the job market in ever increasing numbers despite the promotion of a domestic ideal founded on the complementary nature of the breadwinner-housewife couple. As a result, by the early 1950s married women represented 17% of all women workers in Quebec, whereas they came to almost 32% of the female workforce by the start of the 1960s. Their increased presence on the job market, furthermore, had repercussions on the charitable activities that until then had offered a means of fulfilment for women with time on their hands. Henceforth absorbed by their jobs and domestic responsibilities, fewer women were prepared to become involved in charitable works, as Aline Charles has shown in her study of volunteers in the Sainte-Justine Hospital.

A number of social changes explain this growth in the proportion of married women on the job market. A shorter workweek in factories and offices and the introduction of new domestic technologies that alleviated the burden of household tasks, together with a decline in the fertility rate, certainly contributed, but other factors such as a higher school-leaving age also played a part since, no longer being able to count on their children's wages, many working-class mothers looked for employment. Their desire as parents to ensure a better future for their children by keeping them in school for as long as possible and their wish to participate in the consumer society also induced women to continue working between marriage and the first pregnancy – long enough to accumulate a little nest egg – or to return to work outside the home once the youngest child started school. For, though more and more married women worked during this period, it was less common for them to do so while caring for infants of preschool age, since the absence of child care facilities, the opposition of their husbands, the judgment of their friends and relatives and of society, as well as their own desire to conform to the dominant model, all encouraged them to remain in the home during this stage of their lives.

The employment of married women was also stimulated by the development of the service sector, which was already heavily feminized. In fact the need for workers to fill positions in public and private administrations, businesses, schools, and hospitals, most certainly helped to overcome employers' reluctance to hire women, though large sections of the population continued to condemn working mothers. The way the female workforce was distributed reflected this growth in the service sector: in 1941 manual workers represented almost a quarter of working women in all of Quebec, but twenty years later they amounted to no more than a fifth. Increasingly, it was immigrant women, who in the postwar period arrived in growing numbers, especially from southern Europe, that ended up working in factories. Coming from Greece and Portugal, but above all Italy, these married or single women tried to improve the situation of the families that had immigrated with them by participating in the job market in the same way as men. A high proportion of them entered the garment industry, which was always looking for cheap labour, replacing the Jewish and French-Canadian women who had represented the majority of such employees before the war. In contrast, the proportion of women office workers rose from 14% to 25% throughout the same period, while the proportion of service workers fell from 32% to 21%, mainly because of the declining number of domestic servants. After the Second World War the federal government had again tried to steer Canadian women towards this type of work, but the plan launched by the Selective National Service was a total failure since most ex-servicewomen showed little enthusiasm for domestic service. To fill these jobs, starting in 1947 the Canadian government began to recruit European women refugees from the camps established for them after the hostilities ended. More than 10,000 signed a type of contract that required them to accept low-status and poorly paid jobs for at least a year in return for the granting of immigrant status. For some employers the desperate situation of these solitary women seemed a prime opportunity to acquire a captive workforce, as is shown by the scandal provoked by Ludger Dionne, the Liberal federal MP for Beauce, who in 1947 travelled personally to fetch a hundred Polish women to work in his textile factory in Saint-Georges.

The period between 1940 and 1960 saw a consolidation of female careers in the areas of assistance and of health and the emergence of new career possibilities. Social work, which was developed from the early twentieth century to professionalize the support provided to the poor by female volunteers, had already been taught at McGill University since 1918; on the Francophone side, where charitable organizations were mostly headed by nuns, more time would be required for such courses to become available to young women. In the early 1930s Sister Marie Gérin-Lajoie, the daughter of Marie Lacoste-Gérin-Lajoie and the founder of the Institut Notre-Dame du Bon-Conseil, established the first school to train social workers, but the diploma awarded was merely a certificate, the nature of which was somewhat ambiguous and which failed to gain acceptance. It was finally in 1939 that the University of Montreal's École de Service social opened its doors at the request of the Fédération des oeuvres de charité canadiennes-françaises, an organization created in 1932 by members of the clergy and a group of businessmen to coordinate the fundraising of charitable organizations and rationalize their practices. Until the turn of the 1960s, as Lionel-Henri Groulx informs us, the training provided by the École de Service social, even if the more scientific aspects such as casework were not entirely overlooked, insisted heavily on the vocational aspect of social work, women being considered particularly suitable for this form of Catholic apostleship on account of their intrinsic qualities. It was not until after the 1950s that Francophone social workers demanded real professional standing based on scientific knowledge instead of moral qualities. The fact remains that this new profession, which initially recruited many nuns, still represented a new avenue for laywomen, who were very soon in the majority.

The development of biomedical knowledge and technology also helped to bring women into a variety of auxiliary professions in the health field. Some of these, such as physiotherapy and nutrition, dated back to the time of the First World War. Between 1940 and 1960 speech therapy, audiology, occupational therapy, and psychology were added, while the contribution of lab technicians and radiologists became just as indispensable as that of nurses to the diagnosis and treatment of patients. In 1961 professional women and female technicians represented almost 7% of hospital staff in Quebec, though their presence had been barely noticeable before the war, and in many cases nurses had fulfilled these functions. However, despite their training in specialized institutes, schools created by hospitals, or in some cases universities, these new practitioners had to undertake a lengthy campaign to obtain a professional status that would grant them the exclusive right to practise or at least the exclusive right to their title.

The state of emergency and the full employment resulting from the war provided further encouragement to workers, who in 1944 won legislation guaranteeing the recognition of unions and obliging employers to negotiate in good faith with workers' organizations. The Labour Relations Act, though far from perfect and often ignored by the government of Premier Maurice Duplessis, went some way towards re-establishing the balance of power between employers and unionized workers and encouraged unionization, which jumped from 20% to 27% of all workers between 1941 and 1946 and reached 33% by the mid-1960s. Women were still less unionized than men, but even so one can sense a certain change in the attitude of the unions towards women in paid employment, especially during the 1950s, resulting in the creation of a women's committee by the Catholic Workers Confederation of Canada (CWCC) to study the problems specific to women workers. Without questioning the idea that the basis of the family should be the complementary nature of the female and male roles, or that mothers had the primary responsibility for the children, this committee nevertheless defended some egalitarian positions by agitating for women's right to paid work and equal treatment in job training and wages. The committee's existence, as a result of demands made by women unionists in the same year that the CWCC elected its first female vice-president in the person of Jeanne Duval, shows that the growing presence of women in workers' organizations encouraged collective awareness of the discrimination against them in the employment market.

The unionization of women workers by leading figures such as Madeleine Parent and Léa Roback that began during the Second World War also helped to strengthen women's activism, as is shown by the frequently very difficult textile strikes in Valleyfield, Montreal, Lachute, and Louiseville in the 1940s and 1950s in which these female workers were involved. In 1952 workers at Dupuis Frères, almost 60% of them female, launched a work stoppage to protest against job reductions and claim better wages. The violence used against the picket lines mounted in front of the large French-Canadian department store on St Catherine Street by the members of the CWCC became emblematic of the class relations prevailing in Francophone society, which transcended the National Question on which the elites had always tried to keep the focus. Some years earlier, in 1949, the lay teachers of the Montreal Catholic School Commission, of whom a majority were women, stopped work for a week. Despite the fact that this action was illegal, since public service employees did not have the right to strike, their cause was supported by many parents who also thought that male and female primary school teachers deserved decent salaries. At the beginning of the 1960s it was the turn of the nurses at the Sainte-Justine Hospital to organize a month-long period of "study days" to draw attention to the deplorable working conditions to which they were subjected. This strike by another name, from which they emerged victorious, was a real eye-opener for Quebec society, which was disturbed to see women leaving children to their fate, an action that contradicted the image of the nurse as a devoted, compassionate caregiver.

The strikes by women teachers and nurses were evidence of a new militancy in these two quarters, a consequence of their growing laicization. If in absolute figures the number of nuns continued to grow until the mid-1960s, the proportion of young women choosing to take the veil had been falling continually since the 1940s, while in the 1960s religious communities suffered a decline of 14% in their numbers because many renounced their vows. Combined with the increasing social needs in education and health care, this relative decline in religious personnel forced schools and hospitals to depend on an increasingly numerous lay workforce that was much less ready to sacrifice salaries and working conditions on the altar of a "vocation." Whereas in the past the preponderance of nuns in the hospitals and urban schools had allowed them to impose an apostolic vision on the careers of teachers and nurses according to which devotion to duty and the spirit of charity were meant to prevail over the quest for material gain, in the postwar period lay teachers and nurses, who were now in the majority, demanded recognition for their competence and professionalism and wanted to be paid accordingly. The creation in 1945 of the Corporation des instituteurs catholiques, born of the union of the three existing federations (the Fédération des institutrices rurales, the Fédération des instituteurs ruraux, and the Fédération des instituteurs et institutrices des cités et villes), and the founding in 1946 of the Alliance des infirmières de Montréal, are indicative of this desire to defend their interests more effectively. It should, however, be noted that until 1965, when equal pay legislation was passed, women teachers continued to be paid less than their male colleagues, with male teachers in urban schools sometimes receiving as much as double the salary of women teachers in rural schools.

The 1940s also marked the beginning of the democratization of education in Quebec. An Act enforcing compulsory school attendance, which came into effect in 1943 under the Liberal government of Adélard Godbout, together with the payment of federal family allowances for children up to the age of 16 who were attending school, encouraged a longer period of schooling for the young, even if in poor areas a high percentage still had to sacrifice their studies to help the family. Indeed, the 1951 census shows that 20% of boys and 25% of girls aged 14 and 15 had already left school, and in the case of the latter it was usually to help or replace the mother. In spite of this a larger proportion of young people did continue beyond the primary level, forcing the Francophone school system to adapt, so that towards the mid-1950s the educational authorities introduced a proper secondary program for Francophone Catholics and several public schools opened so-called classic streams, enabling students who lacked the means to attend private colleges to go on to university.

The schools of home economics and the family institutes established by Mgr Albert Tessier in 1938 also underwent a fresh expansion. Fearing a collapse of the family and of traditional values under the impact of "modernity," Church and state formed an alliance to promote this type of training, which unlike that provided by the women's *collèges classiques* (the number of which increased from twelve to twenty-one between 1944 and 1960), was granted generous public funding. From the early 1950s on the teaching of home economics did, however, become the target of numerous criticisms by the nuns in charge of the *collèges classiques*, the Association des femmes diplômées des universités de Québec founded in 1949, and above all, by one of its members, Monique Béchard, a Ph.D. in psychology, who vigorously denounced the essentialist vision of women that underlay it. Rejecting the arguments of male educationalists who claimed to be imbuing girls with a feminine, family culture suited to their maternal "nature" and future role as wives – the only role they considered acceptable – the critics of schools of household economics declared loudly and clearly that motherhood was not the only proper function for women and argued for the right of every individual to an education fitted to her interests and career objectives. In fact this polemic about the purpose of girls' education signified the beginning of the end for schools of home economics and family institutes, for even if their number grew during the 1950s, their clientele represented only a small minority of the female student population.

On the other hand, the number of young women pursuing a university degree increased markedly during the 1940s and especially the 1950s, though this growth did tend to reproduce the already existing divisions along sex lines. For instance, according to the data collected by Johanne Collin, the number of women registered in the twelve professional faculties of the University of Montreal grew from 92 between 1940 and 1944 to over 2,000 between 1960 and 1964. However, while the Faculties of Medicine and Law admitted slightly fewer than a hundred during the latter period, almost 1,500 women were enrolled in programs associated with the paramedical professions such as nutrition, rehabilitation, public health, nursing science, and medical technology. In other words, if women made a breakthrough in the postwar Francophone university world, it was mostly in faculties and schools with a strong female predominance and which, unlike faculties that prepared students to enter the liberal professions, were also accessible to graduates of the public education system. Furthermore, as Collin has noted, the admission of women into certain of these faculties did not necessarily mean access to university-level studies, since some university programs, such as medical technology, would be transferred to the CEGEPs after these were created in the 1960s. Nonetheless, the increase in the number of women students helped to assert their presence on campus. According to Karine Hébert, the women who attended the University of Montreal made their presence more felt in the 1950s when they decried the discrimination and prejudices from which they suffered and demanded the full student status that their sisters at McGill had already achieved. The inclusion of Francine Laurendeau (a future journalist and director with Radio-Canada, the daughter of André Laurendeau, himself a journalist and well-known politician) in the deputation of three University of Montreal students who travelled to meet Maurice Duplessis in Quebec City in 1958 and present to him their complaints about university funding, showed that in future, if it was to claim legitimacy, the student body could no longer ignore its female membership.

Starting in 1964 in the aftermath of the Royal Commission of Inquiry on Education in the Province of Quebec, established by the Liberal government of Jean Lesage, the Quebec education system underwent a thorough reform of its structures and programs. Two women, Sister Ghislaine Roquet and Jeanne Lapointe, a professor of Literature at Laval University, sat on this Commission, whose report recommended the creation of a Ministry of Education, the extension of compulsory school attendance to the age of 16, co-educational classrooms – meaning identical schooling for girls and boys, and the creation of comprehensive schools and general and vocational colleges (CE-

GEPs), putting an end to the reign of the *collèges classiques*. The Parent Report, named after the chair of the Commission, Mgr Alphonse-Marie Parent, also called for equality for girls and boys in education, though it did not question the gendered division of social roles, for if the commissioners thought that education should prepare girls to enter the job market, they also thought that their schooling should develop their ability to look after a home and a family and that for them paid work would represent merely a secondary activity compared with their fundamental destiny as wives and mothers.

And marriage did indeed claim a growing proportion of women in the postwar years. A corollary of the decline in religious vocations was a steadily diminishing rate of female celibacy, while with the help of economic prosperity couples were marrying younger. As a result, the marriage rate, which had fallen to a historic low of 5.2 per 1,000 in 1933, rose to 10 per 1,000 immediately after the war and then remained at more than 8 per 1,000 until 1954. This meant that a growing proportion of the female population experienced motherhood without there being any spectacular increase in the fertility rate, with women giving birth to an average of just under four children between 1946 and the early 1960s. Consequently, the baby boom associated with this period has to be ascribed not so much to an increase in the number of children per mother as to the fact that a higher proportion of women were starting families. Indeed, according to the estimates by the demographer Jacques Henripin, almost 60% of women who married after 1945 resorted to contraception. Among Francophone Catholics, the most common methods were still the Knaus-Ogino, or rhythm method advocated by the

Service de préparation au mariage, an organization created by the Jeunesse ouvrière catholique in 1944, and the so-called symptothermal method advocated by the Service de régulation des naissances (Seréna), an association founded in 1955 by Gilles and Rita Brault.

If women were having fewer children, they were nevertheless encouraged to devote greater attention to them and rear them according to the new norms laid down by psychologists, who experienced a real increase in prestige after the Second World War. The Quebec École des parents, an association founded in 1939 by Claudine and René Vallerand, became one of the main proponents of these psychological theories that, in the context of the Cold War, claimed to produce autonomous individuals imbued with the liberal values dear to Western democracies. The "modern" methods of child-rearing, like those advocated by the École des parents in its magazine and its columns in newspapers and on the radio, were particularly demanding and guilt-inducing for mothers, who were expected to adapt their children's upbringing to their rate of psychological development and so were held responsible for their offspring's slightest behavioural problems or difficulty in adapting to society. Nevertheless, by relating family upbringing to the education of citizens and even to the defence of democracy, the approach of these psychologists stressed the social and even political significance of mothers, increasing their status at a time when motherhood was becoming more widespread.

The École des parents and other organizations associated with the Family Movement that grew rapidly during the 1930s also stressed the importance of fathers in the parenting process. Without abandoning the idea of the complementarity of the feminine and masculine functions, the leaders of this movement advocated a model of the family in which the couple was expected to assume parental responsibility jointly, since the presence of the father was thought to be especially crucial in ensuring psychological balance in boys. To their minds, the male and female psychologies were so dissimilar that boys needed to have a masculine role model if they were to develop normally. This insistence on differentiating the roles and on the specific nature of "normal" female and male personalities did not, however, prevent the Family Movement from advocating equality within the couple and a rather liberal approach to the relations between parents and children, with manifestations of authoritarianism being seen as a barrier to the individual's full development, as required for his or her well-being and for the stability of the family and of society. This new, more egalitarian and democratic family, whose main function was to provide a favourable environment for emotional bonds to develop between its members, also seemed to offer the best defence against the ambient materialism and hedonism that were considered a threat to the nuclear family by inducing individual consumerist desires. The courses offered by the Service de préparation au mariage, which in the diocese of Montreal were taken by almost half the engaged couples between 1955 and 1965, the sex education handbooks published during this period, the Church-sponsored magazines on the subject of the family, as well as the popular press, spread ideas about the woman's place in the family that were innovative but also contradictory. Though this new way of thinking encouraged men to pay more attention to their wives and support them in dealing with family matters, and though it vaunted the intimacy and harmony of the couple, including in sexual matters, and though these media advocated a degree of equality within complementarity, they never doubted that procreation was the primary purpose of marriage or that the father was the natural head of the family, and they often reinforced the most hackneyed prejudices about female psychology and sexuality, of which passivity was considered a fundamental characteristic.

With their well-equipped single-family homes, green spaces, and quiet, homogeneous neighbourhoods, the suburbs that grew up in the postwar period certainly seemed to provide the most favourable habitat for the realization of this family ideal centred on the satisfaction of the emotional needs of the couple and their children. Less pronounced in Quebec than in other regions of North America, the migration of young families towards the periphery of urban centres was nevertheless very real, as shown by the sustained population growth of the municipalities around Montreal and Quebec City between 1941 and 1961. Encouraged by prosperity, but also by the saturation of central neighbourhoods and the deterioration of their housing stock, the acquisition of a suburban home certainly improved families' quality of life, though often at the cost of greater isolation for the woman who spent her time at home. Above all, the suburban housewife, a young, energetic mother, slim, well-dressed, and completely preoccupied with the contentment and well-being of her family, became an archetype that was prominent in women's magazines, radio programs, and soon on television, as well as in the advertising that inundated these media. Newspaper columns, broadcasts, and advertising swamped them with advice about caring for their children and keeping their home, taking no account of the fact that this lifestyle was out of reach for many women, if not for the majority, and that this image of tranquil female domesticity did not necessarily reflect their aspirations.

The women's media in the postwar years therefore helped to spread a rather conformist image of a period during which almost no protests were made and in which the model of the nuclear family, with the woman at its core, was depicted as the universally accepted norm. Yet, as we have already seen, more and more married women were working outside the home, and indeed the very same media were now employing more female journalists, reporters, and program hosts, who projected an image very different from that of a mother solely concerned with her daily household activities. Renée Rowan, who at the end of the 1940s became the first woman to be hired as a general news reporter for *Le Devoir*, Renaude Lapointe, the first female editorialist for *La Presse*, together with Judith Jasmin and Andréanne Lafond, who in the 1950s began hosting current events programs, conducting interviews with political personalities, and commenting on national and international events on radio and television, were some of the pioneers who expanded the representation of women in journalism, providing ample proof that women were just as interested as men in the important issues of the day. Furthermore, some radio programs intended for a female audience, such as *Femina*, hosted by women like Thérèse Casgrain and Solange Chaput-Rolland, which aired from the 1930s to the 1960s, were not afraid to broach social and political issues, while in the advice columns that she wrote for *Le Petit Journal*, Janette Bertrand advised her readers to assert themselves and refuse to tolerate male abuse and violence.

The media also helped to introduce to the public the women writers, actors, singers, and artists, who were more numerous than ever in those careers in the postwar period and some of whom won considerable fame, starting of course with Gabrielle

Roy, who won the Prix Fémina in 1947 for her novel *Bonheur d'Occasion* (*The Tin Flute*). Other women poets and novelists such as Rina Lasnier, Anne Hébert, Germaine Guèvremont, Claire Martin, and Marie-Claire Blais, who in 1966 was awarded the Prix Médicis for *Une saison dans la vie d'Emmanuel*, or dramatists like Françoise Loranger and Jean Desprez (Laurette Larocque), who wrote for stage, radio, and television, also distinguished themselves with occasionally subversive works that made an impression both at home and abroad. Some women headed theatre or dance companies, like Yvette Brind'Amour, who with her partner Mercedes Palomino founded the Théâtre du Rideau Vert in 1948, or Ludmilla Chiriaeff, who created Les Grands Ballets Canadiens in 1955, while much admired singers like Alys Robi and Maureen Forrester pursued international careers. In 1948 seven women artists were among the sixteen signatories of *Refus Global*, a manifesto that denounced the authoritarianism and clericalism of Quebec society and became one of the symbols of protest against the Duplessis regime.

In short, the postwar years, however conformist they may have been, also allowed an occasional dissident female voice to be heard, at least on an individual level. It should also be pointed out that if the feminist groups founded in the early twentieth century seemed to go into decline after women's suffrage was won, many women's associations remained active in the public sphere. During the Second World War the federal government had appealed to all the women's volunteer organizations in the country to help orchestrate campaigns encouraging the purchase of Victory Bonds, to contribute to wartime activities such as those of the Red Cross, and above all to collaborate in implementing the rationing system and distributing ration books. This social and political activism on the part of women did not die away once the war ended – quite to the contrary, women would take advantage of the experience they had acquired to pursue their commitment in numerous fields.

Thus, in 1947, women volunteers who had worked in the consumers' service established by the federal government during the war to unite the volunteers engaged in overseeing prices and rationing founded the Consumers' Association of Canada, an organization that set out to protect consumers and advise public authorities on the subject. Its creation coincided with the federal government's decision to end controls on food prices, stirring discontent among female consumers who had become used to affordable prices during the previous few years. As Magda Fahrni relates, in 1947 and 1948, when inflation returned stronger than ever, housewives in Montreal called for a return of government controls, boycotted a range of products to bring down their price, and campaigned for the legalization of margarine, which was less expensive than butter, bringing their case as far as the Supreme Court of Canada. Such actions show that these women had developed a keen sense of their economic citizenship based on the conviction that it was the government's duty to protect their right to participate in the capitalist economy by preserving their buying power – an idea the government itself had encouraged during the war.

Francophones were a little tardier in joining the Consumers' Association of Canada, but in 1950 it already had twenty-five local branches in Quebec with a total of 1,400 members, both Anglophones and Francophones. Establishing a clear link between the private role played by housewives in the domestic sphere and their public role as consumers, the Association launched an educational effort to help them make better choices, but above all to convince them that by their collective action they were exercising their citizenship and could influence political decisions.

The Consumers' Association tried to draw housewives together around their more traditional function as consumers – an aspect of their role as women in the home that acquired fresh importance in the context of the postwar consumer society. Other organizations, such as various associations of university women, business and career women, and female journalists, founded shortly after the war, became involved in promoting women's educational and professional activities. The collecting and dissemination of information about the role of women in education and the job market were central to the activities of these organizations, which regularly made themselves heard through the media, organized lectures, and exerted pressure on legislators to combat sexual discrimination. To encourage young women to pursue university studies and undertake a career, they also gave talks in schools and convents and provided scholarships for those who could not afford such an education. Long before the feminists of the 1960s, these associations castigated the inferior status of women in society, associating it with a lack of education, a too limited range of career opportunities, and the income and legal inequities from which they suffered. Accordingly, among the claims they expressed were equality of access to education and careers, equal pay for equal work, and the reform of the legal status of married women. Coming mostly from the upper or middle classes, the members of these associations, numbering a few hundred at most, articulated a liberal approach that heralded the egalitarian feminism of the second half of the 1960s.

The Jeunesse ouvrière catholique feminine (JOCF), an organization affiliated with the Catholic Action movement that evolved in Quebec during the 1930s with the aim of rechristianizing society, was another group that offered young women the possibility of involvement in the public sphere. As has been noted by Lucie Piché, if the JOCF, which in the postwar years attracted several thousand members, subscribed to the traditional view of the complementary roles of the sexes in society and the family, it nevertheless allowed its activists to acquire training and assume responsibilities on the organizational and leadership levels that far exceeded those usually entrusted to women, thereby contributing to social change. According to Michael Gauvreau, the courses offered by the Service de préparation au mariage, an initiative of the JOCF, most likely played an important part in the feminist awakening of the 1960s thanks to the personalist philosophy of its teachings on sexuality and contraception, which insisted on individual development rather than just child-bearing and motherhood, and suggested a new, more egalitarian conception of the conjugal relationship, though it was still based on the complementarity of roles. In fact by offering women many opportunities to assert their presence in the public sphere, and by denouncing the clericalism of a retrograde religion that demanded submission from the faithful, groups such as the École des parents, the JOCF, the Service de préparation au mariage, and the Jeunesse étudiante catholique féminine provided prominent platforms from which their members could initiate public debate on issues of concern to them. A number of women who were active in these groups, such as Simonne Monet-Chartrand, Jeanne Duval, Alec Leduc-Pelletier, Jeanne Benoît-Sauvé, and Claudine Vallerand, became significant figures in the Quebec of the 1960s thanks to their social, union, or feminist allegiances.

If the Fédération nationale Saint-Jean-Baptiste and the Montreal Local Council of Women went into a clear decline after the Second World War, this was not the case for the Cercles de fermières du Québec, which continued to prosper. From 27,000 in 1940 their membership reached 49,000 in 1944, an increase not unrelated to the enlistment of rural women in the war effort, which was encouraged by the public authorities. However, this increase in membership did not sit well with the clergy, who feared that the government, as the Cercles' main source of funding, would manipulate the farm women, given that it had recently granted women the right to vote. What is more, the Cercles, which were officially non-sectarian, had just become federated on a territorial rather than a diocesan basis, thus escaping control by the bishops. In 1944, to counteract this threat, the clergy created a rival association, the Union catholique des fermières (a female equivalent of the Union catholique des cultivateurs) and called on the members of the Cercles to abandon their group and join this new organization, which in 1957 changed its name to Union catholique des femmes rurales (UCFR). The clergy had no qualms about ostracizing Cercle members to ensure their compliance, in some parishes going as far as to refuse them communion. In spite of this only 10,000 farm women switched their allegiance, an indication that even outside the large urban centres the Church was losing its power. This initial foundation by the clergy was followed in 1952 by the establishment of the Cercles d'économie domestique (CED) with the objective of uniting village women and women from smaller urban centres. In 1966 the CED and the UCFR, which had moved farther and farther away from the Church to devote more energy to furthering the education of their members about all kinds of social, political, or economic issues vital to women, merged to form the Association féminine d'éducation et d'action sociale.

In 1961 Thérèse Casgrain established a Quebec branch of the Canadian organization called Voice of Women / Voix des femmes in order to oppose the proliferation of nuclear weapons, increasingly a cause of concern for the future of the planet. With some 500 members, Voice of Women was one of the first women's organizations whose militant activities spilled over national frontiers – Thérèse Casgrain was actually arrested during a demonstration in Paris. In the same year as the creation of Voice of Women, the Liberal candidate Claire Kirkland-Casgrain won a by-election in the Jacques-Cartier riding, previously held by her father, who had died a short time before. This trained lawyer, the first woman elected to the Quebec Legislative Assembly and who would be appointed minister of state after her re-election at the Quebec general election of 1962, piloted Bill 16, which became law in 1964, proclaiming spousal equality and putting an end to the legal incapacity of married women. This legislative change, which had long been demanded by the Association des femmes diplômées des universités de Québec, the Association des femmes de carrière du Québec métropolitain, the Fédération des femmes libérales du Québec, and even the Union catholique des femmes rurales and the Cercles d'économie domestique, was not only a successful outcome but also a springboard for feminist struggles to come.

CHAPTER SEVEN

The Feminist Revolution (1966–1989)

The resurgence of the feminist movement is undoubtedly one of the most significant social phenomena to have occurred in the Western hemisphere between 1960 and 1990. Fuelled by the socio-economic changes that had been under way since the Second World War and by the wave of protests that swept over the West at the same time, the Women's Liberation Movement, as it called itself, gave rise to further demands attacking the very foundations of gender relations, leaving an indelible imprint on all the societies it affected. Much more subversive than its early twentieth-century predecessor, which as a general rule accepted the complementarity of roles and functions, this "second wave feminism," as it has also been called, launched a comprehensive denunciation of the inequalities between men and women, of sexual discrimination, and of male domination in both the public and private spheres, and demanded the complete autonomy of women on every level, including, and especially, in matters related to reproduction. The shattering of the model of a housewife living in economic dependency on a provider husband, which had prevailed since the nineteenth century, was undoubtedly one of the main results of this often virulent challenge to the roles and status of women in every domain. At the same time, the face of the family changed radically as a result of a decline in the fertility rate and of marital breakdowns.

The contraction in family size, which had begun well before the 1960s, continued throughout this period. By the end of the decade the fertility rate in Quebec ranked last among the Canadian provinces, at 2.1 (the threshold for generational replacement), and in 1987 it reached a historic low at 1.39 children per woman of child-bearing age. A slight recovery at the end of the 1980s, coinciding with the introduction of the natalist policies of the Liberal government of Robert Bourassa, was more or less maintained, but the average number of children per woman remained below the generational replacement threshold until the early 2010s, making many nationalist observers profoundly uneasy. With an average of 2.6 children per woman, only the Indigenous peoples and certain immigrant groups were recording a fertility rate that ensured their growth.

Such a significant decline in the number of children testifies to couples' massive use of contraception. In fact, according to estimates by Nicole Marcil-Gratton, beginning in the second half of the 1960s, almost 90% of married women in Quebec turned to one or another method of contraception, compared with only 30% before 1946. Furthermore, if in 1970 the pill was the most popular means of contraception, by the middle of the 1970s sterilization, mostly of women, became the most widespread method, despite being almost irreversible. The liberalization of abortion in 1969 also contributed to reducing the number of children per woman, with the proportion of terminated pregnancies equalling 13% of live births in 1976, and 28% ten years later.

Another significant phenomenon during the period was that the proportion of children born to unmarried mothers increased considerably, climbing from 4% to 38% between the early 1960s and the end of the 1980s as Quebec couples tended to prefer de facto relationships to marriage. In the early 1980s this was the case for fewer than 5% of them, but by the end of the decade this figure had already almost doubled. Furthermore, there was an explosion in the proportion of marriages ending in divorce, which rose from a little under 9% in 1969 (the year after the amendments to the federal divorce law) to almost 45% in 1987. This meant that the proportion of single-parent families also increased: standing at 11% in 1961, it reached 20% by the middle of the 1980s, a substantial increase that was attributable to broken relationships rather than to the deaths of husbands. This upsurge is partly explained by the repeal of the Needy Mothers Assistance Act and its replacement by the Social Aid Act, which came into force in 1970 and which did not exclude single mothers, encouraging them to keep their children. This Act also encouraged many to terminate marital situations that had become intolerable.

The growing participation of women in the job market was another indication of the profound upheavals that affected their lives and which may have decided some to separate. Across the board women made up 23% of the total workforce in 1951, while by the end of the 1980s this proportion had nearly doubled, to 43%. This growth, especially noticeable starting from the early

1970s, can be largely attributed to married women who, according to Francine Barry, comprised almost 49% of the female workforce in 1971, compared with only 17% in 1951. By the mid-1980s women's overall participation rate crossed the 50% threshold, compared with 75% for men, while the proportion of married women in employment reached 54%, compared with 22% in 1961. Initially limited mostly to mothers whose children were of school age, the employment of married women later came to include those with very young children. Thus between 1976 and 1990 the participation rate of mothers with a child aged under 3 years rose from 28% to 60%, while that of women aged between 24 and 45 grew from 20% to 70 % between 1951 and 1987.

However, though steadily increasing numbers of women were earning a living, they were largely concentrated in types of employment that can be considered traditional, despite some change in the distribution between different economic sectors. Thus in 1986 fewer than 15% of women were working in manufacturing, compared with 30% in 1951, while by the mid-1980s almost 47% were employed in sociocultural, commercial, and professional services, compared with 39% in the early 1950s. Though they had a greater presence in the tertiary sector, women were still confined to a rather restricted range of professions within which they constituted a substantial majority. For instance, by the mid-1980s 98% of secretaries and 89% of cashiers were women, while the proportion of women in nursing stood at 92%, and in domestic service at 87%. This concentration of female workers in offices, stores, the health sector, and personnel services maintained the salary gap between men and women, even though the latter were generally better educated and a certain proportion of them did have access to well-paid positions or the professions. As a result, by 1986 women in full-time employment earned on average 66% of the wage of men in the same situation, compared with 60% in 1975. When we take part-time work into consideration – beginning in the 1980s it was a rapidly increasing phenomenon in the traditional female areas of employment – the picture was even darker, for while at the start of the decade women workers as a whole (full- and part-time) earned 52% of the men's wage, the figure had fallen to 47% by 1986.

In the 1960s it was not rare for women, even in unionized workplaces, to be paid less than men performing identical tasks – a practice castigated by the feminist groups who were calling at the time for equal pay for equal work. However, the segregation of the job market along sex lines and the systemic devaluation of predominantly female jobs were major obstacles to an increase in women's wages, leading these groups, starting in the 1970s, to call for pay equity. Endorsed by the International Labour Organization in 1951, and ratified by the federal government in 1972, the principle of salary equity led to a re-evaluation of jobs that involved a heavy concentration of both men and women, using "objective" criteria such as the skills required, the degree of responsibility, the physical effort needed, and the working conditions. In Quebec, Section 19 of the Charter of Human Rights and Freedoms, which was passed in 1975 and came into effect in 1976, forbade any form of discrimination on sexual grounds and explicitly recognized the principle of pay equity, though the cumbersome procedures used to rectify inequities and the limited scope of Section 19 have meant that wage differences persisted, as demonstrated by the data given above. Nevertheless, the inclusion of pay equity in the Quebec Charter showed that the society recognized the problem, providing grounds for the feminist and union movements to maintain their pressure for it over the following decades.

Systemic discrimination towards working women came, in the case of immigrants, in addition to the prejudice and racial discrimination that too often restricted them to the worst-paid sectors, whatever their qualifications. It should be remembered that since the early 1970s immigration had become more diversified, with a growing proportion of new immigrants coming from the West Indies and the Caribbean (especially Haiti), Eastern Asia (including Vietnam), South America, and North Africa. The result was a profound change in the ethnic composition of Quebec society, particularly in Montreal, where the great majority of immigrants settled. According to Aleyda Lamotte's analysis of the data from the 1981 and 1986 censuses, 20% of immigrant women held university degrees compared with 13% of native-born women, while 29% of those on the job market held positions as executives and professionals and 31% of the white-collar jobs, compared with 32% and 45% of native-born women. This meant that 40% of immigrant women, compared with 23% of other Quebec women, worked in blue-collar jobs, while they represented 9% of working women overall. In many cases they fulfilled the need for workers in sectors such as garment manufacturing, which was by then in decline, and in which they replaced the immigrants who had arrived soon after the Second World War, but they also worked as cleaners in offices and hotels as well as in the personal services sector – types of work looked down on by female workers born in Quebec or who had immigrated much earlier.

Starting in the early 1980s many domestic helpers arrived in Canada under a federal program that required them to remain with an employer for two years before they could obtain permanent resident status, a period during which they were sometimes at the mercy of unscrupulous bosses. Despite often onerous working conditions and the exploitation to which some were subjected, each year almost 5,000 women, mainly from the Philippines and the Caribbean, took advantage of this federal program after it was introduced in the early 1980s, a sign of the rampant poverty in their countries of origin. For the majority of these women immigration was one of the few means at their disposal to provide a little relief for their families, to whom they would send a portion of their wages while they waited to acquire resident status and could bring them to Canada. Paradoxically, immigrant domestic helpers, who provided a cheap workforce, also freed the middle-class and wealthy women in whose homes they worked from their household duties, allowing them to pursue lucrative professional activities.

Indeed, it was during this period that women were able to invade some formerly male strongholds such as senior management and the liberal professions, positions that required a great deal of availability and were therefore more difficult to reconcile with household and family obligations. Beginning in the 1970s, when women were pursuing university studies in ever increasing numbers, their penetration of certain male preserves continued to grow throughout the following decade. Thus, according to data from the Quebec College of Physicians, the proportion of women in the medical profession grew from 17% to 25% between 1983 and 1993, while it had stalled at 10% in 1976. During the 1980s there were more than twice as many female as male pharmacists, whereas twenty years earlier women amounted to only 19% of the profession. The same was true for women lawyers, engineers, architects, and senior executives. According to

Johanne Collin, major changes taking place within certain of these professions, especially the spread of salaried employment, was likely one of the main causes of their feminization, for as a result men became less attracted to careers that meant a loss of autonomy and social prestige. Even within these professions divisions along sex lines were also seen, for instance, with women being more likely than men to choose family medicine or family law while men remained in the majority in surgery or criminal law. Such disparities, together with the fact that women often worked shorter hours than men in order to have time to look after their families, sometimes resulted in considerable differences in earning power; in 1985, for instance, the remuneration for women doctors, dentists, and other specialists averaged only 47% of that of men. But in spite of everything, the fact that women had broken into the liberal professions was an important step forward, if only because they achieved an enviable status and income that had formerly been beyond their reach.

The constantly growing participation of married women in the job market since the 1950s can be explained not only by the desire of women, often the more highly educated, to have a career and gain some financial autonomy, but also by the need of many households for a second income that would allow them to improve or maintain their standard of living at a time when inflation was eroding their purchasing power. In the 1950s a single breadwinner had been able to ensure the material well-being of the family, but two decades later the ability to afford property and consumer goods required an ongoing financial contribution from the women, who nevertheless continued to perform the majority of household tasks and assume responsibility for the children. Indeed, considerable time would have to pass before men would be prepared to contribute to the housework to the same extent as their wives. Until the 1980s many men considered it was not their place to cook meals, do the laundry, or supervise their children's homework, tasks they considered typically feminine and a threat to their masculinity. It is true that the new household appliances available did lighten the burden of household tasks to a certain extent, but the latter still required planning and not all households owned such appliances, for even in the late 1980s only 43% had a dishwasher and 60% a microwave oven. The sharing of domestic work, a concept that includes not only housekeeping but also caring for the children, therefore became a challenge for many couples and one of the demands of the feminist movement, which throughout this period stressed the social and economic value of this unpaid, invisible work. A fringe of the feminist movement actually called for housewives to receive a wage so that their contribution to the national economy would be fully recognized, while other activists were opposed, fearing that remuneration of that kind would confine women to their roles as mothers and spouses, leaving them restricted to the private realm of the family with no possibility of moving outside it.

Paid maternity leaves and the creation of a network of public child care facilities to support working mothers also figured among the demands that feminists and unionists made of the government. In the early 1970s the federal unemployment insurance program began to make payments to new mothers, but like the unemployed they were still subject to a two-week waiting period and received only 60% of their gross salary for fifteen weeks. Prior to this, the most women could hope for was an unpaid leave granted by their employer. In 1978, to enhance the federal program, the Quebec government agreed to make payments to cover the two-week waiting period, and it also changed the minimum wage legislation, which henceforth guaranteed women the right to take an eighteen-week maternity leave without fearing the loss of their jobs. As for the employees of the Quebec public service, in negotiating their collective agreement they won their full salary for twenty weeks. In 1988 the federal government granted an additional ten weeks of paid leave, to be used by either the mother or father; two years later Quebec legislation on employment standards introduced an unpaid parental leave of thirty-four weeks, which in the case of women could be added to the eighteen weeks already covered by federal unemployment insurance. In theory this change allowed parents to take more time to care for their newborn, but since it was far from covering all the lost salary many couples were unable to take advantage of it.

The issue of daycare facilities also became a social concern in the early 1970s, but the government initially sought above all to regulate the few existing private daycares and create a public system for children with disabilities or who came from a disadvantaged background. In other words, instead of supporting working mothers, which was still a controversial idea at the time, the government considered daycares as primarily a form of "assistance to needy families," as Ghislaine Desjardins has remarked. Working women who needed child care were instead offered a tax deduction for the expense involved, a measure that came into effect in 1972 but fell far short of the entire cost. The creation of community and cooperative daycares, which began in 1972, and their struggle to survive throughout the following years, nevertheless led the Liberal government to draw up an initial daycare policy known as the Bacon Plan, named after Minister for Social Affairs Lise Bacon, who was responsible for it. This plan provided for grants for the creation of new non-profit daycares and for financial assistance to parents who relied on daycare services. However, the criteria for eligibility were such that only poor mothers could take advantage of them. Rather than a collective responsibility, daycare was still, in the government's eyes, a private matter in which it should only intervene to help the most deprived. The arrival in power of the Parti Québécois government in 1976 brought little change in this thinking, even though the subsidies to daycares and parents were increased, for at the end of the 1970s the child care available was still largely insufficient to handle the needs of working women and much too expensive compared with what the average woman earned. It was above all with the creation in 1979 of the Office des services de garde à l'enfance (Office of Child Care Services) that the government took serious action. The legislation creating this body provided that it would subsidize not only non-profit daycares but also private ones and daycares in a family environment, signifying a change in the government policy, which previously had favoured the non-profits. However, in opening the door to public financing of private daycares – a move deplored by several feminist and community groups – this new policy nevertheless explicitly recognized women's right to work and to quality services. Despite a significant increase in the number of places, which rose from 25,000 to almost 60,000 between 1981 and 1987, child care posed a major problem for many working mothers, often obliged to use unlicensed providers who demanded prohibitive rates compared with the wages they earned.

Wage equality and then pay equity, programs for access to equality in employment, maternity leaves, child care, and the removal – with wage compensation – of pregnant women from working environments dangerous for their health were some of the demands supported not only by the feminist movement but also by union organizations, which in the 1970s had added committees on the status of women. The creation of such committees can be largely explained by the increased proportion of women among the union membership which, mainly because of the unionization of the public and quasi-public sectors in which they were heavily represented, rose from a fifth to more than a third from the 1960s to the 1980s, and by a resurgence of feminism. The committees tried to encourage greater participation by women in the union movement and in its various bodies but especially in defending their specific interests, ensuring that collective agreements responded to their requirements and that the latter were not sacrificed at the negotiating table in exchange for salary increases or non-monetary provisions that mostly benefited men. However, if workers were quite ready to support certain demands made by women, such as those for maternity leaves, demands related to the struggle against systemic discrimination in employment and wages or against sexual harassment met with greater opposition, for they represented a more direct threat to male privilege. The election of Monique Simard as vice-president of the Confédération des syndicats nationaux in 1983, and of Lorraine Pagé to head the Quebec Teachers' Corporation in 1988, nevertheless bear witness to the federations' openness to the egalitarian and explicitly feminist objectives that those women advocated. Furthermore, though the difficulty of reconciling domestic responsibilities and activism remained a serious obstacle to women's involvement in union activities, they were always found in the front ranks of strike pickets during the work stoppages by employees of the public and quasi-public services initiated by the common fronts formed by unions in the 1970s and 1980s, for they represented the majority of workers in these sectors.

The participation of nuns in the workforce went into a clear decline starting in the mid-1960s. The drop in recruitment, the numerous renunciations of vows, and the aging of the membership did indeed bring about a dramatic reduction in their numbers, which fell from 43,000 to about 22,000 between 1965 and 1987, a reduction of almost 50%. The secularization of Quebec society and its greater openness to the social and professional aspirations of laywomen have often been invoked to explain this collapse of religious vocations. Those who remained continued to work in the areas of education, health, and social services, though in ever declining numbers because of the retirements and deaths for which new postulants were not numerous enough to compensate. An equally significant fact is that beginning in the 1960s establishments formerly administered by religious communities were being progressively taken over by the government. Thus, according to Micheline Dumont, while in 1960 nuns were in charge of almost 2,000 schools and convents, by 1989 this number had fallen to around fifty. Their exclusion was even more marked in the health field, where they lost their hold over the 105 hospitals they had controlled in 1961. It was the same story in the social services, in which various categories of marginalized individuals (i.e., those with a physical or mental disability, orphans, etc.) became deinstitutionalized and the services deconfessionalized. The evolution towards government control and secularization associated with the Quiet Revolution, which aimed to centralize and standardize programs and modernize their operation, was also accompanied by an increase in the number of men at the head of institutions as nuns were replaced by male administrators appointed by the province. The expertise the nuns had acquired, which had seemed quite adequate as long as they were working for very little financial reward, was considered insufficient as soon as the positions they had occupied came with an enviable salary and government was bent on having things done its way.

Women's work in agriculture also underwent a profound change during this period. The definitive decline of the small farm and its replacement by large, industrial-scale, specialized operations meant that farm women had to adapt to many new technologies that required a higher level of training, whether because of the evolution of biotechnology or the computerization of farming. Also evident was a greater desire of these women for recognition of their contribution to what was still, in spite of everything, a family concern. Under pressure from the feminist movement, which castigated the often precarious situation of women in family businesses (especially following a divorce), and thanks to the studies and awareness-raising work carried out by the Association féminine d'éducation et d'action sociale, the Association des femmes collaboratrices (founded in 1980), and later by the Fédération des agricultrices, the proportion of women who owned a share in agricultural property rose from 4% to 20% between 1981 and 1991. Changes made in 1986 to legislation dealing with the development of farming, raising the settlement allowance to $15,000 and making spousal joint owners eligible to receive it, helped to accelerate this trend.

The education reforms launched in 1964 with the creation of the Ministry of Education were carried on in the second half of the

1960s with the establishment of comprehensive schools and CEGEPs and the expansion of the university system, which admitted a steadily increasing number of students as the baby boom generation reached adulthood. The most flagrant inequities in the education system favouring boys over girls became a thing of the past when the three pillars of the Parent Report reform, co-education, free schooling, and accessibility, ensured that all attended the same establishments and received more or less the same schooling. In practice, however, schools in the 1970s and 1980s tended to reproduce the divisions based on the gender identity that ran through all of society. If in principle all subjects were open to girls, very often the persistence of traditional notions of their role informed the models held up to them and the career choices that they made, at least in the majority of cases.

Textbooks used in primary and secondary schools in the 1970s continued to purvey the most outworn stereotypes of male and female propensities and roles, attributing a largely dominant role to males, doing nothing to change the girls' self-image and little to ignite their ambition where training and careers were concerned. From the second half of the 1970s these sexist representations came under many attacks from feminists and female teachers, who were able to open the eyes of the education establishment. As a result, these images demeaning to women were banished from the new textbooks that were produced beginning in the 1980s. However, the predisposition of adolescents and young women to choose careers as hairstylists or beauticians or to enrol in college and university courses leading to traditionally female professions such as nursing, medical technology, teaching, or social work was more difficult to counteract, for it resulted from a complex web of mutually reinforcing causes. The successes achieved by girls and young women in their studies, and egalitarian feminist thinking, both of which pushed them in the direction of non-traditional and more lucrative trades and professions, were still not enough to counterbalance the social and cultural determinants encouraging them to choose careers considered compatible with the image of femininity instilled in them since childhood, or with their future family responsibilities. However, the 1980s did see some changes in this respect when a number of organizations launched projects encouraging girls to pursue the sciences and to choose non-traditional careers, and when they began to register in greater numbers for technological or university programs in which men predominated.

Indeed, despite the persistence of stereotypes, the advance of women in the universities continued more strongly than ever during this whole period. While they comprised about a third of the student body in the mid-1960s and were mostly concentrated in a limited number of programs, by the end of the 1980s they were in the majority among undergraduates and more numerous than men in the Faculties of Law and Medicine, where they represented 58% and 53% of the students, respectively. In fact with the exception of Engineering, where they came to only a fifth of the enrolments, women comprised almost half of the students in most of the professional faculties such as Administration, Pharmacy, Dentistry, and Architecture. The professoriate was, however, far from becoming feminized at the same rate, for the proportion of women barely exceeded 25% towards the end of the 1980s. This situation partly reflected the lower proportion of female students able to complete doctoral studies, in which they represented only 30% of graduates.

THE FEMINIST REVOLUTION

The advances made by women in the working world and in education throughout this period were backed by the feminist movement, which underwent reorganization in the mid-1960s, while at the same time its resurgence was fuelled by the growing dissatisfaction felt by women about their status and role in society. In other words, if feminism was reborn during this period it was partly because more and more women encountered discrimination and became aware of the inequities they were experiencing, not only in the world of work but within the family, and of their exclusion from the corridors of power. The media, especially the magazine *Châtelaine*, of which Fernande Saint-Martin was editor-in-chief until 1972, the radio program *"Place aux femmes"* (1965–70), hosted by Lise Payette, and especially the TV magazine *Femmes d'aujourd'hui*, which first aired in 1965 and was hosted by Aline Desjardins between 1966 and 1979, helped to bring about this fresh awareness and renewal of activism by dealing with subjects that affected women directly, such as paid employment, the reform of the Civil Code, divorce, contraception, abortion, homosexuality, and conjugal violence.

The genesis of this new "wave" – soon to become a real tsunami – of feminism was marked by the founding in 1966, on the initiative of Thérèse Casgrain, of the Quebec Federation of Women, of the Association féminine d'éducation et d'action sociale that same year, and in the following year by the creation by the federal government, bowing to pressure from numerous women including Laura Sabia, national chair of the Committee for the Equality of Women in Canada, of the Royal Commission on the Status of Women in Canada. If the Quebec Federation of Women, the Association féminine d'éducation et d'action sociale, and the various bodies that appeared before the Commission on the Status of Women, which was chaired by Florence Bird, essentially called for legislative changes – though, it should be said, sometimes quite radical ones – their feminism, which aimed to achieve equality through legislation, soon gave rise to a true women's liberation movement that challenged the patriarchal order and demanded an end to male domination.

Tabled in the House of Commons in 1970, the report of the Royal Commission (known as the Bird Report) included 167 recommendations related to every aspect of women's lives. Compared with a real bombshell by a journalist for the *Toronto Star*, the report documented, with supporting statistics, the often deplorable conditions experienced by women, the inequalities and injustices inflicted on them, and the extent of their needs if they were to participate fully in social, economic, and political life. These included maternity leaves, child care facilities, access to contraception and abortion, wage parity, professional development, the outlawing of sexual discrimination in employment, changes in family law, access to health care, and so on. Widely distributed by all groups with an interest in what was called the "feminine condition," this Report drew up a list of demands around which feminists would rally during the coming decades. In 1988 the Canadian feminist movement found that two of the three aims prioritized by the Bird Commission had been achieved, namely, the decriminalization of abortion and the inclusion of discrimination on sexual grounds in the Canadian Charter of Rights and Freedoms. Only a response to the demand for universal child care was still lacking. The establishment of provincial committees financed by the provinces to advise government on the status of women, such as the Conseil du statut de la femme, which was established in Quebec in 1973, were another outcome of the Commission's work.

If the Bird Report seemed explosive to some, for a portion of the generation of female baby boomers the legislative changes being demanded, while necessary, still fell short. Through their involvement in the social, union, national, and student struggles that characterized the period, these young woman gradually became aware that even in the leftist groups in which they were active it was impossible for them to carve out for themselves a place equal to that of the men, or to have their opinions truly heard. While fighting for the liberation of workers, Afro-Americans, and colonized peoples, and for social justice, they realized that they themselves belonged to an oppressed group – something their comrades in arms refused to recognize or even discuss. From this new awareness was born the women's liberation movement which manifested itself all over the Western world by the creation of single-sex groups in which activists compared their experiences and realized that the difficulties and obstacles they had encountered in their personal and professional lives, far from being due to any personal lack of ability, arose from the power relations between men and women. "The personal is political," they said, meaning that the issue of power lies at the heart of male–female relations, even within the couple and the family. Instead of reforms to the law, the eradication of patriarchy – meaning the domination of women by men in all areas of society, and especially of their bodies – became their objective, along with the abolition of capitalism which, according to their analysis (often inspired by Marxism), profited from the subordination of women. Rejecting the structures and strategies of feminist groups such as the Quebec Federation of Women or the Association féminine d'éducation et d'action sociale, which they considered to be "reformist," they formed a multitude of small groups that functioned informally and preferred tactics similar to those of student or leftist organizations, such as civil disobedience, occupations, and demonstrations. Furthermore, the radical nature of their actions and analyses gave them a great deal of visibility for, more perhaps than the Bird Commission, this radical feminism, though it was not supported by all women, created a dynamic that stimulated reflection in growing numbers of them, finally winning their support for certain specific causes and forcing change.

The Montreal Women's Liberation Movement, created by students at McGill University in 1969, one of the main activities of which was to offer a referral service to women wishing to terminate a pregnancy, was probably the first group in the nebula of the women's movement that came into being in Quebec. In the autumn of that same year some Francophone and Anglophone female students and union members organized a demonstration to protest against the "anti-demonstration" rule that had been introduced by the administration of Mayor Jean Drapeau in the hope that it would be enough to calm the wind of protest blowing through Montreal. Shortly after this event some of them came together to create the Front de libération des femmes du Québec (FLFQ) – a name obviously inspired by that of the Front de Libération du Québec (FLQ). Initially, the FLFQ collaborated with the Montreal Women's Liberation Movement to provide guidance to women wishing to obtain an abortion, distributing the brochure *Pour un contrôle des naissances*, the French version of the *Birth Control Handbook* published by McGill University's student council in 1968 that had become a real bestseller all over North America. In the fall of 1970, however, the Francophones expelled the Anglophones from the group, to the great distress of the latter, alleging that they were exercising too much influence over its ideological direction. At a time when the FLFQ was linking the liberation of women to national liberation for Quebec, Francophone activists considered such an influence a vestige of a colonialist attitude on the part of the Anglophones, who derived their inspiration from an Anglo-Saxon feminist theory that took no account of the particular situation of Quebec. While continuing to provide an abortion referral service to Francophones, the FLFQ then split up into cells, in the same way as the Front de Libération du Québec. One cell agitated for free and open access to abortion, while a second involved itself in the struggle for daycare facilities, and a third, named "Cell X," planned shock tactics. A demonstration in support of abortion that was held on Mother's Day in 1970, the 1971 occupation of taverns (still barred to women), and above all the dramatic gesture they made during the trial of Lise Balcer that same year, brought them considerable publicity. Called as a witness during the trial of the FLQ members accused of the murder of Minister of Labour Pierre Laporte, Balcer refused to testify on the grounds that women could not serve as jurors. Just when she appeared to be sentenced for contempt of court, seven members of Cell X of the FLFQ, sitting in the audience, rushed the jury benches shouting "Discrimination!" and "The law is shit!" and "We're still being raped!" – provoking quite an uproar. They were immediately arrested, sentenced for contempt of court, and imprisoned – though barely three months later the legislation on juries was amended to allow women to serve.

The jurors' affair, and it horrified public opinion, spelled the end of the FLFQ, which was dissolved in the fall of 1971. The Centre des femmes, funded by two former FLFQ activists, took up the baton. Specializing in a referral service for women seeking an abortion, this group also took over the publication of a feminist magazine, *Québécoises Deboutte!* – the first issue of which had appeared in November 1971. However, 1974 marked the end of the Centre des femmes and of this publication, though it did not end the activities of women's collectives trying to provide assistance to women who found themselves in particularly difficult situations. In the following years centres for the support of victims of rape and incest opened their doors in Quebec and Montreal, while just about everywhere in the province other groups set up emergency shelters and safe houses for victims of conjugal violence and associations to defend those who suffered from particularly unequal treatment: mothers of single-parent families, women contributing to a family business, farm women, workers, etc. Women's centres offering a wide variety of services and organizing all kinds of training and information activities on a town or neighbourhood scale also became more numerous, as did women's health centres. By the end of the 1970s these initiatives were plentiful enough to motivate the creation of sectorial groupings: the Réseau des centres d'aide et de lutte contre les agressions à caractère sexuel (1978), the Regroupement des maisons pour femmes victimes de violence conjugale (1979), the Conseil d'intervention pour l'accès des femmes au travail (1984), the Réseau des centres de santé des femmes (1985), and the R [*sic*] des centres de femmes du Québec (1985). Staffed by volunteer or low-paid activists, all these groups constituted what Diane Lamoureux has termed a "service feminism" that complemented or replaced state action. If the government devoted more and more funding to women's centres from the late 1970s on, especially to emergency shelters and safe houses, these were never adequate to fulfil the need, while the activists who staffed them became poorly paid workers forced to devote much more time to their administrative work than to the feminist cause they were defending.

The establishment of centres to combat conjugal violence and sexual assault bears witness to the concern of contemporary feminism for women's control over their own bodies. These phenomena were certainly not new, as is shown by the work of Marie-Aimée Cliche, Kathryn Harvey, Sylvie Frigon, and Raymonde Boisvert on the nineteenth and twentieth centuries, while the founding of the Montreal Society for the Protection of Women and Children in 1882 shows that other groups were concerned about this long before the 1970s. But until then conjugal violence was usually considered a private matter by society and by the judiciary, which blatantly displayed its partiality towards men as the undisputed heads of families, while rape and incest were such taboo matters that most women hesitated to report them. The Civil Code required battered women to prove that their lives were literally in danger if they were to obtain a legal separation on that ground. Exactly as in the case of rape or even incest, in which women were generally suspected of having "provoked" their assailant and needed to prove that their morals were beyond reproach if they were to have any hope of winning their case, victims of physical violence were generally considered responsible for their own misfortune by lacking patience with their husbands; furthermore, from the middle of the twentieth century murders of women were often described in the popular press as "crimes of passion," as if to suggest that they were killings of a special kind, probably inspired by jealousy.

Feminists therefore faced a struggle if they hoped to change minds and the law. Brought into prominence by the repeated demands of women's groups and by the Conseil du statut de la femme, which made it a priority, violence against women nevertheless became an object of public debate in the 1970s: colloquia, awareness campaigns aimed at the population and outreach workers, funding for shelters and safe houses (the number of which grew from fourteen in 1978 to sixty-five in 1989), and legislative changes, most notably the prohibition of harassment that was included in the Quebec Charter of Human Rights and Freedoms in 1982, managed to make such behaviour socially unacceptable, though not to eradicate it. In 1983 a change to the Criminal Code explicitly outlawed conjugal rape and likened sexual abuse to physical assault, putting the emphasis on the violent nature of such acts and the thirst for power underlying them.

Where women's bodies were concerned, however, we can say that the great battle of this period was undoubtedly the struggle for free and open access to abortion, in which even the Quebec Federation of Women eventually played a part. In 1969, responding to the demand of doctors in particular, the federal government finally decriminalized abortion, as it did contraception and homosexuality, though with some severe restrictions, for in order to be legal abortion had to take place in a hospital environment and be recommended by a therapeutic committee of three doctors. Yet hospitals still had to establish such committees, and this was far from happening in Francophone establishments with a Catholic tradition, where many practitioners refused to participate because of their religious convictions. For their part, feminists thought that women should be able to decide for themselves whether they wanted an abortion. The Comité de lutte pour l'avortement libre et gratuit, formed in 1974, spearheaded this battle, organizing numerous demonstrations under the slogan "We will have the children we want," and supporting the actions of Dr Henry Morgentaler, who, starting in 1969, had been performing abortions in his Montreal clinic in defiance of the law. Prosecuted many times, Morgentaler won a number of court cases until in 1988 the Supreme Court of Canada declared Article 251 of the Criminal Code unconstitutional under the Canadian Charter of Rights and Freedoms, which had come into effect in 1982. Despite a few attempts, the Parliament of Canada has to date not been able to pass new abortion legislation that would respect the Charter, so that Canada is one of the few countries with no restrictions on abortion. We know that beginning in 1978, in contravention of the federal law, the Parti Québécois government offered abortion services in the family planning clinics it established. However, these clinics were not accessible to the entire female population, while some became targets for the pro-life movement which, though less active in Quebec than in the rest of North America, nevertheless has a presence there.

Bill 16, which became law in 1964, had put an end to the legal incapacity of married women, though it failed to ensure the full equality of spouses within the couple and the family, another demand made by the feminists of the time. The substitution in 1970 of partnership of acquests for the community of goods as the statutory matrimonial regime, the abolition in 1977 of the father's power in favour of parental authority, the new family law of 1981 recognizing the full equality of spouses, and the 1989 legislation dealing with family assets, which provided for the equal division of certain goods (homes, furniture, automobiles, retirement pensions) between the spouses at the time of a divorce even if the wife has made no financial contribution to the household budget, represent some of the principal legislative changes intended to ensure the equality of men and women within the couple and the family. They were obtained thanks to pressure from feminists, but without encountering very vigorous opposition, except in the last case. It was a different story where the status of Native women was concerned.

In 1967 Mary Two-Axe Earley, a Mohawk from Kahnawake, founded Equal Rights for Indian Women, an association whose main objective was to obtain amendments to the Indian Act, which since the nineteenth century had deprived them of their status and right to live on a reservation if they married a non-Native. Encouraged by Thérèse Casgrain, Two-Axe Earley made a submission on the matter to the Bird Commission, which recommended the repeal of the sections of the Indian Act that sanctioned this discrimination. However, this demand met with strong opposition in the Native communities, for the men feared that non-Natives married to First Nations women might become a majority on the reserves, so that almost two decades of constant pressure were required before the law was changed. The Canadian Charter of Rights and Freedoms, which bans any form of sexual discrimination, finally forced a change in the legislation. In 1985 the Parliament of Canada passed Bill C-31, which restored Indian status to First Nations women married to non-Natives and to their children, allowing them to live on the reservations and make use of the programs and services available.

More than 16,000 women throughout the country took advantage of this right, though it failed to resolve all the problems. The prevalence of conjugal violence and sexual abuse within First Nations communities was another issue to which the Quebec Native Women's Association, founded in 1974, then turned its attention. In 1987, under the presidency of Michèle Rouleau, it launched a major awareness campaign on the theme "Violence Is Tearing Us Apart, Let's Get Together." This was followed in 1995 by a first provincial conference on the issue. In 2003, to coordinate their efforts, the Association created a network of shelters for Native women, of which there are now six in existence.

The feminist ferment of the 1960s and 1970s not only promoted numerous demands, but also encouraged feminist research, creation, and publication, which grew in output throughout the period. In the universities the various disciplines were examined under a gender microscope, while female professors and scholars castigated the sexist bias of the concepts used and the analyses that they produced, and established new centres promoting feminist teaching and research. The Remue-ménage publishing house, founded in 1976 by some feminists, became the forum of choice for the publication of this scholarship. Where artistic creation was concerned many women artists, writers, or singers stood out for their open commitment to feminism and for their abrasive tone, which ruffled many feathers. The production of the play *Les fées ont soif*, by Denise Boucher, a denunciation of the stereotypes of the mother, the virgin, and the prostitute and which scandalized certain Catholic quarters, was probably the most sensational event of the period. But many other theatrical productions, especially those by Les Folles Alliées, the Théâtre des cuisines, the Théâtre expérimental des femmes, Anne-Claire Poirier's films about abortion and violence (*Le Temps de l'avant*, *Mourir à tue-tête*), books like *L'Euguélionne* by Louky Bersianik (Lucile Durand), the monologues of Clémence Desrochers, and the songs of Pauline Julien, along with *La Chambre nuptiale*, an installation by Francine Larivée exhibited in the Complexe Desjardins, were also evidence of this creative outpouring that, sometimes with humour, denounced the subjugation of women and helped to change mindsets. The magazine *La Vie en rose*, which followed numerous other publications in the early 1980s, undertook an analysis of all the news from a feminine perspective, considerably enlarging its scope and influence; however, despite its 40,000 subscribers, it ceased publication in 1987, lacking a solid financial basis.

Quebec feminists of the 1970s and 1980s were obviously attracted by nationalism, for in promoting the self-affirmation and modernization of Quebec, nationalism also held out the promise of their personal emancipation. But the relations between the two movements were also soured by tensions, for the nationalist project went hand in hand with a conception of the place and role of women that was contrary to the feminist vision, especially where women's control over reproduction was concerned. When the members of the FLFQ cried, "Pas de libération des femmes sans libération du Québec. Pas de libération du Québec sans libération des femmes!" they were making it clear that for them the causes of women's liberation and Quebec independence were inextricably linked. But this was far from the case for many nationalists in the 1960s, whose discourse remained thoroughly misogynistic. These people considered women an obstacle to the movement for Quebec independence and, as is shown in a study by Stéphanie Lanthier, they saw Quebec itself like a woman to be vanquished, even by rape. Feminists had been active in the newly created Parti Québécois from the end of the 1960s, but when at a party convention René Lévesque vetoed a proposal in favour of abortion several of them resigned from the committees on the status of women created in the ridings, and formed the Regroupement des femmes québécoises. While still sovereignist, this organization advocated writing in the word "*femme*" on ballots for the 1980 referendum, for they thought that the sovereignist project was far from guaranteeing their emancipation.

Though the Regroupement's strategy did not prevail, the 1980 referendum was nevertheless profoundly influenced by another debate involving women: the so-called Yvette affair. This was provoked by Lise Payette, who was minister of state for the status of women in René Lévesque's government. Criticizing the stereotypes found in schoolbooks, Lise Payette said that the day of the "Yvettes" was over, using the name of the model little girl who appeared in the textbooks, and compared Madeleine Guay-Ryan, the wife of the leader of the Liberal Party and of the "No" side, to an "Yvette," likening federalist women activists to housewives opposed to their own liberation and that of Quebec. This political gaffe, which was all the more clumsy in that Madeleine Guay-Ryan was active in social causes, encouraged Liberal women to mobilize. Defying the advice of party strategists, they organized a brunch in Quebec City and then a large meeting in the Montreal Forum during which they laid claim to the title of "Yvette" in order to defend their political choice more effectively. According to a number of analysts, these activities injected new energy into the "No" campaign, which until then had been limping along, and contributed to its victory on the evening of May 20, 1980. However, in the media the "Yvette affair" was mostly treated from a feminist angle, with several journalists, including Lise Bissonnette in *Le Devoir*, characterizing the rallies not as political activities but as "spontaneous" demonstrations by housewives who were in this way proclaiming their disaffection with feminism. Yet confirmed feminists such as Thérèse Casgrain, Sheila Finestone (at the time president of the Quebec Federation of Women), and Monique Bégin (executive secretary of the Bird Commission who had become minister of health in Ottawa) were among the organizers and invited speakers, and nowhere in their speeches did they denigrate feminism.

The desire of the media to see the Yvettes' political rallies as a reaction against feminism certainly points to the exasperation, and also the angst, felt in certain sectors of Quebec society after a decade of feminist demands. Nine years later two other events occurred as reminders of the extent to which the feminist advances were both fragile and troubling for some. In the summer of 1989 Jean-Guy Tremblay, invoking the rights of the fetus and of the father-to-be, obtained an injunction from the Superior Court forbidding his former partner, Chantal Daigle, to have an abortion. Daigle challenged this injunction, first in the Court of Appeal, which upheld the earlier judgment, and then before the Supreme Court of Canada. In the meantime, unable to wait any longer, she consulted the Women's Health Centre, which in defiance of the decision of the lower-level courts helped her to obtain an abortion in Boston. Simultaneously, in just a few days and in the slowest part of the summer, the Coalition québécoise pour le droit à l'avortement libre et gratuit (Quebec Coalition for the Right to Free Abortion on Demand) organized a demonstration that brought out 10,000 people to defend the unconditional right of women to terminate a pregnancy, a right obtained after a hard struggle just a few years earlier. In the end the Court overturned the earlier judgments on the grounds that, under the law, the fetus was not a human person and therefore could not have any rights, and that a presumed father could not stand in the way of a woman's desire to have an abortion. But the judgment also stated that it was up to lawmakers to decide otherwise, thus leaving the door open to legislative changes unfavourable to women.

The year 1989 ended with an event of unprecedented violence when, on December 6, in Montreal's École Polytechnique, Marc Lépine shot fourteen young women dead and wounded thirteen others before committing suicide. Though he rationalized his act by proclaiming his hate for feminists, and though all the victims were women, the media and public authorities found it very difficult to admit the obvious and associate his murderous rampage with an extreme but real form of anti-feminism; feminists who dared to make the connection were belittled or accused of appropriating the tragic massacre for their own ends. In fact, after two decades, starting from the 1990s, the women's cause still seemed to be met with ever-increasing impatience, and a number of observers would take pleasure in proclaiming the end of a movement that had set out, like so many others, to "change the world."

CHAPTER EIGHT

Women in a Neoliberal Society (1990–2012)

Starting in the 1990s women and the women's movement had to deal with the rise of neoliberalism, an ideology that advocated a return to the free market through deregulation and privatization, lowering taxes on corporations and the wealthiest, and dismantling the welfare state. Beginning in the early 1980s, when a major recession was under way, this trend continued and became amplified over the following decades as government deficits provided justification for the withdrawal of the state from the economy and reducing social programs. Nevertheless, Quebec stood out from its North American neighbours, for the National Question restrained any substantial cuts in state support for the population and even led to the adoption of new social measures of which women were the major beneficiaries. What some have called the "Quebec model" has, however, regularly been put into question by leading conservatives, who consider its "bankruptcy" inevitable, showing that the political right is no less present in Quebec than anywhere else. The feminist movement, which had been carrying on its struggle on several fronts, even though its death had often been proclaimed, therefore became a target for virulent attacks, collective action being considered an anachronism in an age of intense individualism.

Demographically, the 1990s and 2000s were mainly characterized by the increasing diversification of Quebec society. This was especially noticeable in Montreal and the immediately surrounding region. Thus immigrants comprised 11% of the Quebec population in 2006, compared with 8.3% in 1981 – still a low proportion relative to the rest of Canada, where it reached about 20%. Their concentration in the metropolitan region where, according to the 2006 census, immigrants represented a fifth of the population, has further accentuated the cleavage that has always characterized Quebec in this respect. With ever greater numbers coming from the Middle East (especially Lebanon), East Asia, and, after the 2000s, more and more from North Africa (Morocco and Algeria), a greater percentage of these new arrivals now belonged to the so-called visible minorities or to communities whose cultural and religious practices differed substantially from those of the majority group, arousing many fears about their ability to integrate into Quebec society. The question of "reasonable accommodation," a principle laid down by the Charters that aimed to ensure equality by relaxing rules likely to engender indirect forms of discrimination, exercised public opinion to such an extent that the Quebec government was led, in February 2007, to create the Consultation Commission on Accommodation Practices Related to Cultural Differences, commonly known as the Bouchard-Taylor Commission. This Commission, which was asked to draw a picture of the scope of accommodation, analyze what was at stake, and conduct broad public consultation, was extensively covered in the press and provided an opportunity for the expression of frequently xenophobic and sometimes even openly racist sentiments, demonstrating the fear of Quebeckers of French-Canadian descent that their identity would be eroded and revealing the strength of the opposition to a multiculturalism policy that some associated with a federalist policy of assimilation. The treatment of women in Muslim communities, especially in the matter of the so-called Islamic veil, which was seen as the foremost symbol of their domination, was singled out as the flagrant demonstration of an irreconcilable opposition between the majority and certain cultural communities. In the eyes not only of numerous witnesses but also of observers and journalists, religious accommodation, and more broadly the wearing of the veil in the public space, were leading to toleration of practices detrimental to women and posed a threat to the equality of the sexes and to secularism. As Sirma Bilge has noted, this kind of argument proposing a hierarchy of the notions and norms of femininity and masculinity shows how the question of gender relations can be used to assert more easily the superiority of a majority group and thereby define the boundaries of the national community – for never before had public opinion been so passionate in considering the equality of the sexes a characteristic of Quebec society. In other words, the fact that the debate centred on the veil shows clearly that today as in the past women represent a powerful symbol of the specific character of a nation whose boundaries people are seeking to define.

The decline in the birth rate, the concern provoked by the aging of the population, and the need for a workforce to ensure Quebec's economic development go a long way towards explaining the growth in international immigration in the 1990s and

2000s. Though the annual number of births and the composite fertility rate has been rising significantly from early in the twenty-first century, it has nevertheless still fallen well short of the replacement level, even if the fertility rate of Quebec women remains slightly above that in the rest of Canada. According to demographers, this renewed growth of the birth rate, which is sometimes attributed to the introduction of social policies, is due instead to the fact that the cohort of women who reached adulthood towards the end of the 1990s postponed starting a family, so that in 2009 the average age for child-bearing rose to almost 30. The first decade of the twenty-first century, during which the fertility rate rose from 1.4 to 1.7 infants per mother, therefore seems to have been mostly a catch-up period. A majority (over 60%) of these births were now taking place outside marriage, whereas the proportion had stood at under 20% in the early 1980s, reflecting a decline in the marriage rate from 6.9% to 2.9% during the same period. It is worth noting that in Canada as a whole about 30% of babies are born to unmarried mothers, a difference which, according to some observers, is explained by the greater secularization of Quebec society.

From the 1970s on the low birth rate in Quebec, together with its slight recovery in the second half of the 2000s, has been a constant subject of commentaries by observers concerned for the future of Quebec and its place within Canada. For certain politicians, journalists, and intellectuals, the decline in the birth rate is a real "social problem," just as infant mortality used to be, representing a direct threat to national integrity, especially when immigration has been increasing and changing the face of Montreal, where they feel the use of French is in decline. Fuelled by the constitutional crises that marked the turn of the twenty-first century, and by the debates over Quebec sovereignty, these fears have sometimes translated into a condemnation of the rise in abortions, which between 1978 (when clinics for therapeutic abortions, called "Lazure clinics," were created) and 2010 grew from 10 to almost 30 per 100 live births.

While a growing number of women were choosing to terminate their pregnancies, others were instead trying to become pregnant by turning to the new reproductive technologies being developed from the 1980s on, despite the high failure rate and the ensuing health problems for both mother and child. In 2010, in response to the demand from infertile couples but also to counteract the often dramatic effects of premature births caused by the implantation of several embryos, the Quebec government adopted a law regulating the activity of clinics and of research on assisted reproductive technologies and making a certain number of in vitro fertilization (IVF) procedures free under the provincial health insurance. During the first year of the law's application more than 4,000 women underwent this treatment, for a total of 887 pregnancies, while the rate of multiple births related to these procedures fell from 27% to 5%. For the Liberal minister of health, Yves Bolduc, this was a highly positive result, but the fact remains that the new technologies as a whole have raised numerous ethical issues which society, dazzled by scientific progress, has not seemed willing to consider with the degree of seriousness required. If IVF, the donation of eggs, sperm and embryos, artificial insemination, or the use of surrogate mothers now allow many infertile or homosexual couples to have the child they so earnestly desire, some scientists and jurists raise the question of the transformation of this *desire for* a child into the *right to* a child, frequently without any thought for the child's right to know its true parentage.

The medicalization of motherhood, a process that has been under way for several decades, also intensified during this period, with a number of procedures, such as amniocentesis for pregnant women over 35 years of age, the use of epidurals, and the monitoring of the fetus during labour becoming more and more current. Mothers and mothers-to-be also continued to be targeted by advice intended to regulate their behaviour. Thus since the 1970s doctors and other health professionals have placed great stress upon the need for breastfeeding, though they had minimized its importance during the postwar years. In the 2000s they have also condemned the consumption of a single drop of alcohol during pregnancy on the grounds that it can cause fetal alcohol syndrome. If we can certainly agree that breastfeeding is beneficial for the infant and that alcohol can be harmful to it, it has to be recognized that nowadays, as in the past, medical pronouncements often turn out to be alarmist, playing on the guilt feelings and anxiety of mothers in return for increased authority over them. The "pathologization" of pregnancy and birth – quite apart from the fear of losing a portion of their clientele – has also led doctors to oppose the return of midwives who, beginning in the 1970s, have been campaigning for recognition of their profession. In 1999, with the support of the feminist movement, which decried the control exerted by medicine over women's bodies and called for a humanization of the birth process, midwives finally won the legalization of their practice and the creation of a university-level training program. In 2010 fewer than 10% of women were still giving birth with the help of a midwife, but it seems likely that this percentage will increase, if only because the government might be tempted to reduce health costs by encouraging the use of this new group of women professionals who are less generously remunerated than doctors.

Whatever its opponents say about the "Quebec model" being overgenerous in its social policies, it was unable to counteract the most damaging repercussions of the liberalization of trade that, starting in the 1980s, have severely affected the Quebec economy. Faced with what had become worldwide competition, many companies chose to relocate their activities, closing factories in Quebec and opening new ones in parts of the world where taxes, labour standards, and wages allowed them to amass profits large enough to satisfy the insatiable appetites of their shareholders. The relocation of companies has had the greatest effect on the male workforce, the greater proportion of which was in manufacturing, but other phenomena such as a growth in non-standard types of employment (part-time, temporary, or contractual work, self-employment, or holding several jobs), also related to higher productivity and larger profits, have affected traditional areas of female service jobs as well. Since the early 1990s women have recorded a lower unemployment rate than men (6.9% compared with 8.9% in 2010), while more numerous in non-standard types of employment: in 2003 almost 40% of women employees held such jobs, compared with 32% for men, with two-thirds of part-time workers being women. Usually less well paid, non-standard types of employment helped to maintain the gap between men's and women's incomes. In 2007, for instance, lumping together all types of employment, full- and part-time, the average employment income of women came to 76% of that of men while, calculated on an hourly basis, women were earning close to 88% of the male wage. We should also note that part-time, contract, or temporary employees do not enjoy the same benefits as full-time workers, and that it is often more difficult for them to defend their rights. If the proportion of unionized male and female workers is now almost equal, the unionization of areas of employment in which women predominate remains very problematic, as is shown by the closing of the Walmart store in Jonquière in 2004 following an attempt to unionize its employees.

Apart from the greater frequency of non-standard employment among women, their concentration in a limited number of largely female professions (as secretaries, sales clerks, cashiers, educators, office clerks, nurses, teachers, etc.) has been the major factor in maintaining the gap in earnings. According to a study by Marie-Josée Legault, this segregation of the job market on sex lines has been especially unfavourable to women whose occupations require only a minimal educational background, for the largest salary gaps are recorded in the types of job that require the least qualifications. For instance, comparing hourly wages, in 2008 women with a university degree earned 86.5% of the income of men in similar situations, while those without a degree took home barely 76% of the pay of male workers without a degree. The gap was even more considerable if we consider weekly earnings. If, as a group, female workers earned 77% of men's wages, those who had not completed their secondary studies received only 60% of the male wage, since many of them were parttimers. In this way, Legault notes, the job market for women was becoming increasingly polarized, with the better educated being able to catch up on their male counterparts, while for the others this was far from the case. It should be added, furthermore, that immigrant women have been among the most likely to be found in occupations that do not require a degree, such as working in hotels, restaurants, personal services, or manufacturing – and this despite the fact that a greater proportion of immigrant women hold a university degree than do women born in Quebec. As we have already seen, these women are victims of twofold discrimination, sexual and racial, which together restrict them to jobs that require the least qualifications, are the lowest paid, and provide the least security – if indeed it does not shut them out completely from the job market, for in the Montreal region in 2009 the unemployment rate of women workers born outside Canada stood at 13%.

There is, then, no escaping the fact that the laws dealing with pay equity have not yet been able to counteract the systematic devaluation of jobs in which there is a concentration of women. It should be pointed out that it was not until 1996, following pressure exerted by the Coalition pour l'équité salariale, representing forty or so women's groups and unions, that the Quebec government passed a law to correct the situation proactively, at least in part. Previously, redress could be obtained only after lodging a complaint – a very long and complex procedure, as was shown by the case of the professional female employees of the Quebec government who brought their case before the courts in 1981 but had to wait sixteen years to obtain a salary adjustment for some of them. Adopted in 1996, the first Quebec law on pay equity did, however, leave a large number of gaps, especially because it did not apply to employers (including the Quebec state) who had already launched a process to re-evaluate women's pay. Furthermore, according to Marie-Thérèse Chicha, the Pay Equity Commission, created by that legislation to provide guidelines to firms and ensure that their equity program conformed, turned out to be ineffective because of its inadequate budget and a shortage of staff. The way in which salary gaps were calculated, for example by comparing women's jobs with categories of male jobs that were among the lowest paid – a strategy that was challenged by feminist organizations and unions, also helped to maintain pay differentials. In principle employers had until 2001 to carry out a comparative evaluation of the types of employment in which there was a strong concentration of either men or women and to make pay adjustments accordingly, but in 2009 half of them, mostly small and medium-sized companies, had not yet carried out such a study. Forced to react, Jean Charest's Liberal government finally changed the legislation, extending the deadline to allow laggards an additional year either to comply or to pay interest and additional compensation to their employees on top of the stipulated fines. Beginning on January 1, 2011, female workers could lodge a complaint with the Pay Equity Commission, but complete retroactivity (from 2001) was not ensured unless it was received by May 30 of that year. This change therefore threw the burden of initiating proceedings back onto the shoulders of women workers, just like in the early 1980s. It also ran the risk of seriously bogging down the Commission, for the number of complaints had already reached 10,000 by June 20, 2011. In other words, the full effects of the pay equity legislation would be felt only after several years.

Yet the need to settle the question of pay equity seemed all the more flagrant since, on average, women now had a higher educational level than men. Indeed, they were completing their education in greater numbers, whether at secondary school, college, or university, a phenomenon already observed in the 1970s but which has become more pronounced with time. Thus in 1975–76, 22% of girls and 20% of boys obtained a college degree compared with 73% and 54%, respectively, in 2007–08; by the mid-1970s 13% of girls and 17% of boys were completing a bachelor's degree, while thirty years later the proportions stood at 51% and 36%. A slightly larger proportion of women also obtained a master's degree in 2007–08 (10%, compared with 9% for men), and the same proportion (3%) completed a doctorate. But if this breakthrough by women in postsecondary studies has been quite spectacular, the majority have continued to choose areas of study leading to the typically "feminine" careers that are undervalued on the job market.

Since the early 1990s a great deal of ink has been devoted to the academic success of girls, which has drawn attention to the difficulty boys have been experiencing in completing secondary school. However, the boys' dropout rate, which affects about a third of them under the age of 20, should not allow us to forget that 20% of girls are in the same situation. In addition, even if dropout rates have remained very high, they have fallen markedly since the mid-1970s, when barely 50% of boys and 60% of girls obtained this first diploma. It is true that the changes undergone by the Quebec economy and the elimination of many unskilled jobs have made it even more essential for anyone wishing to earn a decent living to remain in school, but the above-mentioned pay differentials between men and women without a degree tend to show that the job market remained more favourable to the former. Furthermore, according to some researchers, the fact that it was easy for boys to find relatively well-paid jobs despite their lack of a secondary school diploma may well be one of the reasons for their higher dropout rate. According to Pierrette Bouchard and Jean-Claude Saint-Amant, the different socialization of boys and girls, particularly in underprivileged environments that are still strongly attached to gender stereotypes, may also explain the higher dropout rate among boys. While many observers claim that school is too "feminine" or excessively "feminized," and maintain that the rigidity of school discipline or an absence of male teachers is mainly responsible for boys' failure, these researchers point instead to the limiting effects of a socialization that leads boys to interpret the demands of school in feminine terms and reject this model as a way of asserting their masculinity.

If on an individual level every boy who drops out certainly represents a human drama, on a collective level there are reasons to question the social hand-wringing it provokes. The fact that a high proportion of boys fail to complete their schooling is actually far from a recent phenomenon, for the available data indicate that it has declined substantially over the past forty years or so. If it gives rise to so many alarmist commentaries today this is clearly because, now that a substantial number of the cultural and institutional obstacles preventing them from pursuing their studies have been removed, girls are outstripping boys, a reversal that seems to threaten male dominance. Rather than any distress about the sad fate that awaits boys who drop out of school prematurely, it is the prospect of an upheaval in gender relations that provokes the greatest concern.

Yet women's access to the real corridors of power has remained limited, for instance, as is shown by their minimal representation in leadership positions in the organizations that determine the really important economic and social directions. For example, in 2005 barely 22% of top executive positions in the private sector were filled by women, and only 11% in the upper administration of a city like Montreal, compared with 38% in the Quebec civil service. Women have also remained in a minority in leadership positions in the sectors of health, social services, and teaching, even though they are a large majority of the workforce. Overall, therefore, the imbalance is still pronounced, even if women are more numerous in university programs that offer management training. According to many researchers, this low representation of women at the highest levels in the hierarchy of organizations can be ascribed to the phenomenon of the "glass ceiling," an expression that describes the obstacles they encounter in rising to the upper echelons, taking the form of the often subtle discriminatory practices that hinder their professional advancement and that become intensified the higher they go. As Isabelle Marchand, Johanne Saint-Charles, and Christine Corbeil have pointed out, the prevailing organizational culture in management circles still clings to stereotypical images of femininity and masculinity that make it easier for it to ascribe competence and power to men and more difficult for women to reach the highest levels of power. In order to have their managerial ability recognized, women are obliged to assume attitudes and behaviour that make them resemble their male colleagues without abandoning their claim to femininity (which could be held against them) and while still coping with the difficult combination of work and family. The way women are socialized, leading them to doubt their competence and turn down promotions that would put them too much into the spotlight, also helps to exclude them from the closed circles of power.

In politics, on the other hand, the representation of women in ministerial portfolios has increased substantially since the mid-

1980s, even surpassing the proportion of female MNAs. While the number of women elected in provincial general elections rose from five in 1976 to more than thirty-five in 2003 and in 2008, and their proportion of MNAs grew from 4.5% to almost 30%, since 1994 the proportion of those becoming government ministers has been much greater than their relative weight: the last Charest Cabinet was almost 50% female. According to Magali Paquin, the pressure exerted by the feminist movement, the expectations of the electorate, and the support of the media help to explain this large number of ministerial appointments. Manon Tremblay and Sarah Andrew note, however, that if women are not entirely absent from the most prestigious ministerial portfolios such as minister of finance, president of the Treasury Board, or deputy premier, for the most part women find themselves in ministries with a social orientation, which are therefore considered more germane to traditional female responsibilities. It should be pointed out that the election of Pauline Marois as leader of the Parti Québécois in 2007 and her election as premier in September 2012 were firsts in the history of Quebec politics. So too was the sharing of the leadership of the Québec Solidaire Party between Françoise David and Amir Khadir, a new egalitarian formula that has, however, provoked a degree of skepticism in many observers.

Has the increased presence of women in politics, especially in Cabinet positions, led to the adoption of more laws favourable to the female population as a whole? Opinions remain divided on this point, for though in several cases women MNAs and ministers have been able to support the demands of the feminist movement, and though it has been possible for alliances to be forged across party allegiances, the fact remains that not all women

MNAs are necessarily feminists and that they are also expected to keep to the party line on certain issues, especially those involving public finances. However, the game of politics is not restricted to the National Assembly, for pressures exerted by the feminist movement and by unions, the support of the population for certain plans, or the desire of the government in power to gain the support of the electorate can also lead it to adopt social measures, even in the face of budgetary restrictions. As was shown by the public debates during the 1990s and 2000s, the fears expressed about the falling birth rate among Francophones and their diminishing relative weight in the Canadian and Quebec populations as a whole have also acted as a powerful inducement to governments to introduce new programs intended to reverse this trend.

Thus in 1988 the Liberal government of Robert Bourassa adopted the first family policy with a strong natalist element, for its main measure consisted in the creation of a system of allowances providing an increased amount with each new birth, the sum disbursed on the arrival of a third child itself rising from $3,000 to $8,000 between 1988 and 1992. The measure came under heavy fire from the feminist movement, which insisted on the need for better support on the birth of the first children instead of encouraging the birth of a third, and the program was terminated in 1997 at the same time as Quebec abandoned the principle of the universality of family allowances, as the federal government had been doing gradually from the late 1970s. To replace it Lucien Bouchard's Parti Québécois government introduced a family allowance for low-income families, created full-time kindergartens for 5-year-olds, and launched a program to establish early childhood centres to provide daycare spaces at $5 a day for all Quebec children. Private daycares did not disappear, but they were required to sign an agreement with the government allowing parents who used their services to benefit from the same rate. Despite the fact that this parental contribution was raised to $7 a day by the Charest government in 2004, that a few tens of thousands of places would be needed to satisfy the demand, and that some government-subsidized private daycares did demand more than the statutory amount, this universal program has nevertheless had no equivalent in North America and actually responded to one of the major demands of the feminist movement since the 1970s.

The Quebec Parental Insurance Plan, which came into effect in January 2006, was another measure that differentiated Quebec from its neighbours. In 2001 the federal government had already improved the parental leave provided through employment insurance by raising from ten to thirty-five the total number of weeks covered at 55% of income, in addition to the maternity leave of fifteen weeks. The new Quebec program provided two options: either a maternity leave of eighteen weeks complemented by a paternity leave of five weeks, plus seven weeks of parental leave (to be taken by the father or the mother), funded at 70% of income, and twenty-five weeks at 55% of income, for a total of thirty-two weeks of parental leave, or fifteen weeks of maternity leave, three weeks of paternity leave, and twenty-five weeks of parental leave at 75% of income. This program thus allowed families to choose between a longer leave paid at a lower rate and a shorter leave with more generous benefits. Above all, and unlike the federal program, this plan covered self-employed and part-time workers as well as same-sex spouses. It also encouraged fathers to play their part in caring for the newborn, since the leave designated for them could not be transferred to the mother. It should, however, be noted that only workers who paid into this plan were eligible; in other cases the provisions of the Employment Standards Act applied, allowing a maternity leave of eighteen weeks and, after 1997, an additional parental leave of fifty-two weeks without pay.

This parental leave, just like the easier access to high-quality child care, has often been linked to the rising birth rate witnessed in Quebec during the 2000s. Furthermore, recent studies have shown that three-quarters of Quebec fathers benefiting from this program have taken advantage of the three- to five-week leave intended for them in addition to using some of the weeks of parental leave that could be shared between both parents, whereas under the federal program only 15% of fathers chose to use some of the parental leave to which couples are entitled. The desire of the Quebec state to encourage men to accept a larger share of responsibility for the care of very young children seems to have begun to bear fruit, encouraging greater equality within the couple. According to Diane-Gabrielle Tremblay, fathers' use of these leaves may even have had a significant knock-on effect, since subsequently men have also seemed more prepared to miss work for family reasons, which in turn may have contributed to a change of attitude in a workplace that had previously been highly resistant to men taking leave to fulfill domestic responsibilities.

Without denying that these two social measures represented substantial step forward for women, some scholars have nevertheless pointed out that the establishment of early childhood centres and of parental leave also served the state's interests. For instance, according to Josée Bergeron and Jane Jensen, the measures regarding early infancy adopted by the Bouchard government at the end of the 1990s were obviously part of a policy to encourage women into employment, since affordable daycare costs appeared to be necessary if mothers on social assistance or earning minimum wage were to re-enter or remain in the workforce. The early childhood centres also fulfilled the purpose of creating new employment in a field of activity – child care – in which undeclared income is very common and deprives the state of tax revenues believed to be significant, so that the government seems to have been motivated to introduce this service by a desire to restore sound public finances as much as to satisfy the long-standing demands of the women's movement. As for the parental leave program, it seems to have emerged at a time of apprehension about an imminent labour shortage that the government was seeking to alleviate by responding to the expectations of young male and female workers. For Nathalie Saint-Amour, therefore, these ostensibly social-democratic policies, represented as measures intended to reconcile employment and family, pursued objectives that were equally compatible with the neoliberal model of encouraging people to find employment and reducing dependency on the state, as is confirmed by the adoption of other measures such as the introduction in 2005 of work premiums for those receiving social assistance.

The Support-Payment Collection Program, introduced in 1995 by the Jacques Parizeau government in response to another demand of the feminist movement, was another example of a progressive measure that the state turned to its own advantage, for the money collected under it would almost all be deducted from the social assistance benefits paid to single mothers. Yet in 1997 support payments for children became tax-exempt because they were not considered income for the parent who received them (usually the mother). However, until the 2010s political pressure and legal action undertaken by a coalition formed in 2007 to stop unjust deductions from child support payments achieved hardly anything, for it was only able to obtain that payments made to women students by a former spouse be excluded from the total amount of loans and scholarships to which they were entitled. It should, however, be noted that in the case of unmarried couples the payment of support applied only to children, for the Civil Code does not recognize any obligation on the part of de facto spouses (who amount to more than a third of Quebec couples) to provide support. In November 2009, in a famous suit involving a billionaire and his former partner who claimed such support in addition to her share of the family assets, the Quebec Appeal Court decided that Article 585 of the Civil Code, which excludes de facto spouses from such protection, was discriminatory, and allowed the government a year to amend it. The government decided instead to challenge this judgment in the Supreme Court of Canada, arguing that couples living in a de facto relationship should not be subject to the same obligations as married couples – an opinion shared by a portion of the population, as shown by the debates provoked by the issue. It is worthy of note that in the other Canadian provinces common-law partners are able to claim support for themselves as well as for their children.

The Quebec feminist movement remained very active throughout the 1990s and 2000s, as is indicated by the adoption of the social measures mentioned above. It is true that these legislative changes beneficial to women and to the equality of the sexes cannot be entirely explained by the pressures exerted by the movement or its campaigns, but the at least partial acceptance of several of its demands prove the vitality of the movement, its ability to organize, to attract widespread support from the population, and to influence decision making on the political level. However, the gains made by feminism remain vulnerable, as is shown by the re-emergence of a certain religious right that has tried to undermine women's reproductive rights just when they are being threatened by the state's disengagement from economic and social matters. During this period the movement has also been rent by numerous controversies, while its ability to make a place for women from immigrant backgrounds has become one of its major challenges, especially at moments when the National Question was monopolizing debates.

One of the earliest public manifestations of tension between groups of women from immigrant communities and Francophone women emerged in the spring of 1990 during the celebrations for the fiftieth anniversary of the granting of women's suffrage in Quebec. This commemoration, named "Femmes en tête" and celebrated in every region of Quebec, ended with a three-day forum entitled "Les 50 Heures du Féminisme" under the honorary presidency of Lise Payette. As a leading figure in Quebec journalism, a feminist, and the former minister for the status of women, Lise Payette, seemed the obvious person to fulfil this role. However, in the preceding months she had collaborated in screenwriting a documentary entitled *Disparaître*, which predicted the disappearance of Quebeckers of French-Canadian descent unless they had larger families and immigrants were selected on the basis of their ability to integrate with Francophone society. Deeply disturbed by the tenor of these remarks, the Collectif des femmes immigrantes, which sat on the organizing committee of Femmes en tête, demanded that Lise Payette be withdrawn and, when the organizers refused, decided to boycott the event.

This painful episode, which turned the spotlight onto the split between women's groups over the National Question, was followed in 1992 by a forum organized by the Quebec Federation of Women and called, "Pour un Québec féminin pluriel." Attended by over 1,000 participants, including several delegates from groups from outside the Federation, this event put the disparities between women on the agenda and encouraged the Federation to redefine its mission in order to concentrate on the problems of women most affected by economic and social inequality, such as immigrant and Native women, lesbians, disabled women, and members of visible minorities. When the new groups then joined the Federation the result was a profound change in the composition of its affiliated membership, so that in 1994 they obtained a review of the Federation's structures, reducing the role of individual members, who were often long-time activists with a strong influence over the organization. In their disappointment several of these activists left the Federation, while it became more diverse and concentrated its efforts on women at the bottom of the social ladder.

Françoise David, who became president of the Federation in 1994, was one of the principal artisans of this change, which revived some of the more forceful strategies of the feminist movement of the 1960s and 1970s. In the first year of her mandate David threw herself into the organization of a demonstration called the "Bread and Roses March," which was held in the spring of 1995. Several thousand women marchers set out from Montreal, Longueuil, and Rivière-du-Loup and converged on

Quebec City, denouncing the poverty affecting women in particular and presenting a list of demands designed to overcome it. Widely reported in the media, the march brought considerable visibility for the women's movement, made it more united, and demonstrated its ability to mobilize not only women's groups but many community groups that were also working to remedy the plight of the most destitute, who had suffered most from the budget cuts made by the state during the previous decade. According to several observers, the Federation's support for Quebec sovereignty in the referendum held by the Parti Québécois government later that year helped it to obtain certain of its demands, particularly a law dealing with the collection of support payments and a law on pay equity, though as we have pointed out these new measures had serious limitations. The government's refusal to raise the minimum wage above $8 an hour, a step considered essential for any effective relief of poverty, showed that employers also had the ear of the state. In the following year, when the Lucien Bouchard government held summits on the economy and employment, the Federation fared no better in its effort to convince it that "zero poverty" should be as absolute a priority as "zero deficit." The neoliberal wave that was washing over Quebec at the time meant that the Federation's objective of reducing poverty was incompatible with those of a government obsessed with balancing the budget and with economic competition from emerging economies.

The Bread and Roses March undeniably marked a new departure in the history of the Quebec Federation of Women, which now turned its thoughts to the effects of globalization on the lives of all women. Recognizing that the deregulation and liberalization of trade increased the poverty of women in the least developed countries while leading to a feminization of poverty in Western countries by encouraging the adoption of neoliberal public policies, the Federation threw itself into organizing the World March of Women, which aimed to create a new North–South solidarity. This worldwide rally, which took place in 2000 and focused on two central themes affecting all women – poverty and violence – brought out several hundred thousand women on five continents and concluded by presenting to the United Nations almost five million cards supporting the objectives of the March. The event was repeated in 2005, on that occasion with the adoption of a Women's Global Charter for Humanity, and again in 2010. For some, however, the emphasis placed by the Quebec Federation of Women on questions related to poverty and the concentration of its energies on actions of global scope risked allowing it to lose sight of other important issues, especially those involving the equality of the sexes. This principle, exactly like the recognition of the reproductive rights of women (including the right to abortion) and of the rights of lesbians, became further subject to compromise when the program of the World March was being written, for women's groups from countries in the South, who were in a substantial majority, were reticent about or even opposed to the idea of endorsing such claims for fear of alienating support.

In fact the recognition of lesbians' right to equality was the main stumbling block in discussions about the organization of the March, showing that this question remained fraught with incomprehension and prejudice. In Quebec, where since 1977 all discrimination on grounds of sexual orientation has been forbidden under the Charter of Human Rights and Freedoms, such total equality before the law was, moreover, very recent, for it was not until 1999 that the legislation recognized same-sex partnerships, while gay marriages were not permitted until 2004 (2005 in the rest of Canada). Previously, in 2002, Quebec legislation had introduced civil unions, thus granting official status to homosexual couples, modified the rules about parentage by allowing two mothers or two fathers to be named on a child's birth certificate, and authorized adoption by same-sex couples. The recognition of these rights was only obtained after a lengthy struggle, the origins of which can be traced back to the 1960s, a period when homosexuality was still considered a crime, or at best a sickness, though some time was needed for the feminist movement to give its full and open support.

Lesbians, who already formed a very vital community in Montreal in the 1950s, though long discriminated against and even ostracized, as Line Chamberland's research has shown, nevertheless quickly entered the feminist ranks in the 1970s. However, their radical analysis of the political and ideological foundations of the oppression of women, which they associated with heterosexuality, did cause numerous tensions within a movement that was dominated by heterosexual women. Furthermore, at a time when the movement was trying to gain legitimacy and respectability, and when homosexuality was still socially stigmatized, the participation of lesbians in the women's movement remained mostly unmentioned, as did the specific problems affecting them. As a result, starting in the 1980s, a number of them left the feminist groups to create their own organizations or formed alliances with gay men; in 1996 they founded the Quebec Lesbian Network, an autonomous group devoted exclusively to the defence of their rights.

The 1990s did, however, see a rapprochement between feminists and lesbians, as was shown in 1995 by the creation by the

Federation of Women of a committee to work for the recognition of gay women. The increased visibility of lesbians and gays in the public arena – a phenomenon not unrelated to the development of the HIV/AIDS epidemic – as well as the more pragmatic direction of their efforts to combat discrimination against homosexuals and gain respect for the rights guaranteed by various charters, encouraged this rapprochement, as did the presence of lesbians within the Federation, which had become much more open to the most marginalized women. Moreover, the Federation participated in a coalition, one that included unions, that campaigned for the recognition of homosexuals' rights, which was gradually obtained, beginning in 1999. However, as is shown by the report of a working group submitted to the minister of justice in 2007, homophobia remains a very present reality in Quebec society, for equality before the law is still not enough to ensure full equality for homosexual, bisexual, and transgendered individuals.

If the National Question and sexual orientation were two important sources of discord within the feminist movement, some other stormy debates took place within it as well. For instance, in the 1990s many feminists wanted pornography to be outlawed because of its degrading and often violent depictions of women and the type of sexual behaviour it portrayed, while others opposed the very principle of censorship, arguing that it could affect sexually explicit cultural productions created by women, especially lesbians. In the 2000s, what has been called the "hypersexualization" of young girls (and, collaterally, of women) gave rise to similar debates, some seeing it as "pornogrifying" mass culture and as a return to the stereotype of the woman as an object of male pleasure, while others denounced what they saw as "moral panic" or spoke instead of an emergent "girl power," referring to the pleasure and even power that girls could derive from their seductive ability. In the same vein feminists also disagreed about female prostitution, considered by one fringe of the movement as the supreme manifestation of the exploitation of women's bodies and by another as a freely adopted form of professional activity. When Stella, a group set up to defend sex workers, joined the Quebec Federation of Women, deep differences emerged over the decriminalization of prostitution.

The wearing of the so-called Islamic veil by certain Muslim women is another example of a controversy that provoked heated debate. Whereas for some feminists, as well as for a substantial proportion of Quebec society, the veil symbolized the alienation of women and their subjection to the men in their religious community and should therefore be forbidden in what was supposed to be a secular public space, others maintained that this would merely isolate women who wore the veil and deprive them of all ability to participate in social life, abolishing at one fell stroke any chance of liberating themselves from it if they so desired. We should mention that this difference of opinion did not only divide White or Christian feminists, for when in May 2009 the Quebec Federation of Women adopted a resolution accepting the wearing of the veil in public institutions, its position was sharply criticized by women of Muslim background, most notably by Djemila Benhabib, the author of *Ma vie à contre-Coran*, who accused the Federation of being in the pay of the organizations Muslim Presence and the Canadian Muslim Council.

All these debates conducted in the name of equality and autonomy show that for feminists women's sexuality and bodies are more than ever fundamental issues that they have found it very difficult to resolve. On the one hand, many remain convinced that the Islamic veil, hypersexualization, or prostitution point to a single issue, namely, the control that patriarchal institutions, whether religious or secular, seek to exert over women, whether by veiling or unclothing them. On the other hand, some insist on the need to take the experiences of these women into account, listen to what they have to say, and recognize them as political subjects, remembering that their stigmatization by feminists serves to reproduce power relations within women's groups even as they fight to rid society of similar relations. Is it possible to be a prostitute, sexually attractive, or wear a headscarf, and still be called a feminist? The question is all the more complex in that it also raises the very definition of feminism, which remains unresolved.

Having become a full-fledged political actor, if not a real institution, feminism acquired legitimacy during the 1990s and 2000s, while at the same time its voice became more moderate. Nevertheless, radical feminism is still very much alive, as is shown by the creation by young women of new groups with provocative names such as Les Sorcières, Les Insoumises, the Blood Sisters, or the pan-Canadian group Toujours RebELLES (Waves of Resistance), organized in Montreal in the fall of 2008, and which has had considerable success, continuing to mobilize young feminists. If, paradoxically, the gains attributed to the feminist movement are often thought to explain why younger generations have lost interest in it, it nonetheless continues to renew itself, proving wrong those who think it has died away or outlived its necessity. Thus the "post-feminist" era has seen the advent of several groups that are again putting questions about patriarchy, capitalism, and also racism and colonialism, at the centre of their political agenda. Could this be a "third wave" of feminism, possibly signalling a break with the past? No, say some young women who, rejecting the very idea that feminism has come in "waves," prefer to see it as continuing the radical tradition that has always survived at the core of the movement while coexisting with its more moderate expression. The vast consultation undertaken in 2011 by the Quebec Federation of Women with a view to organizing a general assembly of the feminist movement in 2013 to take stock of feminist activity, analyze the achievements of the past twenty years, and prepare for future struggles, at least shows that the movement is still on the march.

Conclusion

This short history of women has tried to bring out the roles played by them in Quebec society since the time of the French colonization, the responsibilities that they have undertaken, and their struggles to expand the range of their freedom. It set out to show that the work, living conditions, legal status, and social and political involvement of women can only be understood in the light of a social definition of femininity that has been constructed concurrently with the definition of masculinity, but also taking into account factors such as class, ethnicity, and race that underlie the diversity of women's historical experience. Though women are a heterogeneous group, they still share the fact that they constitute an integral component of a socio-economic organization that, in principle at least, has allotted them a clearly defined place. In practice, as this study has also tried to show, they have also demonstrated their "agency" – in other words, the fact that in many respects, and within the often narrow bounds of the constraints imposed on women and the norms dictating their conduct, they have been able to act in their own interest,

CONCLUSION

exploiting the contradictions of male power in order to push back the restrictions placed on their autonomy. However, the twists and turns of history show that this was not a linear or unambiguous process, for the play of social, economic, and political forces has been just as liable to produce backward as well as forward steps, as is shown by the loss of the vote by women in the nineteenth century and the abolition of the dower.

The changes in modes of production and exchange, the social and political involvement of women, including the feminist movement, as well as the National Question, which for almost a century was intertwined with that of religion, are certainly the main features that help to make sense of the historical experience of Quebec women. During the French regime and the early decades of British rule the family was the basic unit of society, so that despite a division of tasks and responsibilities along sex lines, and despite the authority exerted by husbands, women were at the heart of economic activity and even, where women of the elite are concerned, of political matters. During the nineteenth century, however, the industrial revolution gradually imposed a new organization of labour, marginalizing women's domestic production to the extent that it became invisible to society, despite the fact it was still of crucial importance to the proper functioning of households and to their economic survival, especially the poorest. Then the ideology of separate spheres, which allotted the role of breadwinner to men and that of mother and housewife to women, provided a justification not only for the discrimination from which women suffered in the field of employment, but also for their exclusion from the political arena, from higher education, from the liberal professions, and from the ownership of property (for instance, through the abolition of the dower, restrictions concerning inheritances, and the annulment of Indian status for First Nations women who married non-Natives) – in short, from all the areas in which they might have achieved independence. This consolidation of patriarchy also took the form of restricting women's control over their bodies and reproductive function, as is attested by the adoption of numerous laws in this respect. It was to combat this new sociosexual order that the women's movement grew: from the end of the nineteenth century and for many decades, it would campaign for an end to the legal, social, political, and economic discrimination that kept women in a subordinate condition.

This women's movement was, however, built on a long tradition of social commitment that can be traced back to New France, when nuns established the earliest systems of education and assistance to the poor, the old, the sick, and other marginalized people. Despite those who maintained that women's place was in the home, the nineteenth century witnessed an ever-increasing number of female initiatives of a similar nature, as women tried to respond to the needs of a population reduced to poverty by the expansion of industrial capitalism. Paradoxically, the rhetoric of separate spheres, according to which women's "feminine nature," characterized by compassion and devotedness, made women fit only for domestic life, then served to legitimize this social action which continued to broaden its range as the new liberal capitalist order led to an increase in inequalities of all kinds. This activism in support of the most vulnerable members of society became one of the wellsprings of feminist demands, particularly where women's suffrage was concerned, for it was considered an essential instrument in obtaining the reforms considered necessary. If in the early twentieth century

CONCLUSION

some women used egalitarian arguments to claim political citizenship, the great majority actually justified their demand by asserting that their maternal abilities made them more sensitive to the plight of the poor, especially mothers and children. State initiatives, which became intensified throughout the twentieth century, did not put an end to the social involvement of women, both lay and religious, for it continued to fulfil needs that the public authorities could not or would not satisfy. Following the Second World War, however, it was women's activism, grounded in communities and associations and increasingly political in nature, that came to the fore, preparing the way for a resurgence of feminism in the latter half of the 1960s. The feminist movement would make many demands of the state, but one of its notable features was that it set out to respond to the needs of women by itself offering them a whole range of services (shelters, health centres, etc.) created specifically for them. If these institutions emerged from women's struggle for emancipation and were properly distinguished from women's earlier charitable activities by their militant and even subversive character (an example being the health centres that directed women towards abortion services), it is nevertheless striking that, in our own day as in the past, initiatives intended to counteract the poverty, violence, and exploitation – economic, sexual, or other – of which women are the victims, have most often originated with women themselves.

Finally, it is impossible to understand the history of women in Quebec without considering the impact of the National Question on their lives, their organizations, and their struggles. From the middle of the nineteenth century, when the Catholic Church portrayed itself as the guardian of the nation, and religion was represented as one of the main components of national identity,

CONCLUSION

nationalist discourse persisted in restricting women to their role as mothers, to the exclusion of all others. While several factors, especially the destruction of the old social framework by the pressure of industrial capitalism, encouraged a rise in women's religious vocations, removing a large proportion of women from child-bearing, married women were urged to have large families in order to secure the future of the nation. The "revenge of the cradle," which the Catholic Church and French-Canadian nationalists longed for with all their hearts, would in fact never take place, but this exhortation weighed all the more heavily on laywomen in that nuns had largely taken over the sphere of social, educational, and charitable work that allowed Anglo-Protestant women to make their presence felt in the public domain. It was not that Catholic laywomen were completely absent from it, but they had to adjust to the substantial presence of nuns who competed with them in the areas of teaching and nursing and who, in obedience to their bishops, remained outside the nascent feminist movement, leaving it that much weaker. Many French-Canadian feminists, being both nationalists and fervent Catholics, found themselves torn between their desires, on the one hand to advance the cause of women and on the other to consolidate the nation and respect the dictates of the clergy – a tension that clearly weakened their support for women's rights and diminished the force of their demands. The relationship between feminism and nationalism would remain a thorny question for the women's movement in the late twentieth and early twenty-first centuries, for if a number of militant feminists found it impossible to imagine their own freedom without the freedom of Quebec, conversely, some nationalists viewed women, along with the clergy, as the source of their alienation and found it very dif-

CONCLUSION

ficult to incorporate them into their endeavour to create a more "virile" nation, while others were alarmed to see them abandoning their role as prolific child-bearers. Furthermore, if nationalism was not completely alien to the adoption of some of the most generous social measures benefiting mothers and children in North America, it also gave rise to discord among feminists, for Anglophone women, women from minority ethnic communities, and First Nations women, as well as a portion of Francophone women, did not necessarily support its political aims or, worse, saw it as a source of exclusion.

These three main threads have been our guides in showing that the history of women is unquestionably one of the major currents running through Quebec society on the economic, social, and political levels. Far from being merely anecdotal, it cannot be dissociated from the historical fabric as a whole, for the issues and journeys that it illuminates from a contrasting point of view take us, so to speak, behind the scenes. In fact, the history of women does not merely *add* to our understanding of the past: it is indispensable to a grasp of its many facets and its considerable complexity.

Selected Bibliography

In the course of writing this book, it was necessary to consult a great number of books, articles, and Internet sites too numerous to be listed here in their entirety. In addition, of course, to the authors cited in the text, this bibliography therefore provides only a selection from the most recent of these works. The overview by the Collectif Clio, *L'Histoire des femmes au Québec depuis quatre siècles* (Montreal: Le Jour, 1992), as well as the survey by Gail Cuthbert Brandt, Naomi Black, Paula Bourne, and Magda Fahrni, *Canadian Women: A History*, 3rd ed. (Toronto: Nelson Education, 2011), contain more complete and most useful bibliographies. Also well worth consulting is the bibliography compiled by Diana Pedersen, *Changing Women, Changing History: A Bibliography of the History of Women in Canada*, 2nd ed. (Ottawa: Carleton University Press, 1996), and, for more recent titles, the website of the Canadian Committee on Women's History (http://www.chashcacommittees-comitesa.ca/ccwh-cchf), which covers the literature on Quebec. We would also point out that every issue of the *Revue d'histoire de l'Amérique française* includes a current bibliography and is therefore an indispensable source. It is from that journal, as well as from *Atlantis, le Bulletin d'histoire politique, Canadian Woman Studies / Les Cahiers de la femme, Histoire sociale / Social History, Journal of the Canadian Historical Association / Revue de la Société historique du Canada, Labour / Le Travail, Lien social et Politiques, Recherches féministes, Recherches sociographiques, Sociologie et Sociétés, Canadian Historical Review*, and *Urban History Review / Revue d'histoire urbaine* that we have drawn most of the articles used to document this survey. Among the most consulted Internet sites, we should mention those of the online *Dictionnaire biographique du Canada* (www.biographi.ca/index-f.html), of the Institut de la statistique du Québec (www.stat.gouv.qc.ca), of Statistics Canada (www.statcan.gc.ca/start-debut-fra.html), the websites of the associations and institutions mentioned, as well as those of major daily newspapers.

Bibliography

BAILLARGEON, Denyse. *Babies for the Nation: The Medicalization of Motherhood in Quebec, 1910–1970*. Waterloo: Wilfrid Laurier University Press, 2009 (trans. W. Donald Wilson).

———. "'We Admire Modern Parents': The École des Parents du Québec and the Post-war Quebec Family, 1940–1959." In Nancy Christie and Michael Gauvreau (eds.), *Cultures of Citizenship in Post-war Canada, 1940–1955*, 239–76. Montreal and Kingston: McGill-Queen's University Press, 2003.

———. *Making Do: Women, Family and Home in Montreal during the Great Depression*. Waterloo: Wilfrid Laurier University Press, 1999 (trans. Yvonne Klein).

BARRY, Francine. *Le Travail de la femme au Québec: L'évolution de 1940 à 1970*. Montreal: Presses de l'Université du Québec, 1977.

BEAUGRAND-CHAMPAGNE, Denyse. *Le Procès de Marie-Josèphe-Angélique*. Outremont: Libre Expression, 2004.

BENHABID, Djemila. "Les femmes trahies." *Metropolitain*, May 28, 2009. Available online at www.themetropolitain.ca/articles/view/542. (Consulted July 15, 2011).

BERGERON, Josée, and Jane Jenson. "Nation, natalité, politique et représentations des femmes." *Recherches féministes* 12/1 (1999), 83–101.

BILGE, Sirma. "'... alors que nous, Québécois, nos femmes sont égales et nous les aimons ainsi': La patrouille des frontières au nom de l'égalité de genre dans une 'nation' en quête de souveraineté." *Sociologie et Sociétés* 42/1 (2010), 197–226.

BOISVERT, Raymonde. "L'homicide conjugal à Montréal." *Recherches sociographiques* 35/2 (1994), 237–54.

BIBLIOGRAPHY

BOUCHARD, Gérard. *Quelques arpents d'Amérique: Population, économie, famille au Saguenay, 1838–1971*. Montreal: Boréal, 1996.

BOUCHARD, Pierrette, and Jean-Claude Saint-Amant. "La réussite scolaire des filles et l'abandon des garçons: Un enjeu à portée politique pour les femmes." *Recherches féministes* 6/2 (1993), 21–37.

BOYER, Kate. "'Neither Forget Nor Remember Your Sex': Sexual Politics in the Early Twentieth-Century Canadian Office." *Journal of Historical Geography* 29/2 (2003), 212–29.

BRADBURY, Bettina. *Wife to Widow: Lives, Laws, and Politics in Nineteenth-Century Montreal*. Vancouver: UBC Press, 2011.

———. "Women at the Hustings: Gender, Citizenship, and the Montreal By-elections of 1932." In Mona Gleason and Adele Perry (eds.), *Rethinking Canada: The Promise of Women's History*, 4th ed. Don Mills: Oxford University Press, 2006, 73–94.

———. *Working Families: Age, Gender and Daily Survival in Industrializing Montreal*. Toronto: University of Toronto Press, 1991.

———. "Mourir chrétiennement: La vie et la mort dans les établissements catholiques pour personnes âgées à Montréal au xixe siècle." *Revue d'histoire de l'Amérique française* 46/1 (1992), 143–75.

BRUN, Josette. *Vie et mort du couple en Nouvelle-France: Québec et Louisbourg au XVIIIe siècle*. Montreal and Kingston: McGill-Queen's University Press, 2006.

CARON, Anita, and Lorraine Archambault (eds.). *Thérèse Casgrain: Une femme tenace et engagée*. Sainte-Foy: Presses de l'Université du Québec, 1993.

CHAMBERLAND, Line. *Mémoires lesbiennes*. Montreal: Remue-ménage, 1996.

CHARLES, Aline. *Travail d'ombre et de lumière: Le Bénévolat féminin a l'Hôpital Sainte-Justine, 1907–1960*. Quebec: IQRC, 1990.

CHICHA, Marie-Thérèse. "L'adoption et la mise en oeuvre de la Loi québécoise sur l'équité salariale: L'existence d'un double standard." *Lien social et Politiques*, no. 47 (2002), 85–95.

CLICHE, Marie-Aimée. "Un secret bien gardé: L'inceste dans la société traditionnelle québécoise, 1858–1938." *Revue d'histoire de l'Amérique française* 50/2 (1996), 201–26.

———. "Les filles-mères devant les tribunaux de Québec, 1850–1969." *Recherches sociographiques* 32/1 (1991), 9–42.

COHEN, Yolande. *Femmes philanthropes: Catholiques, protestantes et Juives dans les organisations caritatives au Québec (1880–1945)*. Montreal: Presses de l'Université de Montréal, 2010.

COLLIN, Johanne. *Changement d'ordonnance: Mutations professionnelles, identité sociale et féminisation de la profession pharmaceutique au Québec, 1940–1980*. Montreal: Boréal, 1995.

———. "La dynamique des rapports de sexes à l'université 1940–1980: Une étude de cas." *Histoire sociale / Social History* 19/38 (1986), 365–85.

COOPER, Afua. *The Hanging of Angelique: The Untold Story of Canadian Slavery and the Burning of Old Montreal*. Toronto: Harper Collins, 2006.

D'ALLAIRE, Micheline. *Les Communautés religieuses et l'assistance sociale à Montréal 1659–1900*. Montreal: Méridien, 1997.

DAGENAIS, Michèle. "Itinéraires professionnels masculins et féminins en milieu bancaire: Le cas de la Banque d'Hochelaga, 1900–1929." *Labour / Le Travail*, no. 24 (Fall 1989), 45–68.

DANYLEWYCZ, Marta. *Taking the veil: An Alternative to Marriage, Motherhood, Spinsterhood in Quebec, 1840–1920*. Toronto: McClelland and Stewart, 1987.

———. "Sexes et classes sociales dans l'enseignement: Le cas de Montréal à la fin du 19e siècle." In Nadia Fahmy-Eid and Micheline Dumont (eds.), *Maîtresses de maison, maîtresses d'école: Femmes, familles et éducation dans l'histoire du Québec*, 93–118. Montreal: Boréal, 1983.

DECHÊNE, Louise. *L'État, le peuple et la guerre au Canada sous le Régime française*. Edition prepared by Hélène Paré, Sylvie Dépatie, Catherine Desbarats and Thomas Wien. Montreal: Boréal, 2008.

DEMCZUK, Irène, and Frank W. Remiggi (eds.). *Sortir de l'ombre: Histoires des communautés lesbienne et gaie de Montréal*. Montreal: VLB, 1998.

DESJARDINS, Ghislaine. *Faire garder ses enfants au Québec: Une histoire toujours en marche*. Quebec: Les Publications du Québec, 2002.

DETELLIER, Élise. "'Bonifier le capital humain': Le genre dans le discours médical et religieux sur les sports au Québec, 1920–1950." *Revue d'histoire de l'Amérique française* 62/3–4 (2009), 473–99.

DUFOUR, Andrée. "Les premières enseignantes laïques au Québec: Le cas de Montréal, 1825–1835." *Histoire de l'éducation*, no. 109 (Jan. 2006), 3–32.

DUFOUR, Andrée, and Micheline Dumont. *Brève histoire des institutrices au Québec de la Nouvelle-France à nos jours*. Montreal: Boréal, 2004.

DUMONT, Micheline, *Le Féminisme québécois raconté à Camille*. Montreal: Remue-ménage, 2008.

———. "Les charismes perdus: L'avenir des congrégations religieuses féminines en l'an 2000." *Recherches féministes* 3/2 (1990), 73–111.

DUMONT, Micheline, and Louise Toupin. *La Pensée féministe au Québec: Anthologie [1900–1985]*. Montreal: Remue-ménage, 2003.

BIBLIOGRAPHY

FAHMY-EID, Nadia, et al. *Femmes, santé et professions: Histoire des diététistes et des physiothérapeutes au Québec et en Ontario 1930–1980.* Montreal: Fides, 1997.

FAHRNI, Magda. *Household Politics: Montreal Families and Postwar Reconstruction.* Toronto: University of Toronto Press, 2005.

FERLAND, Jacques, "'In Search of the Unbound Prometheia': A Comparative View of Women's Activism in Two Quebec Industries, 1869–1908." *Labour / Le Travail,* no. 24 (Spring 1989), 11–44.

FRIGON, Sylvie. *L'Homicide conjugal au féminin, d'hier à aujourd'hui.* Montreal: Remue-ménage, 2003.

GADOURY, Lorraine. *La Famille dans son intimité. Échanges épistolaires au sein de l'élite canadienne du XVIIIe siècle.* Montreal: Hurtubise HMH, 1998.

GALLICHAN, Gilles. *Les Québécoises et le Barreau: L'histoire d'une difficile conquête, 1914–1941.* Quebec: Septentrion, 1999.

GAUVREAU, Danielle, Peter Gossage, and Diane Gervais, *La Fécondité des Québécoises, 1870–1970: D'une exception à l'autre.* Montreal: Boréal, 2007.

GAUVREAU, Michael. "The Emergence of Personalist Feminism: Catholicism and the Marriage Preparation Movement in Quebec, 1940–1966." In Nancy Christie and Michael Gauvreau (eds.), *Households of Faith: Family, Gender and Community in Canada, 1760–1969.* Montreal and Kingston: McGill-Queen's University Press, 2002, 319–47.

GIROUARD, Guylaine. "L'admission des femmes à l'Université Laval, 1901–1945: Un compromis entre des objectifs féministes et des objections cléricales." Quebec, Université Laval, Groupe de recherche multidisciplinaire féministe, 1993.

GOSSAGE, Peter. "Les enfants abandonnés à Montréal au 19ᵉ siècle: La crèche d'Youville des Sœurs Grises, 1820–1871." *Revue d'histoire de l'Amérique française* 40/4 (1987), 537–59.

———. *Families in Transition: Industry and Population in Nineteenth-Century Saint-Hyacinthe*. Montreal and Kingston: McGill-Queen's University Press, 1999.

GOSSELIN, Line. *Les Journalistes québécoises, 1880–1930*. Montreal: Collection du RCHTQ ("Études et documents" 7), 1995.

GOUSSE, Suzanne. "Aspects démographiques de la vie des couturières de Montréal au XVIIIᵉ siècle." *Cahiers d'histoire* 29/1 (2010), 145–55.

GRAY, Colleen. *The Congregation Notre-Dame, Superiors, and the Paradox of Power*. Montreal and Kingston: McGill-Queen's University Press, 2007.

GREER, Allan. *Mohawk Saint: Catherine Tekakwitha and the Jesuits*. New York: Oxford University Press, 2005.

GRENIER, Benoît. "Réflexion sur le pouvoir féminin au Canada sous le Régime français: Le cas de la 'seigneuresse' Marie-Catherine Peuvret (1667–1739)." *Histoire sociale / Social History* 42/84 (Nov.–Dec. 2009), 299–326.

GROULX, Lionel-Henri. "De la vocation féminine à l'expertise féministe: Essai sur l'évolution du service social au Québec (1939–1990)." *Revue d'histoire de l'Amérique française* 49/3 (1996), 357–94.

HARVEY, Kathryn. "To Love, Honour and Obey: Wife-Battering in Working-Class Montreal, 1869–1879." *Urban History Review* 19/1–2 (1990), 128–41.

HÉBERT, Karine. "Carabines, poutchinettes, co-eds ou freshettes sont-elles des étudiantes? Les filles à l'université McGill et à l'Université de Montréal (1900–1960)." *Revue d'histoire de l'Amérique française* 57/4 (2004), 593–625.

BIBLIOGRAPHY

HENRIPIN, Jacques. *Naître ou ne pas être*. Quebec: IQRC, 1989.

LACELLE, Claudette. *Les Domestiques en milieu urbain canadien au XIXe siècle*. Ottawa: Minister of Supply and Services, 1987.

LAMOTTE, Aleyda. "Femmes immigrées et reproduction sociale." *Recherches sociographiques* 32/3 (1991), 367–84.

LAMOUREUX, Diane. *L'Amère Patrie: Féminisme et nationalisme dans le Québec contemporain*. Montreal: Remue-ménage, 2001.

———. *Fragments et Collage: Essai sur le féminisme québécois des années 1970*. Montreal: Remue-ménage, 1986.

LAMOUREUX, Jocelyne, Michèle Gélinas, and Katy Tari. *Femmes en mouvement: Trajectoires de l'Association féminine d'éducation et d'action sociale, AFÉAS, 1966–1991*. Montreal: Boréal, 1993.

LANDRY, Yves. *Orphelines en France, pionnières au Canada: Les Filles du roi au XVIIe siècle*. Montreal: Leméac, 1992.

LANTHIER, Stéphanie. "L'impossible réciprocité des rapports politiques et idéologiques entre le nationalisme radical et le féminisme radical au Québec: 1962–1972." Master's thesis (History), University of Sherbrooke, 1998.

LAVIGNE, Marie. "Réflexions féministes autour de la fertilité des Québécoises." In Micheline Dumont and Nadia Fahmy-Eid (eds.), *Maîtresses de maison, maîtresses d'école: Femmes, famille et éducation dans l'histoire du Québec*, 319–38. Montreal: Boréal, 1983.

LEGAULT, Marie-Josée. "La mixité en emploi ... dans l'angle mort chez les moins scolarisés?" *Revue multidisciplinaire sur l'emploi, le syndicalisme et le travail* (REMEST) 6/1 (2011), 20–58.

LÉVESQUE, Andrée. *Making and Breaking the Rules: Women in Quebec, 1919–1939*. Toronto: University of Toronto Press, 2010 (trans. Yvonne Klein).

———. *Éva Circé-Côté: Libre penseuse, 1871–1949*. Montreal: Remue-ménage, 2010.

———. *Red Travellers: Jeanne Corbin and Her Comrades*. Montreal and Kingston: McGill-Queen's University Press, 2006 (trans. Yvonne Klein).

MARCHAND, Isabelle, Johanne Saint-Charles, and Christine Corbeil. "L'ascension professionnelle et le plafond de verre dans les entreprises privées au Québec." *Recherches féministes* 20/1 (2007), 27–54.

MARCHAND, Suzanne. *Rouge à lèvres et pantalons: Des pratiques esthétiques féminines controversées au Québec 1920–1939*. Montreal: Hurtubise HMH, 1997.

MARCIL-GRATTON, Nicole. "Le recours précoce à la ligature des trompes au Québec: Des suites indésirables?" *Sociologie et Sociétés* 19/1 (1987), 83–96.

MARTIN, Michèle. *"Hello Central?": Gender, Technology and Culture in the Formation of Telephone Systems*. Montreal and Kingston: McGill-Queen's University Press, 1991.

MILLS, Sean. "Québécoises Deboutte! Le Front de libération des femmes du Québec, le Centre des femmes et le nationalisme." *Mens* 4/2 (2004), 183–210.

MYERS, Tamara, *Caught: Montreal's Modern Girls and the Law, 1869–1945*. Toronto: University of Toronto Press, 2006.

NOËL, Françoise. *Family Life and Sociability in Upper and Lower Canada, 1780–1870*. Montreal and Kingston: McGill-Queen's University Press, 2003.

NOEL, Jan. *Along a River: The First French-Canadian Women*. Toronto: University of Toronto Press, 2013.

———. "N'être plus la déléguée de personne: une réévaluation du rôle des femmes dans le commerce en Nouvelle-France." *Revue d'histoire de l'Amérique française* 63/2–3 (2009–10), 209–41.

——. "'Femmes fortes' and the Montreal Poor in the Early Nineteenth Century." In Alison Prentice et al., *Canadian Women: A Reader*, 68–85. Toronto: Harcourt Brace, 1996.

——. "New-France: les femmes favorisées?" In Veronica Strong-Boag and A. Fellman (eds.), *Rethinking Canada: The Promise of Women's History*, 23–44. Toronto: Copp Clark, 1986.

PAQUIN, Magali. "Le profil socio-démographique des ministres québécois: Une analyse comparée entre les sexes." *Recherches féministes* 23/1 (2010), 123–41.

PÉLOQUIN, Marjolaine. *En prison pour la cause des femmes: La conquête du banc des jurés*. Montreal: Remue-ménage, 2007.

PICARD, Nathalie. "Les Femmes et le vote au Bas-Canada." Master's thesis (History), Université de Montréal, 1992.

PICHÉ, Lucie. *Femmes et changement social au Québec: L'apport de la Jeunesse ouvrière catholique féminine, 1931–1966*. Quebec: Presses de l'Université Laval, 2003.

POUTANEN, Mary-Anne. "The Geography of Prostitution in an Early Nineteenth-Century Urban Centre: Montreal, 1810–1842." In Tamara Myers, Kate Boyer, Mary Anne Poutanen, and Steven Watt (eds.), *Power, Place and Identity: Historical Studies of Social and Legal Regulation in Quebec*, 55–78. Montreal: Montreal History Group, 1998.

RUDIN, Ronald. "Bankers' Hours: Life Behind the Wicket at the Banque d'Hochelaga, 1901–1921." *Labour / Le Travail*, no. 18 (Fall 1986), 63–76.

SAINT-AMOUR, Nathalie. "Conciliation famille/emploi au Québec: Des objectifs diversifiés." *Informations sociales*, no. 143 (2007), 43–53.

SAINT-MARTIN, Lori. "La chair décevante de Jovette Bernier: Le Nom de la Mère." *Tangence*, no. 47 (1995), 112–24.

SAVOIE, Sylvie. "Les couples séparés: Les demandes de séparation aux 17ᵉ et 18ᵉ siècles." In André Lachance (ed.), *Les Marginaux, les exclus et l'autre au Canada aux XVIIᵉ et XVIIIᵉ siècles*, 45–82. Montreal: Fides, 1996.

SMART, Patricia. *Les Femmes du Refus Global*. Montreal: Boréal, 1998.

TARDIF, Évelyne, and André Bernard. *Militer au féminin dans la Fédération des femmes du Québec et dans ses groupes affiliés*. Montreal: Remue-ménage, 1995.

TREMBLAY, Diane-Gabrielle. "Viser la conciliation emploi-famille au Québec: Des politiques pour les enfants et/ou pour les mères?" *Informations sociales*, no. 160 (2010), 106–13.

TREMBLAY, Manon. *Québécoises et représentations parlementaires*. Quebec: Presses de l'Université Laval, 2005.

TREMBLAY, Manon, and Sarah Andrew. "Les femmes nommées ministres au Canada pendant la période 1921–2007: La loi de la disparité progressive est-elle dépassée?" *Recherches féministes* 23/1 (2010), 143–63.

TREMBLAY, Martine. "La division sexuelle du travail et la modernisation de l'agriculture à travers la presse agricole, 1840–1900." *Revue d'histoire de l'Amérique française* 47/2 (1993), 221–44.

TRUDEL, Marcel. *Deux siècles d'esclavage au Québec*. Montreal: Hurtubise HMH, 2004.

VIAU, Roland, *Femmes de personne: Sexes, genres et pouvoirs en Iroquoisie ancienne*. Montreal: Boréal, 2000.

YOUNG, Brian. *The Politics of Codification: The Lower Canadian Civil Code of 1866*. Montreal and Kingston: McGill-Queen's University Press, 1994.

Index

Abbott, Maude, 89
Abenakis. *See* First Nations
Aberdeen, Lady Ishbel, 87
Abitibi, 108
abortion: criminalization of, 70; Daigle-Tremblay case, xi, 186–87; decriminalization of, 174, 180–81; Depression era, 116; Lazure clincs, 193; liberalization of, 158–59; Parti Québécois veto, 185; pro-life movement, 181; referral services, 176–77
Accueil Bonneau, 64
Act of Union (1840), 60
actors, 149–50
adultery, 69, 105, 127, 128
agency, 217–18

agriculture: British colonial society, 26, 29; and Cercles de fermières du Québec, 123; commercialization of, 77–78; as family business, 170; French colonial society, 8–9; transformation of, 50; women as producers, 77–78
Aird, Janet Finlay, 37
Albani, Emma, 92
Algonkins. *See* First Nations
Algonquians. *See* First Nations
Alliance canadienne pour le vote des femmes, 124–26
Alliance des infirmières de Montréal, 141
Angéline de Montbrun (Conan/Angers), 92

INDEX

Angélique, Marie-Josèphe, 11
Angers, Félicité (Laure Conan), *Angéline de Montbrun*, 92
Anglican Church, 25, 39; on contraception, 113
Anglophone population: cooperation with Francophone organizations, 39; economic domination by, 96; urbanization, 28–29
anti-smoking campaign, 68
architecture, 163, 172
armed forces: nurses, 99, 109, 132–33; women's sections, 132
artisans, 27, 29
Arts, Faculties of, 88
Asian population, 99
Asile de Montréal pour les femmes âgées et infirmes, 38–39
Asile Saint-Jean-de-Dieu, 65
Assistance maternelle de Montréal, 94, 119–20
Association des dames patriotiques du comté des Deux-Montagnes, 45
Association des dames patronnesses de l'hôpital Notre-Dame, 97
Association des femmes collaboratrices, 170
Association des femmes de carrière du Québec métropolitain, 155
Association des femmes diplômées des universités de Québec, 142, 155
Association des femmes propriétaires de Montréal, 126, 127
Association féminine d'éducation et d'action sociale, 155, 170, 173, 176
Atikamekw. *See* First Nations
audiologists, 138
Augustinians: arrival in New France, 6, 17; Montreal General Hospital, 19–20

Baby, Marie-Thérèse, 12
baby boom, 145
Bacon, Lise, 167
Bacon Plan, 166–67
Balcer, Lise, 177, 178
Bank of Hochelaga, 82
Barbel, Marie-Anne, 12
Barrett, H.W., 37
Barry, Robertine, 90, 91
barter system, 10
Beaugrand-Champagne, Denyse, 11
beauticians, 171
Béchard, Monique, 142–43

INDEX

begging, 13
Bégin, Monique, 186
Bell Telephone Company, 81
Benhabib, Djemila, *Ma vie à contre-Coran*, 214
Benoist, Claude, 12
Benoist, Ursule, 12
Benoît-Sauvé, Jeanne, 154
Bergeron, Josée, 205
Bernier, Jovette, *La Chair décevante*, 92
Bersianik, Louky, 184
Berthelet, Olivier, 38
Bertrand, Janette, 149
Bilge, Sirma, 191
Bill 16 (1964), spousal equality, 155, 181–82
Bird, Florence, 174
Bird Commission, 186
Bird Report (Royal Commission on the Status of Women in Canada), 173–75, 182
Birth Control Handbook, 176
birth rate: baby boom, 145; British colonial society, 28; decline in, 191–93; Depression era, 113; French colonial society, 8, 9; generational replacement threshold, 158, 192; rural vs. urban, 75–76
Bishop's University, 88–89

Bissonnette, Lise, 186
Blais, Marie-Claire, *Une saison dans la vie d'Emmanuel*, 150
Blondeau, Angélique, 38
Blondin, Esther, 62
Blood Sisters, 215
boarding houses, 32
bodies, control over, 175, 179–81
Boisvert, Raymonde, 179
Bolduc, Yves, 193
La Bolduc (Mary Travers), 112
Bonheur d'Occasion (Roy), 149–50
La Bonne Parole, 91
Borden, Robert, 98
Bouchard, Gérard, 75
Bouchard, Lucien, 203–4, 206, 210
Bouchard, Pierrette, 199–200
Bouchard, Télesphore-Damien, 126
Bouchard-Taylor Commission, 190–91
Bourassa, Henri, 98, 100
Bourassa, Robert, 158; natalist policy of, 203
bourgeoisie: intolerance of prostitution, 35; Patriot movement, 41–42; role of women, 36
Bourgeoys, Marguerite, 18–19

INDEX

Bourget, Mgr Ignace, 38–39, 40, 62
Boyer, Kate, 83
Bradbury, Bettina, 44, 66
Brault, Gilles and Rita, 146
Bread and Roses March, 209–10
Brind'Amour, Yvette, 150
British colonial society, x; birth rate, 28; domestic servants, 29–32; dower system, 46–48; immigration, 25; Loyalist settlements, 25–26; political structure, 26–28; religious communities, 24; voting rights, 27–28, 42–45
Buhay, Becky, 108
Buller, Annie, 108
business, women in French colonial society, 9–10, 12–13

Cadron-Jetté, Rosalie, 62
Canadian Alliance for Women's Suffrage, 127
Canadian Council on Child Welfare, 119
Canadian Jewish Chronicle, 91
Canadian Muslim Council, 214
Canadian Patriotic Fund, 99
La Canadienne, 104
capitalism: abolition of, 175; industrial expansion, 73–74; monopolies, 73

care givers, women's role as, 94–96
Casgrain, Thérèse, 124, 125, 134, 149, 155, 173, 182, 186
cashiers, 160
Catholic Action movement, 153
Catholic Church: on Americanization of culture, 104; Christian feminism, 97, 153–55; French-Canadian identity, 96–97; and French colonial society, 24; inequality of sexes, 4–5; influence on gender relations, vii–viii, x; and national identity, 220–21; opposition to contraception, 75, 113, 147; patriarchal authority of, 1, 13–14, 60–63, 154–55; social involvement, 62–68; view of feminism, 97; women's suffrage, 96–97, 101, 125–26
Catholic Women's League, 104
Catholic Workers Confederation of Canada (CWCC), 139–40
CEGEPS, 144–45, 171
"Cell X," 177
Central Board of Catholic Examiners, 85
Centre des femmes, 178
Cercles d'économie domestique (CED), 155

INDEX

Cercles de fermières du Québec, 101, 154; opposition to suffrage, 122–24

La Chair décevante (Bernier), 92

La Chambre nuptiale (Larivée), 184

Le Chaînon (The Link), 116

Chamberland, Line, 212

Chaput-Rolland, Solange, 149

Charest, Jean, 198, 204; ministerial appointments, 202

charities. *See* social assistance organizations

Charles, Aline, 135

Charon brothers, 19

Charpentier, Yvette, 108

Charter of Human Rights and Freedoms (Quebec, 1976), 161, 180, 211

Charter of Rights and Freedoms (Canada, 1982), 174, 181, 182

Châtelaine, 173

Cherrier, Rosalie, 46

Chicha, Marie-Thérèse, 197

child birth: concealment of, in criminal law, 69–70; maternity leave, 165–66, 174, 204–5; medicalization of, 118–20; Montreal Lying-in Hospital, 66; paternity leave, 166, 204–5

child care: Canadian Council on Child Welfare, 119; Child Welfare Division, 119; early childhood centres, 204, 205, 206; infant care clinics, 119; parental leave, 166, 204–5, 206; psychological theories of, 146–48; role of fathers in parenting process, 146–48; *salles d'asile*, 64; sharing of domestic work, 164–65. *See also* daycare

children: abandonment of, 13, 63; adoption by same-sex couples, 212; custody of, 69; as factory workers, 53; family size, 75–76; as family workforce, 8, 9, 28; "Goutte de lait" clinics, 93, 117–18; illegitmate births, 116; infanticide, 69–70; infant mortality rate, 8, 63, 87, 93, 117; inheritances of, 16; in matrilineal indigenous society, 3, 4; orphanages, 17, 20, 37–38, 120, 121; as purpose of marriage, 11; *right* vs. *desire* for, 193; school attendance, 33, 142, 144; Support-Payment Collection Program, 206–7

INDEX

Chiriaeff, Ludmilla, 150
cinemas, 83
Circé-Côté, Éva ("Julien Saint-Michel"), 91
citizenship: male definition of, 45; and property ownership, 41, 42
Civil Code: adoption of, 48; adultery, 127, 128; on battered women, 179; changes to, 68–69, 71; legal status of married women, 126, 127; principle of paternal rule, 134; support payments to de facto spouses, 207
civil disobedience, 176
civil law, 24, 25
civil rights, Dorion Commission, 126–28
civil unions, and same-sex partnerships, 212
class relations, moralizing attitude towards, 95
clerical workers, 81–83
Cliche, Marie-Aimée, 31, 179
clothing depots, 64, 65
Coalition pour l'équité salariale, 197
Coalition québécoise pour le droit à l'avortement libre et gratuit, 186–87
Coderre, Louis, 114

Le Coin du feu, 91
Collectif des femmes immigrantes, 208–9
Collège Marguerite-Bourgeoys, 89
College of Physicians (Quebec), 90
collèges classiques, 58, 89, 142
Collin, Johanne, 143–44, 164
Coloured Women's Club of Montreal, 94
Comité de lutte pour l'avortement libre et gratuit, 181
Comité provincial pour le suffrage féminin, 101
Committee for the Equality of Women in Canada, 173
Committee of Sixteen, 114
common law, 25
community of goods, 14–15, 126, 181–82
Company of One Hundred Associates, 6
Complexe Desjardins, 184
Conan, Laure (Félicité Angers), *Angéline de Montbrun*, 92
Confédération des syndicats nationaux, 168
Congregation of Notre Dame, 19, 23, 82, 89
Congregation of the Holy Names of Jesus and Mary, 62

Congregation of the Sisters of Providence, 39
conscription, 98
Conseil d'intervention pour l'accès des femmes au travail, 178
Conseil du statut de la femme, 174, 180
Constitutional Act (1791), 27–28
Constitutional Party, 46
construction, 107
Consultation Commission on Accommodation Practices Related to Cultural Differences, 190–91
Consumers' Association of Canada, 151–52
consumer society: development of, 129; participation in, 135–36; transition to, 103–4
contraception: access to, 174; birth control pill, 158; breastfeeding, 11; Church opposition, 75; criminalization of, 70, 71–72; decriminalization of, 180; and family size, 113, 158–59; Knaus-Ogino method, 113, 145–46; rhythm method, 113, 145–46; sterilization, 158; sympto-thermal method, 146; withdrawal method, 113

Cooper, Afua, 11
Corbeil, Christine, 201
Corbin, Jeanne, 108
Corporation des instituteurs catholiques, 141
corruption: police corruption inquiry (1924), 114
Cotté, Gabriel, 38
Couagne, Thérèse de, 11
County Health Units, 117, 118
coureurs de bois, 6
crafts: Cercles de fermières du Québec, 123; First Nations, 2
Crèche d'Youville, 37–38, 63, 64
Cree. *See* First Nations
Criminal Code: conjugal rape, 180
criminal law: abortion, 70–71; infanticide, 69–70
Cuvillier, Austin, 44

Dagenais, Michèle, 82
Daigle, Chantal, 186–87
Daigle-Tremblay case, xi, 186–87
Dalhousie, Lady, 40
Dames de la Charité, 38, 39
Dames de l'Asyle des Orphelins Catholiques Romains, 38
Danylewycz, Marta, 57
Daveluy, Marie-Claire, 92
David, Françoise, 202, 209
daycare, 174, 204; associations

with communism, 131; Bacon Plan, 166–67; demand for, 165, 166–67, 178; financial assistance, 167; Montreal Day Nursery, 67; *salles d'asile*, 64; unlicensed, 167; wartime facilities, 131, 133

day labourers, 32

Dechêne, Louise, 22

delinquency, juvenile, 65–66, 95; of girls, 114–15. *See also* Juvenile Delinquents Court

demographics: 1941 census, 131–32; contraception use, 145–46; employment of servants, 30; female occupations, 1835 census, 31–32; female workforce, 78, 106–7; immigrant women, 162, 196–97; male/female education levels, 198–99; New France male–female ratio, 6–7. *See also* population

dentists, 172

Derick, Carrie, 98

Desaulniers sisters, 12

Desjardins, Aline, 173

Desjardins, Ghislaine, 166

Desprez, Jean, 150

Desrochers, Clémence, 184

Detellier, Élise, 105

Le Devoir, 100, 149, 186

De Witt, Emily F., 67

diet, and food supply: First Nations, 2–3, 4; food riots, 22–23; French colonial society, 9; Montreal Diet Dispensary, 67, 93; rationing, 132, 151; soup kitchens, 38, 65; in urban areas, 55

dietetics, 84

Dionne, Ludger, 137

discrimination: awareness of, 173; female students, 144; ideology of separate spheres, 218–19; against immigrants, 162–63, 197; people of African descent, 94; racism, 191, 197; reasonable accommodation, 190–91; sexual discrimination, 152, 157, 161, 174; in the workplace, 57–58

diseases and epidemics: cholera, 38, 39; First Nations societies, 4; tuberculosis, 87; typhus, 39

Disparaître (documentary), 208

divorce, 3, 105, 158, 159

doctors: female physicians, 88–90, 164; pregnancy and child care, 118–20

domestic helpers, immigrants as, 162–63

domestic servants, 136–37, 160; British colonial society, 29–32; decline in, 52–53, 84,

107; French colonial society, 10–11, 16; immigrant women, 29–30; sexual abuse, 31; working conditions, 30–31
Dominion Textile Inc, 73
Donalda, Pauline, 92
Dorion, Charles-Édouard, 126
Dorion Commission, legal reforms, 126–28
dowers: abolition of, 46–48; as inheritance, 15–16; legal registration of, 68
Drapeau, Jean, 176
Drummond, Grace Julia, 94
Dufour, Andrée, 33, 34
Dumont, Micheline, 34, 169
Duplessis, Maurice, 111, 121, 129, 139, 144
Dupuis Frères, 140
Durand, Lucile, *L'Euguélionne*, 184
Durocher, Eulalie, 62
Duval, Jeanne, 139, 154

Eastern Townships, 26, 88
École de Service social, 138
École des parents, 146, 153
École ménagère agricole, 83–84
École Polytechnique (Montreal massacre), xi, 187
écoles de rang, 56–57, 59, 86
education: accessibility, 171; CEGEPs, 144–45, 171; classic streams, 142; co-educational classrooms, 144, 171; comprehensive schools, 171; compulsory attendance, 142, 144; controversy over girls' education, 142–43; convent schools, 17–18; dropout rates (boys), 199–200; education tax, 58; Francophone secondary program, 142; government role in, 33; high school, 58; male/female comparisons, 198–99; Ministry of Education reforms, 144, 170–72; Montreal Catholic School Board, 57; Parent Report, 129, 144–45, 171; period of schooling, 135, 142; post-secondary. *See* universities; primary, 58; Protestant school system, 57–58; public education system, 58–59; scholarships, 152; social debate over, xi; teacher training, 57; textbooks, sexist representations in, 171–72. *See also* schools; teachers
elderly and disabled, care of, 38–39, 64, 65
elections, British colonial structure, 27–28
employment: blue-collar jobs, 162; female occupations,

1835 census, 31–32; female workforce, 78–83, 131–32, 134–37, 159–60; immigrant women, 29–30, 162, 196–97; and industrialization, x, 49–51; male labour, 29; male unemployment, 107, 111–12; manufacturing, and industrial development, 49–51, 73; of married women, xi, 54, 107, 129, 130–32, 134–37, 160; non-standard, 195; office work, 74, 100; seamstresses, 10; seasonal unemployment, 56; Selective National Service, 130, 137; service sector, 107–8, 136–37; traditional/non-traditional occupations, 32, 160, 171–72; urbanization of workforce, 50–51, 75; wage disparity, 51, 78–79, 82, 160–61; white-collar jobs, 81, 162; working conditions, 161; World War II, 130; of young women, 83, 84, 106–7

Engineering, Faculties of, 172
engineers, 163
England, Grace Ritchie, 89, 98
equal pay legislation (1965), 141
Equal Rights for Indian Women, 182
ethnic diversity, 74, 162, 190–91
ethnicity, as marker of identity, viii
executives, senior, 163; "glass ceiling," 200–201

Fabre, Mgr, 97
factories: female workforce, 53–54, 78–79, 107; hiring age, 79; munitions, 99, 130; workforce growth, 49, 73; work-week restrictions, 79
Fahrni, Magda, 151
Fair Wage Act (1937), 111
family: de facto relationships, 159, 192; family law reforms, 181–82; family size, 75–76, 113, 158–59; female entrepeneurship, 12–13; feminism as threat to, 97; and French Canadian identity, 96–97, 122, 134; French colonial society, 5–6, 8–9; honour of, 69–71; housewives contribution to family income, 55–56, 112–13, 131–32; identification of women with, 51–52, 54–55; impact of industrialization, 51–54, 84; nuclear family model, 149; parental equality, 147, 181; paternal rule of, 106, 134; postwar roles of women, 133–34;

post–World War II, 129–30; republican view of women's role, 41–42; "revenge of the cradle," 221; second income, need for, 164; sharing of domestic work, 164–65; single-parent families, 159; spousal equality, 155, 181–82; women as caregivers, 94–96

family allowance, 120–22, 134, 142, 203

Family Movement, 146–48

family planning clinics, 181

farm women: butter and cheese making, 77–78; Cercles de fermières du Québec, 122–23; home economics education, 83

Fédération catholique des institutrices rurales, 109

Fédération des agricultrices, 170

Fédération des femmes libérales du Québec, 155

Fédération des instituteurs et institutrices des cités et villes, 141

Fédération des instituteurs ruraux, 141

Fédération des institutrices rurales, 141

Fédération des oeuvres de charité canadiennes-françaises, 138

Fédération nationale Saint-Jean-Baptiste, 83–84, 91, 154; activism by, 95; Canadian Patriotic Fund, 99; Dorion Commission and, 126; Provincial Franchise Committee, 101; women's suffrage, 97, 98, 123, 124

Les fées ont soif (Boucher), 183

Female Benevolent Society, 36–37, 39

Female Compassionate Society, 40, 66

Femina, 149

femininity: American influence on, 104; male–female power relations, viii, 217; new model of, 104–5; social and cultural determinants of, 171–72; women as caregivers, 94–96

feminism, x, 91; anti-feminism, 187; Bread and Roses March, 209–10; "Cell X," 177; Christian feminism, 97, 153–55; demands, 95–96, 167–68, 174; equality through legislation, 174; family law reforms, 203–7; growth of, 96–98; impact on gender relations, 157–58; Islamic veil, 214; legal status, 126–28; and

INDEX

lesbian community, 212–13; and nationalism, xi, 97, 177, 184–86, 208–10, 218, 221–22; nationalist response to, 98, 100–101; and patriarchal control, 215; pornography, and pornogrifying mass culture, 213–14; in professional associations, 152–53; and prostitution, 214; radical feminism, 124–25, 175–79, 215–16; redefinition of, xi; and the religious right, 208; resurgence of, xi, 173–75, 220; Royal Commission on the Status of Women in Canada, 173–75; scholarship, 183; second wave, 157; service feminism, 178–79; theatre, and artistic creation, 183–84; third wave, 216; view of Church on, 97; Yvette affair, 185–86. *See also* suffrage

Femmes d'aujourd'hui (magazine), 173

"Femmes en tête" commemoration, 208–9

fertility rate: decline in, x, 113, 135, 158; French colonial society, 7, 8; generational replacement threshold, 158, 192; rural vs. urban, 75–76

fetal alcohol syndrome, 194

"Filles de la congrégation," 18–19

filles du roy, 5, 7

"filles-mères," 62

Finestone, Sheila, 186

First Nations: arrival of Europeans, ix–x, 4–5; conversions to Catholicism, 5, 17; craftwork, 77; equality of sexes, 1–2; government assimilation policy, 72; Indian status, 72, 182–83; inheritance rights, 72; linguistic groups, 2; loss of land, 77; loss of status, 5; mixed marriages, 6, 72; religion, 3, 4; sexual freedom of, 3, 4; societal organization, 1–4; voting rights, 99; women's work, 2–3, 4

fishing, 76

flappers, as emancipated women, 104

Les Folles Alliées, 183

food supply. *See* diet, and food supply

footwear industry, 50, 53, 130

forestry, 76, 77

Fornel, Jean-Louis, 12

Forrester, Maureen, 150

Forrestier, Marie, 17

France: emigration from, 6–7; Royal letters patent, 18, 20

Francoeur, Joseph-Napoléon, 107

INDEX

Francophone population: access to post-secondary education, 89–90; cooperation with Anglophone organizations, 39; nationalism of, 96–98; Quebec Act, 25

free market: impact on workforce, 195–98; and welfare state, 189

French Canadian identity, 96–97, 122, 129, 134, 191, 220–21

French Canadians, migration of, 96

French colonial society, ix–x; British Conquest, 22–24; community of goods, 14–15; comparison to First Nations societal organization, 1–2; coureurs de bois, 6; employment, 10; family, 5–6, 8–9; fertility rate, 7; filles du roy, 5, 7; fur trade, 5–6; marriage age, 7–8; population growth, 6–7; Quebec Act, 25; religious communities, 16–22; remarriage, 8, 10; role of upper-class women, 11–12; village women, 9–10

Frigon, Sylvie, 179

Front de libération des femmes du Québec (FLFQ), 176–78, 184

Front de libération du Québec (FLQ), 177, 178

fur trade, 10; and First Nations societies, 4, 5–6

garment industry, 136, 162; strikes, 108; sweating system, 53–54

Gaudreault, Laure, 108–9

Gauvreau, Michael, 153

gender relations: Church influence on, vii–viii; Civil Code restrictions, 68–69; and feminism, 157–58; First Nations societies, 1–2, 4; and gender identity, 171; hierarchy of feminine/masculine norms, 191; impact of industrialization, 51–54; income inequality, 152; legal status of married women, xi, 14–15, 68–69, 152; lifestyle changes, 103; patriarchal missionary teachings, 4–5; post–World War II, 129–30; post–World War I transitions, 105–6; prejudice against women, 41–42; and sexual identity, viii

gender stereotypes, 200

Gérin-Lajoie, Marie, 137

Gibb, Eleanor, 36

Girls' Cottage Industrial School, 115

"glass ceiling," 200–201

INDEX

Gleason, Anne-Marie ("Madeleine"), 91, 93
Globensky, Hortense, 46
Godbout, Adélard, 125–26, 142
Gossage, Peter, 53, 63
Gosselin, Line, 90
Gouin, Lomer, 98
Gousse, Suzanne, 10
"Goutte de lait" clinics, 93, 117–18
governesses, 32
government: Bacon Plan on daycare, 166–67; Depression relief programs, 111–12; family allowance, 120–22, 134, 203; health agencies, 119; income tax law, changes to, 130–31, 133; unemployment insurance program, 133–34; war effort, 99–100, 106
Les Grands Ballets Canadiens, 150
Grant, Captain David, 39
Gray, Colleen, 23
Great Britain: acquisition of New France, 22–24, 25–26; Royal Proclamation (1763), 25; Seven Years War, 22
Great Depression: economy during, 108–11; family economy, housewives contribution to, 112–13; family size, 113; living conditions, 112–13; male unemployment, 111–12; relief programs, 111–12
Grenier, Benoît, 12
Grey Nuns, 19–20; Crèche d'Youville, 63; membership, 38; Notre Dame Hospital, 65; Royal letters patent, 20; Salle Nazareth (later as Nazareth Institute), 64–65; social assistance by, 37–38, 39, 64
Groulx, Henri, 138
Grunet, Marie, 17
Guay-Ryan, Madeleine, 185
Guèvremont, Germaine, 150
Guyart, Marie (Marie de l'Incarnation), 7, 17

Hadassah, 124
hairdressers, 171
Hall Gauld, Bella, 108
harassment, prohibition of, 180
Harvey, Kathryn, 179
health care: access to, 174; Assistance maternelle de Montréal, 119–20; auxiliary professions, 138–39; County Health Units, 117; of elderly and disabled, 38–39, 64; Faculties of Medicine, 88–90; "Goutte de lait" clinics,

93, 117–18; prevention and education, 87; public health services, 87–88, 118; and reproductive technologies, 193; social assistance organizations, 36–40, 92–96; Victorian Order of Nurses (VON), 87, 93; women's health centres, 178. *See also* hospitals

heavy industry, male unemployment, 107

Hébert, Anne, 150

Hébert, Karine, 144

Hébert, Louis, 6

History of Emily Montague, The (Moore Brooke), 91–92

home economics education, 83–84; essentialist vision of women, 143; expansion of, 142; as preparation for motherhood, 84; public funding, 142

homes and shelters, 65; Accueil Bonneau, 64; conjugal violence victims, 178, 179, 180; elderly and disabled, 64; Hospice Saint-Charles, 64; Ladies' Protestant Home, 66; Magdalene Homes, 67; Maison de la Providence, 38–39; Native women, 183; Notre-Dame de la Protection (Le Chaînon/The Link), 116; safe houses, 178, 179, 180; St Bridget's Asylum, 66; for young women, 116; Young Women's Christian Association (YWCA), 116

homophobia, 213

homosexuality: decriminalization of, 180; right to equality, 211–13; same-sex partnerships, 212

Hospice Saint-Charles, 64

hospitals: apprenticeship of student nurses, 86; auxiliary health care professions, 138–39; Hôtel-Dieu de Montréal, 11, 18, 37–38; maternity hospitals, 71; McGill University Health Centre, 37; Miséricorde Hospital, 116; Montreal Foundling and Baby Hospital, 93; Montreal General Hospital, 19–20, 37, 64, 86; Montreal Lying-in Hospital, 66; Notre Dame Hospital, 65, 86; Sainte-Justine Hospital, 94, 140

Hôtel-Dieu de Montréal, 11, 18, 37–38

housewives: activism by, 100, 151; contribution to family income, 55–56, 112–13, 131–32; economic citizenship of, 151–53; home economics education, 84; suburban housewife archetype, 148–49; World War II war effort, 132–33. *See also* married women

Hull, 50, 74

Hurons (Wendat). *See* First Nations

hydroelectric dams, 77

hypersexualization of girls, 213–14

immigrants and immigration: assimilation of, 208–10; British colonial society, x, 25, 28; Caribbean, 162, 163; China, 74; discrimination against, 162–63; diversification of, xi; domestic helpers, 162–63; East Asia, 162, 190; England, 28; filles du roy, 5, 7; Greece, 136; integration of, 124; Ireland, 28; Italy, 74, 136; Jewish population, 74; Loyalist refugees, 26; Middle East, 190; North Africa, 162, 190; Philippines, 163; Poland, 137; Portugal, 136; reasonable accommodation, 190–91; Scotland, 28; service sector employment, 136–37; South America, 162

immorality, and female delinquency, 114–15

incest, 178, 179

income: housewives' contribution to family income, 55–56, 112–13, 131–32; tax law, 130–31, 133. *See also* wage disparity

Indian Act, 182

Indian status, 72, 182–83

industrialization, 49–72; devaluation of female activities, 5; expansion of capitalism, 73–74; factories, 49–50; impact on traditional family, 84; Manufacturers' Act (1885), 79; railways, 49; rural migration, 50–51; social exclusion of the marginalized, 65–66. *See also* employment

infanticide, 69–70

infant mortality rate, 8, 63, 87, 93

inflation, 132, 164; housewives boycotts, 100, 151

Les Insoumises, 215

Institut des sourdes-muettes, 65

Institute of the Sisters of Mercy, 62–63

Institut Notre-Dame du Bon-Conseil, 137

INDEX

Institut Sténographique Perreault, 82
International Labour Organization, 161–62
Inuit, 2
in vitro fertilization (IVF) procedures, 193
Iroquoians. *See* First Nations
Iroquois, 2, 17, 20, 22, 26
Islam. *See* Muslims

Jasmin, Judith, 149
Jensen, Jane, 205
Jesuits, 21
Jeunesse étudiante catholique féminine, 153
Jeunesse ouvrière catholique, 146
Jeunesse ouvrière catholique feminine (JOCF), 153
Jewish population, 74, 89; Hadassah, 124; National Council of Jewish Women, 123–24; Pioneer Women, 124
Jonquière, 196
Le Journal de Françoise, 91
journalism, 90–91, 149; pseudonyms, 91
Julien, Pauline, 184
jurors' affair, 177–78
Juvenile Delinquents Court, 95, 114–15

Kahnawake, 182
Khadir, Amir, 202
King, Mackenzie, 133
Kingston Women's Medical College, 89
Kirkland-Casgrain, Claire, 155
Knights of Labour, 79

labour movement: Catholic Workers Confederation of Canada (CWCC), 139–40; concerns over female employment, 79; exclusion of women, 80; pay equity, 161–62; union organization, 79; women's involvement in, 139–41, 168–69; workforce activism, 108–10; work stoppages and strikes, 80, 108, 168–69
Labour Relations Act (1944), 139
lab technicians, 138
Lacelle, Claudette, 30
Lachine Canal, 29, 35, 49
Lachute, 140
Lacoste-Beaubien, Justine, 94
Lacoste-Gérin-Lajoie, Marie, 97, 98, 101, 124, 137
Ladies Benevolent Society, 66
Ladies' Protestant Home, 66
Lafond, Andréanne, 149
laicization of workforce, 141

INDEX

Lamothe-Thibodeau, Marguerite, 97
Lamotte, Aleyda, 162
Lamoureux, Diane, 178
land: availability, 8; clearing, 8–9, 76; inheritance of, 16; Loyalist grants, 26; ownership of through marriage, 14–15; seigneurial system, 7, 8, 25
Landry, Yves, 7
language: English, 82; French, 24
Lanthier, Stéphanie, 185
Lapointe, Jeanne, 144
Lapointe, Renaude, 149
Laporte, Pierre, 177
Larivée, Francine, 184
Larocque, Laurette, 150
Lasnier, Rina, 150
La Société compatissante des Dames de Québec, 40
laundresses, 32
Laurendeau, André, 144
Laurendeau, Francine, 144
Laval, Mgr de, 18
Laval University, 144; Faculty of Medicine, 89–90
La Vie en rose (magazine), 184
Lavigne, Marie, 75
law: bar admittance, 88; Faculties of, 59, 88, 143, 172; Paris Custom, 14, 16

lay communities: charitable works, 19–20. *See also* social assistance organizations; Congregation of Notre Dame, 19; financial support, 20–21; Grey Nuns, 19–20; Montreal Sisters of Charity, 19
laywomen, status of, 61
Lazure clincs, 193
League for Women's Rights, 124–26
leather, 49, 50
Lebel, Léon, 122
Leclerc Hamilton, Caroline, 94
Leduc-Pelletier, Alec, 154
legal profession, 163, 164
Legardeur de Repentigny, 12
Legault, Marie-Josée, 196
legislation: Bill 16 (1964), 155, 181–82; Bill C-31, 182–83; Charter of Human Rights and Freedoms (Quebec, 1976), 161, 180, 211; Charter of Rights and Freedoms (Canada, 1982), 174, 181, 182; Constitutional Act (1791), 27–28; Employment Standards Act, 205; equal pay legislation (1965), 141; Fair Wage Act (1937), 111; family law reforms, 181–82; Indian

Act, 72, 182–83; Labour Relations Act (1944), 139; Manufacturers' Act (1885), 79; Needy Mothers Assistance Act (1937), 121–22, 159; pay equity, 197–98; Social Aid Act (1970), 159; Support-Payment Collection Program, 206–7
Legislative Assembly (Quebec), 90, 155; suffrage pilgrimage, 125
Legislative Assembly (Upper Canada), 27–28; Rebellions (1837–1838), 40
Lemoine, Alexis (Monière), 10
Le Moyne, Marie-Charles-Joseph, 39
Lépine, Marc, 187
Lesage, Jean, 144
lesbians, 211–13
Le Temps de l'avant (Poirier, film), 184
L'Euguélionne (Bersianik/Durand), 184
Levasseur, Irma, 90, 94
Lévesque, Andrée, 114, 116
Lévesque, René, 185
Lewis-Landau, Regina, 89
Liberal Party (Quebec), 125, 155, 185, 193, 198, 203
Liberal Women's Club, 125

Ligue des droits de la femme, 124–26
logging industry, 29
Loranger, Françoise, 150
Louiseville, 140
Louis XIV, 7
Lower Canada: birth rate, 28; British immigration, 28; creation of, 28; as pre-industrial society, 29–46
Loyalists, 25–26

MacDonald Langstaff, Annie, 88, 90
MacMurchy, Helen, 119
"Madeleine" (Anne-Marie Gleason), 91, 93
Magdalene Homes, 67
Maison de la Providence, 38–39
Maisonneuve, Yvonne, 116
Maliseet. *See* First Nations
management, professional faculty of, 172
Mance, Jeanne, 18
Manufacturers' Act (1885), 79
manufacturing, 160; and industrial development, 49–51, 73
Marchand, Félix-Gabriel, 97
Marchand, Isabelle, 201
Marchand, Joséphine, 91, 97
Marcil-Gratton, Nicole, 158
margarine, legalization of, 151

INDEX

Marie de l'Incarnation, 7, 17

Marois, Pauline, 202

marriage: age, in French colonial society, 7–8; community of goods, 14–15, 126, 181–82; de facto relationships, 159, 192; divorce, 3, 109, 158, 159; dower system of inheritance, 15–16, 46–48; egalitarian conception of, 153; home economics education, 83–84; legal separation, 69, 71; love-based, 106; in matrilocal indigenous society, 3; as natural state of women, 13; post–World War II rate, 145; remarriage, 8, 10

married women: economic dependency of, 12–13, 14–16, 157–58; employment of, xi, 54, 107, 129, 130–32, 134–37, 160; legal incapacity of, 14–15, 68–69, 126–28, 155, 181; legal status of, xi, 96, 122, 152; public merchant status, 15; second income, need for, 164; spousal equality, 155, 181–82; subordination of, 68–69; unemployment insurance program, 133–34. *See also* housewives

Martin, Claire, 150

Martin, Michèle, 81

Marxism, 108, 175

masculinity: and dropout rates (boys), 200; male–female power relations, viii, 217

maternity leave, 165–66, 174, 204–5

matrilineal society, 3, 4

Mauricie, 77

Ma vie à contre-Coran (Benhabib), 214

McGill Normal School, 85

McGill University, 98, 144, 176; access to, 58–59, 88; Faculty of Arts, 88; health care programs, 87; merger with Bishop's Faculty of Medicine, 89; social work, 137

McGill University Health Centre, 37

media: magazines, 104; role in renewal of activism, 173; suburban housewife archetype, 149. *See also* journalism

medical technology, 143–44

Medicine, Faculties of, 59, 88–90, 143, 172

men: breadwinner role, 51, 54; dominance of, 179; double standard, 13, 35, 69–72, 127,

128; public sphere of, viii; sharing of domestic work, 164–65
mentally ill, care of, 65
Methodists, 39
Metropolitan Life Insurance Company, 87
middle class, employment of domestic help, 52–53
midwives and midwifery, 119; British colonial society, 32; French colonial society, 10; professional recognition, 194–95
Mi'kmaq. *See* First Nations
mining, 77
Ministry of Agriculture: Cercles de fermières du Québec, 101; home economics schools, 83
Ministry of Education, 144
Miséricorde Hospital, 116
missionaries: on gender relations in indigenous societies, 1–2, 4; male dominance of, 4–5; view of interracial marriage, 6
model schools, 57, 58
Mohawk. *See* First Nations
Monet-Chartrand, Simonne, 154
Le Monde Ouvrier, 91
Mon magazine, 104
Montagnais. *See* First Nations
Montpetit Commission, 120–22
Montreal: 1832 by-election conflict, 43–44; 1835 census, 32; Anglophone/Francophone cooperation, 39–40; Anglophone population, 25, 28–29; Coloured Women's Club of Montreal, 94; Department of Health, 116, 117, 118; domestic servants, 53; École ménagère agricole, 84; ethnic diversity, 74, 162; female occupations, 1835 census, 31–32; female workforce, 78, 106–7; food riots, 22–23; garment industry strikes, 108; "Goutte de lait" clinics, 93, 117–18; industrialization, 50; male/female ratio, 52; Montreal Local Council of Women, 95, 97; Montreal Park and Playground Association, 94; population growth, 74; prostitution, 35, 114; *salles d'asile*, 64; shipyard, 29; social assistance organizations, 36–39, 62–68; suburban growth, 148; urban migration, 51; work stoppages and strikes, 140

INDEX

Montreal Catholic School Board, 57, 59
Montreal Catholic School Commission, 140
Montreal Day Nursery, 67
Montreal Diet Dispensary, 67, 93
Montreal Foundling and Baby Hospital, 93
Montreal General Hospital, 19–20, 37, 64; male administration of, 40; school of nursing, 86
Montreal Labour College, 108
Montreal Ladies' Benevolent Society, 37, 93
Montreal Local Council of Women, 95, 97, 123–24, 126, 127, 154
Montreal Lying-in Hospital, 66
Montreal massacre, xi, 187
Montreal Park and Playground Association, 94
Montreal Sisters of Charity, 19
Montreal Society for the Protection of Women and Children, 179
Montreal Suffrage Association, 98
Montreal Women's Liberation Movement, 176
Montreuil, Gaétane de, 91

Moore Brooke, Frances, *The History of Emily Montague*, 91–92
morality: and chastity, 13, 70–71, 115–16; double standard for, 13
Morgentaler, Henry, 181
motherhood: breastfeeding, 194; maternity leave, 165–66; medicalization of, 118–20, 194–95; public concern with, 116–17; unemployment insurance program, 165–66. *See also* unwed mothers
Mourir à tue-tête (Poirier, film), 184
Mullins-Leprohon, Rosanna, 92
multiculturalism, reasonable accommodation, 190–91
murders, as crimes of passion, 180
Muslims: Canadian Muslim Council, 214; Islamic veil, 191, 214; Muslim Presence, 214
Myers, Tamara, 114–15

Napoleonic Wars, and British emigration, 28
Naskapi. *See* First Nations
National Council of Jewish Women, 123–24

INDEX

National Council of Women of Canada (NCWC), 97

nationalism, and nationalists: Americanization of culture, 104; child care, and family integrity, 131; and class relations, 140; family allowance, 134; and feminism, x, xi, 177, 184–86, 208–10, 218, 221–22; in Francophone population, 96–98; French Canadian identity, 129; influence on gender relations, viii, 220–21; and neoliberalism, 189; and religion, 218; response to women's suffrage, 98, 100–101

National Question. *See* nationalism, and nationalists

natural resources: development and exploitation of, 73, 77; male unemployment, 107

Nazareth Institute, 64–65

Needy Mothers Assistance Act (1937), 121–22, 159

neoliberalism, and the Quebec model, 189

New France: borders of, ix; British Conquest, 22–24; immigration to, 6–7; Iroquois threat, 22; Paris Custom, 14, 16; Seven Years War, 22–23

Nielson, John, 44

Nightingale, Florence, 86

Noel, Jan, 23

Le Normand, Michelle (Marie-Antoinette Tardif), 92

Notre-Dame de la Protection (Le Chaînon/The Link), 116

Notre Dame Hospital, 65; school of nursing, 86

novelists, 91–92

nuclear family model, 149

nuclear weapons, opposition to, 155

nuns: Augustinians, 6; choir sisters, 21; classes of, 21–22; convent schools, 58; decline in, 141, 169; government control of social services, 169–70; numbers of, 21, 60–61; nursing sisters, 18, 141; patriarchal hierarchy of Catholic Church, 61, 62–63; schooling by, 17–18; social services provided by, 40, 62–68, 221; status of, 61; as teachers, 33, 141; Ursulines, 6, 7, 17–18

nursing and nursing profession, 86–88, 160; Graduate Nurses' Association of the Province of Quebec, 109; nursing sisters, 18, 141; private home care, 86–87, 110; professional association, 109–10; public health services, 87–88, 110; "registered nurses," 109; training and certification, 86; Victorian Order of Nurses (VON), 87, 93; work stoppages and strikes, 140; World War I, 98, 99

occupational therapists, 138
Oeuvre de la soupe, 65
Oeuvre du dépôt, 65
Office des services de garde à l'enfance, 167
Office of Child Care Services, 167
office workers, 74, 100, 105, 136
Ontario, as Upper Canada, 28
Opera Guild of Montreal, 92
organizational culture, 201
orphanages, 17, 20, 64, 65, 66, 71; Crèche d'Youville, 37–38, 63, 64; Dames de l'Asyle des Orphelins Catholiques Romains, 38; and family poverty, 120, 121; infant mortality rate, 8, 63; Orphelinat Catholique, 38; Protestant Orphan Asylum, 37
Orphelinat Catholique, 38
O'Sullivan's Business College, 82

Pagé, Lorraine, 168
Palestre nationale, 105
Palomino, Mercedes, 150
Papineau, Louis-Joseph, 44
paramedical professions, 143
Parent, Madeleine, 140
Parent, Mgr Alphonse-Marie, 145
parental equality, 147, 181
Parental Insurance Plan, 204–5
parental leave, 204–5, 206
Parent Report, 129, 144–45, 171
Paris Custom, 14, 16, 46, 126
Parizeau, Jacques, 206–7
Parliament: abortion legislation, 181; Bill C-31, 182–83; on Indian status, 72, 182–83
Parti Québécois, 167, 181, 185, 202; 1980 Referendum, 185; social programs, 203–4
paternity leave, 166, 204–5
paternity suits, 69
La Patrie, 90, 93
patriarchy: family honour, 69–71; and feminism, 215; in French colonial society, 13–16; ideology of separate spheres, 51–52, 218–19; Quebec as matriarchal society, myth of, vii; sexual double standard, 13, 35, 69–72, 127, 128; subordination of married women, 68–69

INDEX

Patriot movement, 44; abolition of dower system, 47–48; boycott of British imports, 45; view of women in politics, 41–42; women's associations, creation of, 45
pay equity. *See* wage disparity
Pay Equity Commission, 197–98
Payette, Lise, 173, 185, 208–9
Pelland, Marthe, 89
Perrault, Marie-Claire, 44
Pesotta, Rose, 108
Le Petit Journal, 149
Peuvret, Marie-Catherine, 12
pharmacists, 163, 172
physiotherapists, 138
Picard, Nathalie, 42
Piché, Lucie, 153
Pioneer Women, 124
pioneer women, roles of, 26
"*Place aux femmes*" (radio program), 173
Poirier, Anne-Claire, 184
political activism, 150–51
politics: British colonial society, 26–28; exclusion of women, 28, 41–42; female participation, 202–3; ministerial portfolios, 201–2; sexual immorality of female participation, 41
Pontbriand, Mgr, 19

population: Anglophone population, 25, 28–29; ethnic diversity, 74, 162, 190–91; international immigration, 191–92; New France, 5, 7; urban migration, 50–51, 52. *See also* demographics
pornography, and pornogrifying mass culture, 213–14
Pour un contrôle des naissances, 176
Pour vous Mesdames, 91
Poutanen, Mary Anne, 35
poverty: Bread and Roses March, 209–10; care of by lay communities, 19–20, 66–67; as feminist issue, xi; feminization of, 210–11; La Bolduc (Mary Travers), 112; moralizing attitude towards, 95; and prostitution, 13, 34–35, 114; social assistance organizations, 36–40, 62–66; of widows, 13; World March of Women, 211
power of attorney, 23
power relations: conjugal violence, 179–80; in male–female spheres of activity, viii, 175; post–World War I transitions, 106
pregnancy: alcohol during, 194; amniocentesis, 194; conceal-

ment of, in criminal law, 69–70; fetal monitoring, 194; and loss of employment, 31; medicalization of, 118–20; and reproductive technologies, 193

pre-industrial society, 29–46; resource economy of, 29

prejudice. *See* discrimination

La Presse, 149

Presbyterians, 39

private sphere: of domestic female respectability, 68; interrelationship with public sphere, viii, 151–53; women in politics, 41–42

professional associations: access to, 59; nursing and nursing profession, 109–10; social activism by, 152–53

professions, liberal, 163–64

prohibition movement, 67–68

pro-life movement, 181

property ownership: community of goods, 14–15, 126; and the dower, 15–16, 46–48; spousal joint owners, 170; and voting rights, 27–28, 42–43, 126

prostitution, 20; bawdy houses, 114; brothels, 35; Committee of Sixteen, 114; and feminism, 214; growth of, 114; and immorality of female political participation, 41; and loss of employment, 31; and poverty, 13, 34–35; rehabilitation, 67

Protestant Central Board of Examiners, 86

Protestant Orphan Asylum, 37; male administration of, 40

Protestants, 39

Provincial Franchise Committee, 101, 124

psychologists, 138, 146

Public Assistance Act (1921), 120

public health services: nursing and nursing profession, 110; private clinics, 118

public sphere: exclusion of women, 28; interrelationship with private sphere, viii, 151–53; social/political involvement, 92–96; women in politics, xi, 41–42

Quebec, Province of: as British colony, 25–26; Constitutional Act (1791), 27–28; ethnic diversity, 74, 162, 190–91; as Lower Canada, 28; matriar-

INDEX

chal society myth, vii; and New France, ix; Parental Insurance Plan, 204–5

Quebec City: 1835 census, 32; Anglophone population, 25, 28–29; convents in, 6, 7, 17; demographic stagnation, 51; female workforce, 78; food riots, 22–23; footwear industry, 50; French colonial society, 6–7; "Goutte de lait" clinics, 94; homes and shelters, 66; male/female ratio, 52; normal schools, 85; prostitution, 35; *salles d'asile*, 64; shipyard, 29, 50; social assistance organizations, 37, 39–40; suburban growth, 148; voting rights of widows, 43

Quebec Coalition for the Right to Free Abortion on Demand, 186–87

Quebec College of Physicians, 163

Quebec Federation of Women, 173, 176, 180, 186, 216; feminization of poverty, 210–11; "Pour un Québec féminin pluriel" forum, 209; prostitution, 214; recognition of homosexual rights, 213

Quebec Lesbian Network, 212

Quebec model, xi; impact of free market, 195–98; and neoliberalism, 189

Quebec Native Women's Association, 183

Québécoises Deboutte!, 178

Québec Solidaire Party, 202

Quebec Teachers' Corporation, 168

Quiet Revolution, 169

race, as marker of identity, viii

racism, 191, 197

radical feminism, 124–25, 175–79, 215–16; civil disobedience actions, 176

radiologists, 138

railways, 49

Ramezay, Louise de, 12

rape, 70, 71, 179; conjugal rape, 180; support centres, 178

rationing, 132

R des centres de femmes du Québec, 178

reasonable accommodation, 190–91

Rebellions (1837–1838), 60; role of women, 40–42, 45–46

Red Cross, 99, 150

Referendum (1980), Yvette affair, 185–86

reform schools, 115
Refus Global, 150
Regroupement des femmes québécoises, 185
Regroupement des maisons pour femmes victimes de violence conjugale, 178
Relations of the Jesuits, 1–2
religion: Anglophone/Francophone cooperation, 39–40; decline of, 129; and ethnic tensions, 40; First Nations societies, 3, 4; influence on gender relations, vii–viii; and nationalism, 218; patriarchal inequality of sexes, 4–5; as patriarchal organization, 1; ultramontanist ideology, 40. *See also* Catholic Church
religious accommodation, 190–91
religious communities, 16–22, 24, 40; charitable works, 65–66; decline in, 141; social involvement of, 62–68; socio-economic factors for joining, 60–61. *See also* social assistance organizations
religious right, 208
Remue-ménage publishing, 183
reproductive technologies, 193
republicanism, role of women, 41–42
Réseau des centres d'aide et de lutte contre les agressions à caractére sexuel, 178
Réseau des centres de santé des femmes, 178
La Revue Moderne, 91, 104
Ritchie England, Grace. *See* England, Grace Ritchie
Roback, Léa, 140
Roberval, 83
Robi, Alys, 150
Rollet, Marie, 6
Roman Catholic Church. *See* Catholic Church
Roquet, Ghislaine, 144
Rouleau, Michèle, 183
Rousselot, Victor, 64
Rowan, Renée, 149
Roy, Gabrielle, *Bonheur d'Occasion* (*The Tin Flute*), 149–50
Royal Commission of Inquiry on Education in the Province of Quebec (Parent Report), 144–45
Royal Commission on the Relations of Labour and Capital, 79
Royal Commission on the Status of Women in Canada, 173–75, 182

Royal Victoria College, 88
Rudin, Ronald, 82
rural population: standard of living, 76–77; urban migration, 50–51, 75, 130
rural women, employment of, 54

Sabia, Laura, 173
safe houses, 178, 179, 180
Saguenay, 75
Saint-Amant, Jean-Claude, 200
Saint-Amour, Nathalie, 206
Saint-Charles, Johanne, 201
Sainte-Justine Hospital, 94, 140
Saint-Hyacinthe, 50, 53, 64
Saint-Jean, Idola, 101, 124, 125
Saint-Joseph-de-la-Flèche, 18
Saint-Martin, Fernande, 173
Saint-Martin, Lori, 92
"Saint-Michel, Julien" (Éva Circé-Côté), 91
Saint-Pascal-de-Kamouraska, 83, 84
Saint-Père, Agathe de, 12
Saint-Vallier, Mgr de, 18
Salle Nazareth (later as Nazareth Institute), 64–65
salles d'asile, 64
same-sex partnerships, 212
Savoie, Sylvie, 15
School of Household Science, 84

schools, 89, 142; academies, 58; boarding schools, 34; CEGEPs, 144–45, 171; *collèges classiques*, 58, 89, 142; comprehensive schools, 171; convent schools, 17–18, 58, 59; *écoles de rang*, 56–57, 59, 86; education tax, 58; funding of, 59; home economics, 83–84, 142–43; model schools, 57, 58; normal schools, 85; public education system, 58–59; reform schools, 115; trustee schools, 34. *See also* education; teachers
seamstresses, 10, 32, 53–54; strikes by, 108
secretaries, 81–83, 160
seduction: abduction, 70–71; civil suits, 69
seigneurial system, 7, 8, 25
Selective National Service, 130, 137
separate spheres, ideology of: charitable work of middle-class women, 36–40; employment of women, 55–56; impact of industrialization, 51–54; male definition of citizenship, 45; male domination, 157; maternalist

ideology vs. patriarchal discourse, 94–96; post–World War I transitions, 106–7; relationship between public/private spheres, viii, 151–53, 218–19; rural/urban dichotomy, 122–23; social/political involvement, 92–96; women in politics, 41–42
Seréna, 146
servants. *See* domestic servants
Service de préparation au mariage, 146, 147; personalist philosophy of, 153
Service de régulation des naissances (Seréna), 146
service feminism, 178–79
service sector, 160, 162; growth in, 107–8, 136–37
settlements: land grants, 112; settlement nurses, 110; standard of living, 76–77, 112–13
settlers: Loyalist settlements, 25–26; women's responsibilities, 76
Seven Years War, 22–23
sexual abuse, 180, 183; domestic servants, 31; and morality of victim, 71
sexual assault, 179–80
sexuality: contraception use, 145–46; double standard, 13, 35, 69–72, 127, 128; flapper as emancipated woman, 104; hypersexualization of girls, 213–14; identity as social construct, viii
sexual orientation, discrimination against, 211–13
Shane, Bernard, 108
Sherbrooke, 50, 74, 93
shipyards, 29, 50
Siegler, Ida, 91
Simard, Monique, 168
single-parent families: family allowance, 120–22
single women: seduction of, as civil suit, 69; urban migration of, 52
Sisters of Providence, 40, 62, 65
Sisters of St Anne, 62
Sisters of St Joseph, 37–38
Sisters of the Good Shepherd, 62
Sisters of the Good Shepherd of Angers (reform school), 115
slaves and slavery: French colonial society, 10–11; Loyalist refugees, 26
Smith, Donald, 88
social activism, 150–51
Social Aid Act (1970), 159
social assistance: for blind children, 64–65; of Catholic laywomen, 66–68; chari-

table work of middle-class women, 36–40, 66–68; child care (*salles d'asile*), 64; clothing depots, 64; homes and shelters, 38–39, 64; ideology of separate spheres, 219–20; by religious communities, 18–21, 62–68; soup kitchens, 38, 64, 65

social assistance organizations, 36–40, 135; Anglophone/Francophone cooperation, 39–40; Asile de Montréal pour les femmes âgées et infirmes, 38–39; Assistance maternelle de Montréal, 94, 119–20; Coloured Women's Club of Montreal, 94; Congregation of the Holy Names of Jesus and Mary, 62; Crèche d'Youville, 37–38; Dames de la Charité, 38, 39; Dames de l'Asyle des Orphelins Catholiques Romains, 38; Female Benevolent Society, 36–37, 39; Female Compassionate Society, 40, 66; ideology of separate spheres, 92–96; Institute of the Sisters of Mercy, 62–63; Ladies Benevolent Society, 66; La Société compatissante des Dames de Québec, 40; Maison de la Providence, 38–39; Montreal Diet Dispensary, 67, 93; Montreal Ladies' Benevolent Society, 37, 93; Orphelinat Catholique, 38; private charities, 39; Protestant Orphan Asylum, 37; Salle Nazareth (later as Nazareth Institute), 64–65; Sisters of Providence, 39, 40, 62, 65; Sisters of St Anne, 62; Sisters of the Good Shepherd, 62; Société des dames de la Providence, 38–39; Young Women's Christian Association (YWCA), 66–67, 93, 105. *See also* health care; hospitals

social class, as marker of identity, viii

social exclusion of marginalized population, 65–66

social insurance (Montpetit Commission), 120–22

social workers, 137–38

Société des dames de la Providence, 38–39

Sorel, 64

Les Sorcières, 215

soup kitchens, 38, 65, 67

speech therapists, 138

INDEX

sports, participation in, x, 104–5
St Bridget's Asylum, 66
Stein, Amy, 124
Stella, 214
stereotypes, 183, 185
St Paul University (Minnesota), 90
suburbs: suburban housewife archetype, 148–49; and urban growth, 148
suffrage, xi, 91, 124–26; Alliance canadienne pour le vote des femmes, 124–26; Cercles de fermières du Québec, 122–23; civics courses offered, 124; demand for, 96, 97, 219; eligibility, and electoral procedures, 42–45; exclusion of women, 44–45; federal granting of, 99; Fédération nationale Saint-Jean-Baptiste, 97, 98, 123, 124; "Femmes en tête" commemoration, 208–9; Ligue des droits de la femme, 124–26; Montreal Local Council of Women, 123–24; National Council of Jewish Women, 123–24; temporary voting rights, 98; Woman's Christian Temperance Union, 68. *See also* voting rights

Sulpicians, 20, 21, 38, 64
Support-Payment Collection Program, 206–7
sweating system, 53–54

Talon, Jean, 8
Tardiff, Marie-Antoinette (Michelle Le Normand), 92
Taschereau, Louis-Alexandre, 101, 120
Tavernier-Gamelin, Émilie, 38, 65
teachers: Francophone teachers, 57, 85; high school, 58; lay teachers, 32, 33–34; morals of, 56; nuns as, 57, 59–60; primary teachers, 56; salaries, 34, 140; training and certification, 85–86; training of, 57; unionization of, 108–9; wage disparity, 57–58; work stoppages and strikes, 140. *See also* education; schools
teaching profession: and feminine sphere, 56; feminization of, 34; as preparation for marriage, 34, 56; training and certification, 85–86
technicians, medical, 138
Tekakwitha, Catherine, 5
telephone operators, 81
Tessier, Frances Barnard, 94
Tessier, Mgr Albert, 142
textile industry, 12, 53, 130;

Dionne scandal, 137; growth of, 49, 50; monopolies in, 73; work stoppages and strikes, 80, 140
Théâtre des cuisines, 183
Théâtre du Rideau Vert, 150
Théâtre expérimental des femmes, 183–84
Thirteen Colonies, 25
tobacco, 53
Toronto Star, 174
Toujours RebELLES, 215
tourism, 123
trade unions, and female workforce, 106
Travers, Mary (La Bolduc), 112
Tremblay, Diane-Gabrielle, 205
Tremblay, Jean-Guy, 186
Tremblay, Martine, 77–78
Trois-Rivières, 50, 74
Trudel, Marcel, 11
trustee schools, 34
Two-Axe Earley, Mary, 182

ultramontanist ideology, 40
unemployment: and free market, 195; male unemployment, 107, 111–12; seasonal unemployment, 56; World War II, 130
unemployment insurance program, 133–34; payments to new mothers, 165–66

Une saison dans la vie d'Emmanuel (Blais), 150
Union catholique des cultivateurs, 154
Union catholique des femmes rurales (UCFR), 154–55
Union catholique des fermières, 154
unionization: and female workers, 79, 139–40; garment industry, 108; Walmart, 196. *See also* labour movement
United Nations, 211
United States: influence of, 104, 129; population migration, 50–51
universities: access to, 58–59, 88–90; Bishop's University, 88–89; expansion of, 171; Faculty of Law, 59, 88; Faculty of Medicine, 59, 88; female enrolment, 143–44, 172; funding of, 144; Kingston Women's Medical College, 89; Laval University, 89–90, 144; McGill University, 58–59, 87, 89, 144; Royal Victoria College, 88; University of Montreal, 87, 89, 143–44
University of Montreal: École de Service social, 138; Faculty of Law, 143; Faculty of Medi-

cine, 143; female enrolment, 143–44; health care programs, 87, 89
unmarried women: employment of, x, 54; nuns, 16–22
unwed mothers: care of, 20; de facto relationships, 159, 192; family honour of, 69; "*filles-mères*," 62; infanticide, 69–70; social disapproval of, 13, 62–63
Upper Canada, creation of, 28
upper-class women, role of, 11–12
urbanization: Anglophone population, 28–29; and ethnic diversity, 74; impact on traditional family, 84; "modern" female role models, x; and moral depravity, 122–23; rural migration, 75; of workforce, 50–51
Ursulines, 7; arrival in New France, 6, 17; home economics schools, 83; normal schools, 85; as teachers, 33, 57

Vallerand, Claudine and René, 146, 154
Valleyfield, 50, 140
Verchères, Madeleine de, 22
Veuves Benoist et Makarty, 12
Viau, Roland, 5

Victoria, Queen, 41
Victorian Order of Nurses (VON), 87, 93
Victory Bonds, 99, 150
Viger, Jacques, 31, 35
Villeneuve, Cardinal Rodrigue, 125
violence: and alcohol, 67; awareness campaign, 183; conjugal, 14, 15, 67, 178, 179–80, 183; École Polytechnique, xi; male abuse, 149; World March of Women, 211
visible minorities: reasonable accommodation, 190–91
Voice of Women (Voix des femmes), 155
voting rights: electoral procedures, 42–43; exclusion of women, 44–45; property qualification, 27, 42–43; temporary, 98. *See also* suffrage

wage disparity, 51, 78–79, 82, 160–61; equal pay legislation (1965), 141; factory workers, 53–54, 78–79; income inequality, 152; liberal professions, 164; non-standard vs. traditional employment, 195–96; and pay equity, 161–62, 174, 197–98; teach-

ers, 57–58, 141; Women's Minimum Wage Act (1919), 110–11
water, municipal supply, 56
Waves of Resistance, 215
Wendat (Huron). *See* First Nations
widows: dower system, 15–16, 46–48; employment of, 10, 54, 131–32; as entrepreneurs, 12–13; federal pension, 96, 120, 121; property ownership, 27, 43, 127; remarriage, 8, 10; voting rights, 27, 43
Woman's Christian Temperance Union, 67–68
Women's Global Charter for Humanity, 211
Women's Health Centre, 186
Women's Liberation Movement, 157
Women's Minimum Wage Act (1919), 110–11
Women's Minimum Wage Commission, 110–11
wood, as export product, 29, 50
workforce: feminization of, 78–83; growth of, 49; impact of free market, 195–98; laicization of, 141; marginalization of women, 51–52; militancy of female workers, 80; redeployment of female labour, 107–8; service sector, 107–8, 136–37; urbanization, 50–51. *See also* employment
working class: Great Depression, 112–13; home economics education, 84; wages, 54
work stoppages and strikes, 80, 108, 140, 168–69
work week: restrictions, 79; shortened length of, 135
World March of Women, 211
World War I: conscription, 98; dietetics, 84; nurses, 99, 109; postwar American influence, 103–4; temporary voting rights, 98; women's contributions to war effort, 99–100, 106
World War II, 130–34; rationing, 132, 151; refugees, 137; war effort, 132–33, 150–51, 220
writers, 91–92, 149–50

Young Women's Christian Association (YWCA), 66–67, 93, 105, 116
Youville, Marguerite d', 19
Yvette affair, 185–86
YWCA (Young Women's Christian Association), 66–67, 93, 105, 116

**Books in the Studies in Childhood and Family in Canada Series
Published by Wilfrid Laurier University Press**

Making Do: Women, Family, and Home in Montreal during the Great Depression by Denyse Baillargeon, translated by Yvonne Klein • 1999 / xii + 232 p/ ISBN 0-88920-326-1 / ISBN-13: 978-0-88920-326-6

Children in English-Canadian Society: Framing the Twentieth-Century Consensus by Neil Sutherland with a new foreword by Cynthia Comacchio • 2000 / xxiv + 336 p/ illus. / ISBN 0-88920-351-2 / ISBN-13: 978-0-88920-351-8

Love Strong as Death: Lucy Peel's Canadian Journal, 1833–1836 edited by J.I. Little • 2001 / x + 229 p/ illus. / ISBN 0-88920-389-x / ISBN-13: 978-0-88920-389-230-x

The Challenge of Children's Rights for Canada by Katherine Covell and R. Brian Howe • 2001 / viii + 244 p/ ISBN 0-88920-380-6 / ISBN-13: 978-0-88920-380-8

NFB Kids: Portrayals of Children by the National Film Board of Canada, 1939–1989 by Brian J. Low • 2002 / vi + 288 p/ illus. / ISBN 0-88920-386-5 / ISBN-13: 978-0-88920-386-0

Something to Cry About: An Argument against Corporal Punishment of Children in Canada by Susan M. Turner • 2002 / xx + 317 p/ ISBN 0-88920-382-2 / ISBN-13: 978-0-88920-382-2

Freedom to Play: We Made Our Own Fun edited by Norah L. Lewis • 2002 / xiv + 210 p/ ISBN 0-88920-406-3 / ISBN-13: 978-0-88920-406-5

The Dominion of Youth: Adolescence and the Making of Modern Canada, 1920–1950 by Cynthia Comacchio • 2006 / x + 302 p/ illus. / ISBN 0-88920-488-8 / ISBN-13: 978-0-88920-488-1

Evangelical Balance Sheet: Character, Family, and Business in Mid-Victorian Nova Scotia by B. Anne Wood • 2006 / xxx + 198 p/ illus. / ISBN 0-88920-500-0 / ISBN-13: 978-0-88920-500-0

A Question of Commitment: Children's Rights in Canada edited by R. Brian Howe and Katherine Covell • 2007 / xiv + 442 p/ ISBN 978-1-55458-003-3

Taking Responsibility for Children edited by Samantha Brennan and Robert Noggle • 2007 / xxii + 188 p/ ISBN 978-1-55458-015-6

Home Words: Discourses of Children's Literature in Canada edited by Mavis Reimer • 2008 / xx + 280 p/ illus. / ISBN 978-1-55458-016-3

Depicting Canada's Children edited by Loren Lerner • 2009 / xxvi + 442 p/ illus. /ISBN 978-1-55458-050-7

Babies for the Nation: The Medicalization of Motherhood in Quebec, 1910–1970 by Denyse Baillargeon, translated by W. Donald Wilson • 2009 / xiv + 328 p/ illus. / ISBN 978-1-5548-058-3

The One Best Way? Breastfeeding History, Politics, and Policy in Canada by Tasnim Nathoo and Aleck Ostry • 2009 / xvi + 262 p/ illus. / ISBN 978-1-55458-147-4

Fostering Nation? Canada Confronts Its History of Childhood Disadvantage by Veronica Strong-Boag • 2011 / x + 302 p/ ISBN 978-1-55458-337-9 *Cold War Comforts: Maternalism, Child Safety, and Global Insecurity, 1945–1975* by Tarah Brookfield • 2012 / xiv + 292 p/ illus. / ISBN 978-1-55458-623-3

Ontario Boys: Masculinity and the Idea of Boyhood in Postwar Ontario, 1945-1960 by Christopher Greig • 2014 / xxviii + 184 p / ISBN 978-1-55458-900-5

A Brief History of Women in Quebec by Denyse Baillargeon, translated by W. Donald Wilson • 2014 / xii + 272 p / ISBN 978-1-55458-950-0